GERTRUDE STEIN AND THE MAKING OF LITERATURE

Gertrude Stein and the Making of Literature

Edited by

SHIRLEY NEUMAN

and

IRA B. NADEL

Northeastern University Press
BOSTON

Northeastern University Press 1988

First published 1988 by The Macmillan Press Ltd

Printed and bound in Great Britain

Library of Congress Cataloging-in-Publication Data
Gertrude Stein and the making of literature.
Originally published: Basingstoke, Hampshire :
Macmillan Press, c 1987.
Includes index.
1. Stein, Gertrude, 1874–1946 – Criticism and interpretation.   I. Neuman, S. C. (Shirley C.)
II. Nadel, Ira Bruce.
PS3537.T323Z615   1988   818'5209   87–22122
ISBN 1–55553–025–7

Contents

List of Plates

Acknowledgements

One of the pleasantest moments in the preparation of *Gertrude Stein and the Making of Literature* is this one, in which the editors can at last acknowledge the personal and professional kindnesses from friends, colleagues and scholarly organisations that helped make it possible. Chief among these we want to thank Dr David Schoonover and his staff at the Collection of American Literature, the Beinecke Rare Book and Manuscript Library, for their unfailing and friendly helpfulness to Shirley Neuman in her research there. This and other research on Stein was funded by a Research Time Release grant to Shirley Neuman from the Social Sciences and Humanities Research Council of Canada, which has been invaluable to the project, and by a Central Research Fund grant from the University of Alberta.

Professor Karen Rowe, Director of the Center for the Study of Women, University of California at Los Angeles, most generously provided us with information about essays from the UCLA Conference 'Considering Gertrude Stein: The Importance of her Writing and her Influence on Literature and Art', sponsored by the UCLA Extension Program, the UCLA Research Library, and the UCLA Center for the Study of Women and organised by herself and by Professor Martha Banta and Jim Hartzell.

We also gladly thank Jorge Frascara for turning his professional talents to designing a cover that is both meaningful and attractive for this volume, and Cameron Laux for volunteering to compile the index.

The editors and the authors of essays in this volume also wish to make grateful acknowledgement to the following:

David S. Lake Publishers, Belmont, California (formerly Pitman Publishing), for permission to quote from Gertrude Stein, *What are Masterpieces*, copyright 1970.

The Estate of Gertrude Stein for permission to quote from Gertrude Stein, *Last Operas and Plays*, ed. Carl Van Vechten (New York: Random House, 1949).

Random House Inc., for permission to quote from Gertrude Stein, *Ida A Novel* (New York: Random House, copyright 1941 by Random House, Inc.).

Random House, and the Estate of Gertrude Stein for permission to quote from Gertrude Stein, *The Autobiography of Alice B. Toklas* (New York: Harcourt Brace, copyright Harcourt Brace and Company, 1933); from Gertrude Stein, *Everybody's Autobiography* (New York: Random House, copyright 1937 by Random House, Inc.); and from Gertrude Stein, *Lectures in America* (New York: Random House, copyright 1935 by the Modern Library, Inc.).

Yale University Press for permission to quote from Gertrude Stein, *Four in America* (New Haven: Yale University Press, copyright 1947 by Alice B. Toklas).

The Estate of Gertrude Stein and the Collection of American Literature, the Beinecke Rare Book and Manuscript Library, Yale University, for permission to quote from the following Gertrude Stein manuscripts: early notebooks for *The Making of Americans*; manuscript notebook of the play *The Five Georges*; manuscript notebook of *Stanzas in Meditation*; manuscript notebooks of *Ida*; manuscript of 'Arthur and Jenny'; typescript of 'Portrait of Daisy'; manuscript notebook and scenarios of *Doctor Faustus Lights the Lights*; manuscript fragments pertaining to *Ida* and *Doctor Faustus Lights the Lights*.

The Estate of Gertrude Stein and the Collection of American Literature, the Beinecke Rare Book and Manuscript Library, Yale University, for permission to publish the following pieces by Gertrude Stein: 'American Language and Literature', 'A Poem about the end of the war', 'Realism in Novels'; and for permission to quote from the following letters: letter from Louis Solomons to Gertrude Stein, 27 February 1898; letter draft from Gertrude Stein to Bernard Fay, n.d.; letter from Emily Dawson to Gertrude Stein, 27 December 1908; letter from Gertrude Stein to Robert Haas, 17 May 1937; letter from Gertrude Stein to Thornton Wilder, 8 December 1937; letter from Gertrude Stein to Thornton Wilder, 11 May 1938.

The Estate of Gertrude Stein, the Beinecke Rare Book and Manuscript Library, Yale University, Virgil Thomson, and the Yale Music Library Archives, Yale University, for permission to quote manuscript materials from the Gertrude Stein and the Virgil Thomson collections.

The Estate of Carl Van Vechten, Joseph Solomon, Executor, and the Collection of American Literature, the Beinecke Rare Book and Manuscript Library, Yale University, for permission to reproduce the photograph of Gertrude Stein by Carl Van Vechten which is used on the cover of this volume.

List of Abbreviations

In this collection, references to the following works by Stein or to collections of her writings are identified by abbreviations in the text and notes. First editions of Stein's works are used except where later editions are both as accurate and more accessible than first editions. Where some other edition than the first is used, the first date given is that of original publication.

ABT   *The Autobiography of Alice B. Toklas* (New York: Harcourt Brace, 1933).

AWD   *An Acquaintance with Description* (London: Seizin Press, 1929).

B&W   *Brewsie and Willie* (New York: Random House, 1946).

BTV   *Bee Time Vine and Other Pieces [1913–1927]*, vol. III of the Yale Edition of the Unpublished Writings of Gertrude Stein (New Haven, Conn.: Yale University Press, 1953; repr. New York: Books for Libraries Press, 1969).

CE   *Composition as Explanation* (London: Hogarth Press, 1926).

DF   *Doctor Faustus Lights the Lights*, in Gertrude Stein, *Last Operas and Plays*, ed. with an introduction by Carl Van Vechten (New York: Random House, 1949; repr. New York: Vintage Books, 1975) pp. 89–118.

EA   *Everybody's Autobiography* (New York: Random House, 1937; repr. New York: Cooper Square, 1971; repr. with index added, New York: Vintage Books, 1973).

FIA   *Four in America* (New Haven, Conn.: Yale University Press, 1947).

G&P   *Geography and Plays* (Boston, Mass.: Four Seas Company, 1922; facsimile, New York: Something Else Press, 1968).

GHA   *The Geographical History of America or the Relation of Human Nature to the Human Mind* (New York: Random House, 1936; repr. with new introduction by William H. Gass, New York: Vintage Books, 1973). Although the text of the Vintage edition has not been reset, the addition of Gass's introduction means that the pagination is not the same as that of the 1936 edition. References in this collection of essays are to the 1973 printing, unless otherwise specified.

GS–CVV   *The Letters of Gertrude Stein and Carl Van Vechten*, ed. Edward Burns (New York: Columbia University Press, 1986) 2 vols.

HTW   *How To Write* (Paris: Plain Edition, 1931; repr. New York: Something Else Press, 1973; repr. with new introduction by Patricia Meyerowitz, New York: Dover, 1975).

HWW   *How Writing Is Written*, vol. II of the Previously Uncollected Works of Gertrude Stein, ed. Robert Bartlett Haas (Los Angeles: Black Sparrow Press, 1974).

Ida   *Ida A Novel* (New York: Random House, 1941; repr. New York: Cooper Square, 1971; repr. New York: Vintage Books, 1972).

LGB   *A Long Gay Book*, in *Matisse Picasso and Gertrude Stein with two shorter stories* (Paris: Plain Edition, 1933; repr. Barton, Berlin and Millerton: Something Else Press, 1972).

LIA   *Lectures in America* (New York: Random House, 1935; repr. with introduction by Wendy Steiner, Boston, Mass.: Beacon Press, 1985).

MOA   *The Making of Americans* (Paris: Contact Editions, 1925; repr. New York, Frankfurt-am-Main and Villefranche-sur-mer: Something Else Press, 1966).

MOUA   *The Mother of Us All*, in Gertrude Stein, *Last Operas and Plays*, ed. with an introduction by Carl Van Vechten (New York: Random House, 1949; repr. New York: Vintage Books, 1975) pp. 52–88.

N   *Narration* (Chicago: University of Chicago Press, 1935; repr. 1969).

NTY   *A Novel of Thank You*, vol. VIII of the Yale Edition of the Unpublished Writings of Gertrude Stein (New Haven, Conn.: Yale University Press, 1958; repr. New York: Books for Libraries Press, 1969).

O&P   *Operas and Plays* (Paris: Plain Edition, 1932).

PL   *Painted Lace and Other Pieces [1914–1937]*, vol. v of the Yale Edition of the Unpublished Writings of Gertrude Stein (New Haven, Conn.: Yale University Press, 1955; repr. New York: Books for Libraries Press, 1969).

P&P   *Portraits and Prayers* (New York: Random House, 1934).

QED   *Q. E. D.* [first published in 1950 as *Things as They Are*], in *Fernhurst, Q. E. D., and Other Early Writings* (New York: Liveright, 1971).

RAB   *Reflection on the Atomic Bomb*, vol. I of the Previously Uncollected Writings of Gertrude Stein, ed. Robert Bartlett Haas (Los Angeles: Black Sparrow Press, 1973).

SIM   *Stanzas in Meditation and Other Poems [1929–1933]*, vol. VI of the Yale Edition of the Unpublished Writings of Gertrude Stein (New Haven, Conn.: Yale University Press, 1956; repr. New York: Books for Libraries Press, 1969).

TB   *Tender Buttons* (New York: Claire Marie, 1914; repr. New York: Haskell House, 1970).

TI   'A Transatlantic Interview – 1946', in *A Primer for the Gradual Understanding of Gertrude Stein*, ed. Robert Bartlett Haas (Los Angeles: Black Sparrow Press, 1973) pp. 15–35.

WAM   'What Are Master-pieces and Why Are There So Few of Them', in *What Are Masterpieces* (Los Angeles: Conference Press, 1940; repr. with added afterword, New York: Toronto, London, Tel Aviv: Pitman, 1970) pp. 81–95.

WIHS   *Wars I Have Seen* (New York: Random House, 1945).

YCAL   Yale Collection of American Literature, Beinecke Rare Book and Manuscript Library, Yale University.

YGS   *The Yale Gertrude Stein*, ed. Richard Kostelanetz (New Haven, Conn., and London: Yale University Press, 1980).

Notes on the Contributors

Charles Caramello teaches English and Comparative Literature at the University of Maryland. He has also been a fellow of the National Humanities Center and of the Center for Humanities at Wesleyan University. He is co-editor of *Performance in Postmodern Culture* (1977) and author of *Silverless Mirrors: Book, Self and Postmodern American Fiction* (1983). His 'Reading Gertrude Stein Reading Henry James: Eros is Eros is Eros is Eros' appeared in the *Henry James Review*, 6, 3 (Spring 1985).

Marianne DeKoven teaches English at Rutgers University. She is the author of several articles on twentieth-century literature and of *A Different Language: Gertrude Stein's Experimental Writing*.

Ulla E. Dydo has taught at Vassar College and at Brooklyn College and is now Professor of English at Bronx Community College, City University of New York. 'Composition as Meditation' is from the book she is writing about Stein's work from 1923 to 1932. She has published 'How to Read Gertrude Stein: The Manuscript of *Stanzas in Meditation*', *Text: Transactions of the Society for Textual Scholarship*, I (1981) 271–303; 'To Have the Winning Language: Texts and Contexts of Gertrude Stein', in Diane Middlebrook and Marilyn Yalom (eds), *Coming to Light: American Women Poets of the Twentieth Century*, 58–73; 'Must Horses Drink? or, "Any Language is Funny if You Don't Understand It"', *Tulsa Studies in Women's Literature*, IV, 2 (Fall 1985) 272–80; and '*Stanzas in Meditation*: The Other Autobiography', *Chicago Review*, 35, 2 (Winter 1985) 4–20.

Susan E. Hawkins, Assistant Professor of English at Oakland University, Rochester, Michigan, has published articles on critical theory, contemporary poetry and the prose poem. Her contribution to this volume will be included in a larger work in progress, *On the Border: The Prose Poem in Postwar America*.

Alan R. Knight is Assistant Professor of English at McGill University. He has published articles and read conference papers on contemporary Canadian literature and on Gertrude Stein. He is now revising for publication his *Explaining Explaining: Refiguring Gertrude Stein's Lectures.*

Robert Martin is Professor of English at Concordia University in Montreal. He is the author of *The Homosexual Tradition in American Poetry* (1979) and *Hero, Captain, and Stranger: Male Friendship, Social Critique, and Literary Form in the Sea Novels of Herman Melville* (1985). He co-edited, with Judith Scherer Herz, *E. M. Forster: Centenary Revaluations* (1982).

Ira B. Nadel, Professor of English at the University of British Columbia, is the author of *Biography: Fiction, Fact and Form* (1984). He has published essays on Dickens, George Eliot, Victorian autobiography and Joyce, and co-edited *The Victorian Muse* (1986). He is writing a study of Joyce and his Jewish circle.

Shirley Neuman is Professor of English at the University of Alberta. She has written articles on autobiography and on modern British and Canadian literature. She is the author of *Gertrude Stein: Autobiography and the Problem of Narration* (1979) and of *Some One Myth: Yeats's Autobiographical Prose* (1982), and co-editor (with Smaro Kamboureli) of *A Mazing Space: Writing Canadian Women Writing* (1986). She is working on a study of Stein's 'novels' to be published by Macmillan.

bpNichol is a poet, prose-writer, and playwright who lives in Toronto. His earlier essay about Gertrude Stein, titled 'some beginning writings on GERTRUDE STEIN'S THEORIES OF PERSONALITY', appeared in *Open Letter*, 2nd ser., 2 (Summer 1972) 41–8.

Marjorie Perloff is Professor of English and Comparative Literature at Stanford University. She has published widely on the subjects of twentieth-century American literature and painting. Her most recent books include *Frank O'Hara: A Critical Introduction* (1977), *Frank O'Hara: A Poet Among Painters* (1977), *The Poetics of Indeterminacy: Rimbaud to Cage* (1982), *The Dance of the Intellect: Studies in the Poetry of the Pound Tradition* (1985) and *The Futurist Moment: Avant-Garde, Avant-Guerre, and the Language of Rupture* (1986).

Henry M. Sayre, whose PhD is in American literature, now teaches Art History at Oregon State University, where he is Assistant

Professor. He writes about cultural history and is the author of *WCW: The Visual Text of William Carlos Williams* (1980) and of *The Object of Performance: The American Avant-Garde since 1970* (1987). He is also co-editor of a forthcoming anthology, *The Line in Postmodern Poetry*.

Neil Schmitz is Professor of English and American Literature at the State University of New York at Buffalo, and has also taught at the University of Sussex. He is the author of essays on contemporary fiction and on nineteenth-century literature as well as of several essays on Gertrude Stein. His *Of Huck and Alice: Humorous Writing in American Literature* (1983) principally considers Mark Twain and Gertrude Stein.

Stephen Scobie, poet and critic, is Professor of English at the University of Victoria, where he teaches Canadian Literature and Modern Literature. He is the author of *Leonard Cohen* (1978), of *bpNichol: What History Teaches* (1984), and of *Sheila Watson and her Works* (1985). He is now working on a study of the connections between experimental painting and writing in the twentieth century.

Introduction

SHIRLEY NEUMAN AND IRA B. NADEL

From 1902–3, when she began drafting passages of *The Making of Americans* and writing *Q. E. D.*, to 1946, when she completed *The Mother of Us All*, Gertrude Stein made literature: many portraits (and perhaps an occasional prayer), short stories, children's stories and detective stories, novels, poems, operas and plays, essays and lectures, geography, art criticism, autobiographies and diaries, and even a nightclub skit and a valentine. Writers as various as Ford Madox Ford, E. M. Forster, Robert Graves, James Joyce, Wyndham Lewis, T. S. Eliot, and Edith Sitwell, Ernest Hemingway, Sherwood Anderson, Scott Fitzgerald, Thornton Wilder, Dashiell Hammett, Mina Loy, Laura Riding and Edmund Wilson acknowledged – sometimes gladly, sometimes grudgingly, and with varying combinations of admiration, bewilderment and malice – the energy and influence she exerted on modernism. Yet, when we look to the interest publishers showed in her work during most of her life, to her sales, or to her critical reception, we are hard put to document that influence. Indeed, Gertrude Stein is among the very best examples of her own assertion that 'Those who are creating the modern composition authentically are naturally only of importance when they are dead' for only then will the audience's understanding have caught up with the artist's perception (*CE*, pp. 8–9). Her contemporaries, she thought, were seldom her contemporaries; most of them were fifty years behind.

Which is not to say that Gertrude Stein has not continually exerted influence during the last fifty years: among those for whom her work is central are, in the United States, William Carlos Williams, Robert Duncan and David Antin, Virgil Thomson, John Cage and the musicians and dancers connected with Judson Church, Willem de Kooning and Robert Rauschenberg; and, in Canada, Marshall McLuhan, bpNichol, George Bowering and *The Four Horsemen*. Nor can it be said that she has not always had perceptive critics, even when she was alive; one can cite Thornton Wilder's introductions to *The Geographical History of America* and *Four in America*, or Marcel Brion's 'Le Contrepoint poétique de Gertrude Stein', written during her lifetime, and Donald Sutherland's

Gertrude Stein: A Biography of her Work,[1] written in the years immediately following her death. But it is true to say that, while some poets, musicians, dancers and painters have known how to read Stein and have used that reading to further their own work, most critics have not known how to deal with Stein. They have written to justify negative and uncomprehending reactions to her work, or they have focused on the more 'comprehensible' pieces – *Three Lives* and *The Autobiography of Alice B. Toklas* – or they have decided instead to write about one of the canonised modernists, about Joyce or Eliot, about Hemingway or Faulkner.

This began to change markedly during the 1970s, fifty years after the middle decade of Stein's literary career: Leon Katz's 1963 PhD dissertation studying Gertrude Stein's notebooks for *The Making of Americans* began to be widely cited by a growing group of Stein scholars and became an index of the importance of manuscript research to Stein studies; Richard Bridgman undertook to reassemble all of Stein's many works in a chronological critical reading that demonstrated the interconnectedness of their literary preoccupations; Edward Burns edited *Gertrude Stein on Picasso* and there were major museum catalogues evaluating Stein's position among cubist painters; and James Mellow gave us the most extensively researched biography of Stein we have to date.[2] This scholarship proved doubly effective in dispelling a good deal of the atmosphere of hermeticism that had always clung to Stein's work. It gave us essential information about how Stein wrote and about the ostensible referential content, the objects and people and events, that surface so discontinuously in her work. But at the same time, with that information available to her readers and critics, they became less distracted by the ostensible references of her writing, and freer to turn their attention to her actual subject, her long meditation on language and writing, freer both to situate her within the major cultural movements of her time and to begin to describe her poetics. That new freedom shows itself not only in the works just cited, but also in many other studies from the same period: by the end of the decade David Lodge had re-evaluated Stein's place in the metaphor/metonymy typology of modernist and postmodernist fiction; Wendy Steiner had written a major study, bringing together archival research and Russian formalist criticism, of Stein's literary portraits; Paul Alkon, James Breslin and Shirley Neuman had variously read the autobiographies as attempts to dismantle concepts of identity and the subject; Neil Schmitz had presented

Stein as a postmodernist; and Jane Rule, Catharine Stimpson and Elizabeth Fifer had given us important feminist readings of Stein's *oeuvre* and her literary reputation.[3]

What made these new looks at Stein possible, however, was not only scholars' new and growing body of information about her life, her milieu and her writing practices, but the new critical discourse that was becoming current. Since the early 1970s, three trends in criticism and theory – all three of which figure in major ways in this collection – have helped us immeasurably in understanding Stein. One is the contribution of feminist criticism and theory to recent Stein studies: it provides a context in which to understand the domestic and personal aspects of her writing, it has enabled us to approach some of the evasions and concealments of her work, and, by politicising our analyses of the relationship of language, cultural power and gender, it has contributed to our understanding of the reasons for her critical reception among the other modernist writers.[4]

A second aid to Stein studies has been our relatively recent familiarity with the work of twentieth-century linguists. Ferdinand de Saussure, early in Stein's career, had turned his attention from *what* words signify to *how* they signify. By focusing on semiotics rather than on semantics, by positing the sign as a relationship of signifier to signified in which the signified was a concept and in which every sign pointed to another sign rather than to an origin, Saussure called referentiality into question. Or, as Henry Sayre says in this collection about Stein: 'the structure of representation . . . [and] not what is represented itself' became Saussure's subject and one we now recognise as also Stein's. Had scholars had Saussure's work available to them before its publication in the 1950s, and had the linguistic observations of the Russian formalists not had to wait for the mediation of Roman Jakobson for their impact on Western literary criticism, we would certainly have been much quicker to articulate Stein's relation to language.[5]

The third factor in our rereading of Gertrude Stein's work is the dissemination of poststructuralist theory and practice in all the arts. That theory has given critics a conceptual framework and a terminology with which to talk about what had seemed most frustratingly unnameable in Stein's work. Not a few of us, confronted with the deferral of meaning postulated by a linguistic theory which sees the sign as endlessly displaced by another sign, and with the poststructuralist subversion of the subject into a series of distinctive linguistic events, have had an experience of *déjà vu, déjà lu*, have realised that the theory was not as new as it sounded, that 'Stein did that!' What poststructuralist theory did was let us begin to *name* what has seemed most problematic in Gertrude Stein's writing: her distinction between human nature and the human mind, her refusal to write plots that go somewhere, the flagrant discontinuousness and repetitiveness of much of her writing, the fact that the beauty of her work cannot be found in 'wholeness, harmony and radiance'.[6] In Wendy Steiner's words, 'the training in paradoxical thinking that pop art and deconstruction recently have provided tends to normalise Stein's writing to a striking extent'.[7] We no longer read Stein as an isolated genius or as an eccentric; instead, we begin to understand not only her relation to cubism but also her connections to the movements in literature and the visual arts which preceded her and which came after her. We discover that 'modernism' is more varied than we had previously believed, and that the distinctions between modernism and postmodernism are not nearly so sharp as those contemporary writers and artists rebelling against their 'modernist' precursors would have us believe. In short, we discover another tradition of modernism and enlarge our understanding of both literary history and of the writers who created that other tradition.[8]

Gertrude Stein and the Making of Literature attests, by its very existence, to the fact that the Stein scholarship and the critical theory of the 1970s and 1980s have changed the reception of her work. More than fifty years after Stein became famous for publishing a work her readers *could* understand, even though the fact that she had written it troubled *her*, a major press has published, for the first time in the history of her critical reception, a collection of new essays about her work.[9] This volume of essays itself comes out of three prior discussions from among the many in which Gertrude Stein now figures as central. The first of these was a conference, the programme of which was planned by Professors Martha Banta and Karen Rowe, that was held at the University of California at Los Angeles in November 1984. Titled 'Considering Gertrude Stein: The Importance of her Writing and her Influence on Literature and Art', it was the occasion for which the essays of Henry Sayre, Marjorie Perloff and Neil Schmitz, now collected here, were written. Six weeks later, at the 1984 Modern Language Association meetings in Washington, Marianne DeKoven and Ira B. Nadel first presented their essays, collected here, at a session organised by the present editors and devoted to Gertrude Stein. And Stein figured prominently at another MLA session, titled 'Postmodernism' and held in Chicago in 1985, at which Charles Caramello presented the paper that opens this collection.

These essays, and the others collected here, share in that scholarly knowledge and literary theory which has increasingly enabled us to understand how we must *read* Stein and at the same time add to that gratifying understanding. What Stein meant by *writing* – the ways she worked, her relationship to the language she used, and the ways the work itself demands to be read – is the subject of Ulla E. Dydo's essay 'Composition as Meditation' (Ch. 4). Marjorie Perloff (Ch. 5) and Marianne DeKoven (Ch. 2) each confront the Stein myth with the Stein *oeuvre* so as to demonstrate *how not* to read her as well as *how* to read her. Comparing passages in the autobiographies with Marty Martin's play *Gertrude Stein Gertrude Stein Gertrude Stein*, Marjorie Perloff also reads Stein with scrupulous attention to the style of the autobiographies and the nuanced information it conveys. Marianne DeKoven confronts earlier versions of the persistent myths surrounding Stein in order to account for the reception of her work and to resituate it in the contexts of modernism and feminism.

The issues of literary history and literary theory, raised in the context of literary canons by Marianne DeKoven, reappear in other contexts in many of the essays. Where Ira B. Nadel, for example (in Ch. 6), presents Henry James as Stein's precursor, other contributors concern themselves with her relation to the cultural movements initiated by *her* contemporaries and with her influence on *our* contemporaries: Charles Caramello (Ch. 1) discusses her relationship to modernism and postmodernism; Stephen Scobie, in his discussion of *A Long Gay Book* (Ch. 7), re-examines the metaphor/metonymy distinction and the influence on Stein of cubism; and Henry M. Sayre (Ch. 3) first places her work in relation to cubism and then places contemporary trends in American music, dance and visual art in relation to her work.

Each of the scholarly and critical developments noted above figures in these essays. Attention to Gertrude Stein's manuscripts and to the order of their composition underlies Ulla E. Dydo's reading of an interrelated group of Stein texts from the late twenties and early thirties; it also lets Shirley Neuman (Ch. 11) reconstruct the relationship of *Doctor Faustus Lights the Lights* to *Ida A Novel*. Feminist theory leads to particular insights in nearly all these essays and it provides a large part of the conceptual framework, the discursive practice and the critical insights of the essays by Marianne DeKoven, Susan E. Hawkins (Ch. 8) and Robert K. Martin (Ch. 13). The importance of semiotic analysis to our understanding of Stein is reinscribed in different ways in three essays: Stephen Scobie uses Roman Jakobson's metaphor/ metonymy distinction in a reconsideration of the relation of Stein's writing to cubism; Alan R. Knight (Ch. 10) uses Peirce's speech-act theory in combination with recent work on the manifesto as genre to provide a context for the discussion of Stein's lectures; and the issues of representation and *re*-presentation foregrounded by Saussure's analysis of the function of the sign are essential to Henry Sayre's positioning of Stein in relation to cubism and to postmodernism. The configurations of poststructuralist theory, like those of feminism, repeatedly inform the insights of these essays and are also the subject of Charles Caramello's essay 'Gertrude Stein as Exemplary Theorist' and of the meditation on the concept of *difference* which is central to the arguments of Neil Schmitz (Ch. 9) and of Henry M. Sayre, both of which present Stein as a postmodernist writer.

Several of this volume's critics give us detailed readings of individual Stein works: Susan E. Hawkins looks at the syntax of *Tender Buttons*; Stephen Scobie discusses passages from *A Long Gay Book*; Neil Schmitz shows us the differing pleasures of garden verse in *Stanzas in Meditation*; Alan R. Knight reads 'What Are Masterpieces and Why Are There so Few of Them' as a manifesto; Shirley Neuman interprets *Doctor Faustus Lights the Lights* in relation to other works of the same period from which it was drawn and to the Faust tradition in opera; bpNichol (Ch. 12) reads the first pages of *Ida A Novel* as Stein always asked to be read, word by word, with concentration; and Robert K. Martin places *The Mother of Us All* in the context of Gertrude Stein's understanding of American history and feminism.

Finally, Gertrude Stein herself has the last word (Ch. 14). 'Realism in Novels' and 'American Language and Literature', published here in their entirety and in English for the first time, present some of the literary-historical conclusions she drew from *her* reading. 'A Poem about the end of the war', previously unpublished, leaves you the readers, beginning again, differently reading Gertrude Stein's words. As she herself so often wrote, 'Welcome'.

Notes

1. Thornton Wilder, Introduction to Gertrude Stein, *The Geographical History of America Or The Relation of Human Nature to the Human Mind* (New York: Random House, 1936) pp. 7–14, and Introduction to *FIA*, pp. v–xxvii; Marcel Brion, 'Le Contrepoint poétique de Gertrude Stein', *Echanges*, III (June 1930) 122–8; Donald Sutherland, *Gertrude Stein: A Biography of her Work* (New Haven, Conn.: Yale University Press, 1951).

2. Leon Katz, 'The First Making of *The Making of Americans:* A Study Based on Gertrude Stein's Notebooks and Early Versions of her Novel (1902–08)' (Ph.D. dissertation, Columbia University, 1963); Richard Bridgman, *Gertrude Stein in Pieces* (New York: Oxford University Press, 1970); Edward Burns (ed.), *Gertrude Stein on Picasso* (New York: Liveright, 1970); *Four Americans in Paris: The Collection of Gertrude Stein and her Family* (New York: Museum of Modern Art, 1970); *Gertrude Stein and Picasso and Juan Gris* (Ottawa: National Gallery of Art, 1971 [courtesy of the Museum of Modern Art, New York]); James R. Mellow, *Charmed Circle: Gertrude Stein and Company* (New York: Praeger, 1974).

3. David Lodge, 'Gertrude Stein', *The Modes of Modern Writing: Metaphor, Metonymy, and the Typology of Modern Literature* (Ithaca, NY: Cornell University Press, 1977) pp. 144–55; Wendy Steiner, *Exact Resemblance to Exact Resemblance: The Literary Portraiture of Gertrude Stein* (New Haven, Conn.: Yale University Press, 1978); Paul K. Alkon, 'Visual Rhetoric in *The Autobiography of Alice B. Toklas*', *Critical Inquiry*, 1, 4 (June 1975) 849–81; James E. Breslin, 'Gertrude Stein and the Problems of Autobiography', *Georgia Review*, 33, 4 (Winter 1974) 901–13; S. C. Neuman, *Gertrude Stein: Autobiography and the Problem of Narration*, English Literary Studies, 18 (Victoria, BC: University of Victoria, 1979); Jane Rule, 'Gertrude Stein', *Lesbian Images* (1975; repr. New York: Pocket Books, 1976) pp. 64–76; Neil Schmitz, 'Gertrude Stein as Post-Modernist: The Rhetoric of *Tender Buttons*', *Journal of Modern Literature*, 3 (1974) 1203–18; Catharine R. Stimpson, 'The Mind, the Body, and Gertrude Stein', *Critical Inquiry*, 3, 3 (Spring 1977) 489–506; Elizabeth Fifer, 'Is Flesh Advisable? The Interior Theater of Gertrude Stein', *Signs*, 4, 3 (Spring 1979) 472–83.

4. Gertrude Stein figures in a great many contemporary discussions of women's literature; see particularly Stimpson, 'The Mind, the Body, and Gertrude Stein', *Critical Inquiry*, 3, 3; Fifer, 'Is Flesh Advisable?', *Signs*, 4, 3; Carolyn Burke, 'Gertrude Stein, the Cone Sisters, and the Puzzle of Female Friendship', *Critical Inquiry*, 8, 3 (Spring 1982) 543–64; Cynthia Secor, 'Gertrude Stein: The Complex Force of her Femininity', in Kenneth W. Wheeler and Virginia Lee Lussier (eds), *Women, the Arts, and the 1920s in Paris and New York* (New Brunswick), NJ: Transaction Books, 1982) pp. 27–35; Cynthia Secor, 'The Question of Gertrude Stein', in Fritz Fleischmann (ed.), *American Novelists Revisited: Essays in Feminist Criticism* (Boston, Mass.: G. K. Hall, 1982) pp. 299–310; Susan Hastings, 'Two of the Weird Sisters: The Eccentricities of Gertrude Stein and Edith Sitwell', *Tulsa Studies in Women's Literature*, 4, 1 (Spring 1985) 101–23; Catharine R. Stimpson, 'The Somagrams of Gertrude Stein', *Poetics*

Today, 6, 1–2 (1985) 67–80, and 'Reading Gertrude Stein' (review essay), *Tulsa Studies in Women's Literature*, 4, 2 (Fall 1985) 265–72.

5. See Lodge, *The Modes of Modern Writing*, and Steiner, *Exact Resemblance to Exact Resemblance*; also Marianne DeKoven, *A Different Language: Gertrude Stein's Experimental Writing* (Madison: University of Wisconsin Press, 1983); Randa Dubnick, *The Structure of Obscurity: Gertrude Stein, Language, and Cubism* (Chicago and Urbana: University of Illinois Press, 1984); and Jayne L. Walker, *The Making of a Modernist: Gertrude Stein from 'Three Lives' to 'Tender Buttons'* (Amherst: University of Massachusetts Press, 1984).

6. For poststructuralist criticism of Stein see references in DeKoven, *A Different Language*; Dubnick, *The Structure of Obscurity*; and Walker, *The Making of a Modernist*. See particularly the chapters on Gertrude Stein in Neil Schmitz, *Of Huck and Alice: Humorous Writing in American Literature* (Minneapolis: University of Minnesota Press, 1983) pp. 160–240, and Wendy Steiner, Introduction to *LIA*, pp. ix–xxvii.

7. Steiner, Introduction to *LIA*, p. xi.

8. Marjorie Perloff, *The Poetics of Indeterminacy: Rimbaud to Cage* (Princeton, NJ: Princeton University Press, 1981) p. 33; this book is a reassessment and extension of our understanding of modernism to take account of writers such as Stein.

9. One mainstream academic journal, *Twentieth Century Literature*, has devoted a special issue to Gertrude Stein (24, Spring 1978), as have several avant-garde and 'little' magazines: *Widening Circle*, 1, 4 (1973); *white pelican*, 3 (Autumn 1973); *Lost Generation Journal*, 2 (Winter 1974); and *In 'Hui*, 5 (automne 1978) and 0 (1983), supplement titled *Gertrude Stein, Encore*, ed. Jacques Darras. The most interesting of these, in terms of present Stein scholarship and critical theory, are the *white pelican* issue and the two issues of *In 'Hui*. Michael Hoffman (ed.), *Critical Essays on Gertrude Stein* (Boston, Mass.: G. K. Hall, 1986) includes some new essays about Stein and reprints some of the more important essays previously published in journals.

1

Gertrude Stein as Exemplary Theorist

CHARLES CARAMELLO

Gertrude Stein's work presents an acute case of the tension between referentiality and reflexivity that has haunted formalist aesthetics in music, painting and literature for more than a century; and it presents an acute case of the dialogic situation inherent in all literature and salient in modernist literature. One must wonder, then, why a generation of moderns would direct such animus toward Stein and, in effect, direct a generation of critics and reviewers to share in it. One must wonder why the moderns who found Henry James admirably difficult found Stein only obscurely so; why an Eliot would characterise James as having 'a mind so fine that no idea could violate it', by which he meant to compliment James's 'superior intelligence',[1] while a Leo Stein would characterise his sister Gertrude as being 'practically inaccessible to ideas', by which he meant to soften without retracting his judgement of her basic 'stupidity'.[2] One must wonder why sympathetic critics and reviewers such as Edmund Wilson almost invariably would declare Stein's work 'important' but still unreadable;[3] why those unsympathetic would produce exhalations such as this, from a review of her *Four in America*: 'Well, James and Joyce and Sterne are sometimes hard reading, but they make sense for the hard-working reader' – an invocation meant to suggest that Stein makes only, as the review is titled, 'Nonsense'.[4] Although answers are various, we might consider briefly Stein's ideas and her sense of tradition, for both reflect her distance from her fellow moderns.

Stein doubtless would have approved Mallarmé's riposte to Degas, quoted with approval by Valéry, that 'one does not make poetry with ideas, but with *words*'.[5] But she was no ideologue of the autonomous verbal artifact, and she doubtless would have disapproved of MacLeish's dictum that 'A poem should not

1

mean / But be'. Stein meant her works to mean, but she meant them to mean only those ideas won through her struggle with writing itself. As a poet and portraitist, she was committed to exact representation of the object or person observed, and, as a writer of narrative prose, to exact representation of the event or behaviour observed; in each genre, she sought to avoid the intervention of 'remembered' conventions, of constituted knowledge, of what often pass for ideas. But Stein understood representation to mean representation of the thing *being* observed and to entail a reflexive presentation about that observing and about the writing of it. On the one hand, then, Stein was committed to unmediated mimesis; but, on the other hand, she perceived mimesis as a mediation and undertook simultaneous analysis of the mimetic act. On the one hand, she chose the concrete over the abstract and thus seemed devoid of ideas except those she derived from observing things; but, on the other hand, she wrote things that were analysis of that observing and of themselves as writing and that thus appear abstractionist. Stein found in cubism the method that would serve her both as means of representation and as mode of reflexive analysis. She found in it her method not only for developing the ideas she derived from observing things but also for generating and conveying the ideas she was simultaneously developing about the very process in which she was engaged.

This attitude toward ideas reflects the kinds of ideas that Stein tended to develop. She had a coherent view of human psychology derived largely from William James; and she had a coherent view of social relations consistent with it. But Stein the literary practitioner developing ideas about the human psyche and about social relations never departed from Stein the theoretician attempting to derive and to demonstrate the fundamental principles of the strictly contemporaneous twentieth-century writing she determined cubism to be. And this duality of purpose, in turn, reflects the duality of artistic lineage Stein claimed for herself. On the one hand, she announced that 'one can only have one métier as one can only have one language. [My] métier is writing and [my] language is english' (*ABT*, p. 94); she regarded Henry James 'quite definitely as [my] forerunner, he being the only nineteenth century writer who being an american felt the method of the twentieth century' (p. 96); and she often seemed to consider herself the extension of what Leavis eventually would style the 'great tradition' of the English novel. On the other hand, Stein identified three crucial, lateral influences on her work: Flaubert's self-conscious artfulness, Cézanne's attention to 'the realism of the composition' (*TI*, p. 16), and Picasso's analytical reflexivity. In short, Stein placed herself in the lineage of Anglo-American realism, but she also claimed that her French tutors had instructed her in extending that lineage toward a still realistic but highly reflexive cubistic writing.

Without labouring the point, we can say that Stein's attitude toward ideas, the ideas she developed, and the lineage she claimed form a nexus that distinguishes her from her fellow moderns. At once referential and reflexive, Stein's cubism constitutes a method of generating and conveying ideas and conduces to the particular kinds of ideas she developed most fully in her poetry, portraiture and narrative prose. Her cubism thus shares basic functions with the modernist symbolism she repudiated; but it differs fundamentally from it in conception and execution. And Stein's repudiation of modernist symbolism as a compositional basis, in turn, reflects her repudiation of the cultural tradition claimed by the modern symbolists. She rejected the 'mind of Europe' as Eliot explicitly, Pound and Joyce implicitly, understood that entity; and she rejected Eliot's influential model of the individual talent absorbing the vast European tradition and extending it, in theory at least, through an impersonalised, public writing. Stein not only dwelled on the personal and the private, but also refused appeal to a tradition that, needless to say, offered little welcome to a Jewish-American lesbian. In fact, Stein portrayed such appeals as decidedly unmodern and as reasons for the accessibility and the acceptability of the work of her rivals. In *The Autobiography of Alice B. Toklas*, she quotes with approval Picasso's characterisation of Braque and Joyce as 'the incomprehensibles whom anybody can understand' (*ABT*, p. 260), and, extending the characterisation to Hemingway, she specifies the reason for that intelligibility: 'he looks like a modern and he smells of the museums' (p. 266). To smell of the museums is to remember the cultural storehouse of symbols rather than to write what one observes; it is to invoke one's prior knowledge and that of one's audience rather than to develop knowledge by writing; it is to practice cultural conservationism rather than to advance a program of strict contemporaneity.

It does not surprise, then, that Stein's fellow moderns directed animus toward her and, especially, toward her works of imaginative literature. She rejected a broad European tradition in order to claim her place in a narrow Anglo-American lineage of realism, and she repudiated the symbolism she associated with the former in order to practice the cubism she saw as extending the latter. Moreover, she argued aggressively that a woman, herself, could write so importantly with that cubism that she would number among the three geniuses of Alice B. Toklas's acquaintance and among the four geniuses of the twentieth century. What does surprise is our residual animus toward Stein, an animus not entirely mitigated by recent and excellent work on her. One must wonder, that is, why our postmodern generation, theory its collective obsession, esteems Stein's experimentation with received literary genres and with original generic hybrids but continues, by and large, to deem her a muzzy thinker who expounded idiosyncratic opinions from an acoherent theoretical point of view. One must wonder why we accord such privilege to Stein's self-theorising works of imaginative literature but continue to undervalue her self-practising works of literary theory. One must wonder why we have yet to investigate fully Stein's theory of writing as she systematically developed and articulated it in the series of works that begins with her statement of method, *Composition as Explanation* (1926), and her pragmatics of writing, *How To Write* (1931); that continues through her studies in genre and its relation to reception, *Lectures in America* and *Narration* (both published 1935); and that culminates in the sophisticated meditations on aesthetics, psychology and ideology that constitute *Four in America* (composed 1931–4, published posthumously 1947) and *The Geographical History of America or The Relation of Human Nature to the Human Mind* (1936). Although answers are various, we might note briefly their proximity to those we have already considered.

Stein maintained that 'real thinking is conceptions aiming again and again always getting fuller, that is the difference between creative thinking and theorising'.[6] Vintage Stein, this initially opaque remark actually reduces to etymological clarity: 'creative thinking' means the *growth* of ideas through the constant struggle to express concretely not only the meaning of the thing being observed but also the meaning of the manner of observation and the meaning of the mode of its presentation; 'theorising' means the adoption of a *spectatorial*, if not voyeuristic, distance from the thing being observed and from the process of observation and inevitably issues in an abstractionism that Stein regarded as pornographic.[7] The difference is between an iterative process of cognition and a reiterative process of recognition; between an observation of phenomena independent of culturally determined conventions and an observation of phenomena within such 'remembered', and often pernicious, conventions; between a relentless interrogation not only of every concept employed but also of every formulation deployed, down to the merest phoneme and grapheme, and an accedence if not to received concepts then to received formulations that surreptitiously perpetuate these concepts. As Stein eventually would put it, the difference is between, on the one hand, understanding that 'something means anything' and determining which anything a given something might come to mean, and, on the other hand, believing that 'anything means something' and already having determined by one's conceptual or linguistic biases which something a given anything will come to mean.[8] Stein chose 'creative thinking' over 'theorising' in developing her ideas about writing, and she pursued the implications of her choice in ways that have led us to mistake her coherently anti-theoretical programme as simply a theoretically acoherent programme.

Stein's choice, that is, reflects the scientific and philosophical lineage she claimed for herself; and this lineage, in turn, implied to her a method not only for thinking about writing but also for writing about writing. In *Everybody's Autobiography*, Stein notes that William James had taught her that 'science is not a solution and not a problem it is a statement of the observation of things observed' (*EA*, p. 242). As a literary practitioner, Stein was a close observer of sharply delineated phenomena; as a literary thinker, she was a scientific experimenter working within the tradition of American pragmatism. In this limited sense, she was an anti-theoretical theoretician. She perceived writing not as an abstract phenomenon she was observing and analysing from a distance but as the concrete phenomenon she was simultaneously observing, theorising about and practising. She concluded that 'creative thinking' about literature entailed an equally 'creative' writing, a method of composition in which observation and its statement would *develop* simultaneously and, moreover, simultaneously on two levels: experimenter's observation and experimenter's statement of observation made; experimenter's observation of manner of observation and mode of statement and experimenter's statement of manner employed and mode deployed. Such a method would be continuously representational with respect to its creation and continuously reflexive with respect to itself as creation; the theoretical discourse issuing from that method would thus remain wholly concrete, notwithstanding its appearance of abstractionism. On this basis, Stein declared that 'expository writing is so dull because it is all remembered' (*WAM*, p. 90); on this basis, she rejected exposition as a discursive mode just as she rejected symbolism as an expressive mode; on this basis, she practised cubist composition in her theoretical writing just as she practised cubist composition in her imaginative literature.

In sum, Stein claimed an intellectual lineage of experimentalism and pragmatism, and she devised for her works of literary theory a method of composition she thought required by her extension of that lineage. She was not promulgating with this method an abstract metaphysics of writing but was struggling with it to understand and to explain how writing made sense – and was made to make sense – within the concrete socio-historical conditions of her epoch. And this struggle both informed and reflected her gender-based analysis of 'why [it is] that in this epoch the only real literary thinking has been done by a woman' (*GHA*, p. 218). Stein did not aver gratuitously that 'Einstein was the creative philosophic mind of the century and I have been the creative literary mind of the century' (*EA*, pp. 21–2); rather, she associated 'theorising' with patriarchy, with 'too much fathering going on', with fathers 'looming and filling up everything' (*EA*, p. 133) rather than determining through 'creative thinking' and creative writing how a given something comes to mean anything.[9] This feminist aspect of her programme adds ideological point to her claim that she found it 'impossible to put [words] together without sense. I made innumerable efforts to make words write without sense and found it impossible. Any human being putting down words had to make sense out of them' (*TI*, p. 18). Among other things, Stein meant that words carry conventional meanings and that the culturally and politically disenfranchised had best learn precisely how those in power go about constituting and enforcing those meanings. Only by 'creative thinking' can one do so, and only by creative writing can one then make words stop making conventional sense and start making a difference. Until we learn to start making better sense of Stein's words, we shall abet through our conventions for literary theory, our orthodoxies and neo-orthodoxies, one such disenfranchisement of her: the moderns will have dismissed Stein's poetry, portraits and narrative prose as self-regarding obscurantism; we postmoderns will continue to dismiss her theoretical writing as unsystematic rambling, if not quite nonsense.

Notes

1. T. S. Eliot, 'Henry James', *Little Review*, 1918; excerpted in *Selected Prose of T. S. Eliot*, ed. Frank Kermode (New York: Harcourt Brace Jovanovich/ Farrar, Straus and Giroux, 1975) p. 151.
2. Leo Stein, *Journey into the Self*, ed. Edmund Fuller (New York: Crown, 1950); see pp. 142, 149, 298.
3. See, for example, Edmund Wilson's comment on *The Making of Americans* in his *Axel's Castle: A Study in the Imaginative Literature of 1870–1930* (New York: Charles Scribner's Sons, 1931) p. 239.
4. L. A. Sloper, 'Nonsense' (review of *Four in America* by Gertrude Stein) *Christian Science Monitor*, 22 Nov 1947, p. 17.
5. Paul Valéry, 'Poetry and Abstract Thought', *The Art of Poetry*, tr. Denise Folliot, vol. vii of the *Collected Works of Paul Valéry*, Bollingen Series 45 (New York: Pantheon Books, 1958) p. 63.
6. Quoted in Leon Katz and Edward Burns, 'They Walk in the Light', foreword to Gertrude Stein, *Picasso: The Complete Writings* (1970; Boston, Mass.: Beacon Press, 1985) p. 15.
7. See *EA*, p. 127: 'The minute painting gets abstract it gets pornographic.' I would maintain that Stein felt the same way about thinking and about writing.
8. In *Brewsie and Willie*, Stein's last sustained work of prose, two characters propose as the lesson of psychoanalysis and of science that 'anything means something'; one of them, however, rethinks his position: 'Perhaps, said Donald Paul, something means anything, perhaps it's more like that' (*B&W*, p. 58).
9. I am inferring this association from the parabolic discussion of 'avarice', 'nutting', and 'fathering' that occupies pp. 128–39 of *Everybody's Autobiography*.

2

Gertrude Stein and the Modernist Canon

MARIANNE DeKOVEN

In his Introduction to *The Yale Gertrude Stein*, Richard Kostelanetz says that 'no other twentieth-century American author had as much influence as Stein' (*YGS*, p. xxx). However, outside the growing body of academic Stein criticism, Gertrude Stein's public presence, her reputation in any segment of the culture which is aware of her at all, seems to have little to do with her work. Unlike the writers and artists with whom she is generally grouped, she is still perceived as not so much a writer as a 'personality', the centre of one of those nodes of celebrity which are equated with the avant-garde in highbrow mythology. Moreover, the most widely accepted myth of the history of Stein's reputation is less interested in *her*, even as a personality, than in her association with important men: William James, Picasso, Matisse, Apollinaire, Hemingway, Fitzgerald, Wilder, Anderson. This myth begins its narrative with Stein at Harvard, working under James and Hugo Münsterberg. It follows her as she follows brother Leo to Paris and to the early joint purchases of the famous post-impressionist paintings, then to her friendships with Matisse, Picasso, Gris, and the other great male modern painters (Marie Laurencin might also be included these days, last name on the list).

It is easy to imagine a Hollywood Life of Gertrude Stein. We should see her walking through the Paris streets to sit for Picasso in Montmartre, as he painted the famous portrait. She would look pensive, observing the low life of Pigalle, registering the details which she would weave that night into the story of Melanctha. We would see her writing late at night in the atelier at the rue de Fleurus, surrounded by The Paintings; the camera would pan to the Cézanne portrait on the wall and then down to the French schoolchild's composition book in front of her, where the words of *Melanctha* would be scribbled rapidly by her so greatly inspired hand. Almost

8

every biography of Stein, including her own in the voice of Alice Toklas, from which so many of the rest derive, evokes these scenes – Great Moments of Modern Culture – aglow with the sheen of idealised memory.

The myth continues its narrative with the growing fame of the Steins' paintings, the establishment of the Saturday Evenings at the atelier at 27 rue de Fleurus as the most important salon in Paris, the cultural centre of the Western world. As we move through time we see a new generation of post-war American expatriates flocking to Paris (somehow they always flock) and congregating around Gertrude and Alice. We see Gertrude influencing their writing and dubbing them, via Hemingway, 'lost'. The myth jumps another ten years to 1932, when Gertrude writes Alice's famous *Autobiography* – she has been writing steadily all this time but the myth doesn't think it has amounted to much – goes home to America for the first time in thirty years and is a great success: now that she is famous, says the myth, she can drop the defensive posture of unintelligibility and make sense for a change.

In another ten years she dies, widely loved if not entirely respected, with her last words resuscitating the devotion of her post-1932 admirers: 'What is the answer?' she asks on her deathbed. 'But then what is the question?' she replies. That dying statement is an ideal summation and apotheosis of Gertrude Stein in the terms of an official myth, with its stoic courage and devotion to the pursuit of truth, its aphoristic abstraction and epistemological honesty. It has echoes of both William James and eternity, and is such a perfect climax to the Hollywood Life of Gertrude Stein that it is difficult to believe she actually said it, until one remembers her own late concern with public self-creation.

In spite of this myth, it is Stein's work, much more importantly than her influential friendships, that one might think would locate her at the centre of modern literary and intellectual history. To survey the movements with which Stein's work affiliates her is to survey twentieth-century Western culture. Her encoding of lesbian sexual feeling in her experimental work, her undoing of patriarchal portraiture in *The Autobiography of Alice B. Toklas*, the buried anger at female victimisation in *Three Lives*, and her overall, lifelong commitment to freeing language from the hierarchical grammars of patriarchy have made her profoundly important to contemporary feminist experimental writers, represented in journals such as *HOWever* in San Francisco, and to critics working from both

Anglo-American and French feminist perspectives.[1] Her radical experimental writing, again because of its attempts to confront and reform essential structures of conventional language, has lately been of interest also to structuralist critics and to poststructuralists, language critics and poetics theorists.[2] Her connections to modern art, not just to modern artists, have informed a substantial body of criticism.[3] We know from the biographies how important she has been to mainstream American modernism and to American expatriation in Paris. Richard Kostelanetz and Jerome Rothenberg, among others, have documented Stein's crucial role in the development of the avant-garde.[4] Books such as Allegra Stewart's *Gertrude Stein and the Present* and Norman Weinstein's *Gertrude Stein and the Literature of Modern Consciousness*[5] have also demonstrated the centrality to major currents of twentieth-century philosophy of Stein's psychological, linguistic, epistemological, phenomenological and metaphysical thought.

The theoretical concerns which inform her art, no less than her philosophical speculation, put her at the very heart of progressive twentieth-century literature. Her preoccupations with time, language, the relationship between subject and object, the nature of consciousness and knowing, and the ways in which writing can be a model of authentic experience are the primary concerns of both modernism and postmodernism. Crudely, her earliest work is modernist and her later work, as Neil Schmitz and others have shown, is prophetically postmodernist.[6] *Three Lives* and *The Making of Americans* have much in common with the major texts of modernism, concerned as they all are with consciousness-in-time, with individual consciousness set against social backgrounds, and with literature as a large synthesising force. They all alter the form of narrative to coincide with new conceptions of time, consciousness, subjectivity and perception, but they all retain some version of plot, character and theme. In all of them, language is equally an autonomous artistic medium and a system of communication.

In her abolition of the censoring authorial ego, Stein has an important connection to surrealism, which we might put somewhere between the modern and the postmodern. Although Stein rejects both the Freudian subconscious and the idea of automatic writing, and in that sense is anti-surrealist, she does see her writing as proceeding from a state of trance or meditation, and therefore from depths of the mind which are capable of purer, more profound vision than the shallows of 'normal' consciousness. This notion of meditation is also central to experimental theatre, and to the work of American writers such as Kerouac, Burroughs and Baraka.

In her later work, Stein shares with these and other postmodernists a vision of extreme fragmentation, abstraction, non-selectiveness, open-endedness, randomness, flux. She also shares the preoccupation of the *nouveau roman* and of American postmodernists such as William Burroughs with the question of literary mediation: the way in which conventional writing, through its familiarity, prevents instead of enables vision. Stein undertook *matte* or 'zero-degree' writing half a century before Sarraute or Robbe-Grillet, and her verbal collages anticipate Burroughs' efforts to scramble habitual verbal associations by means of what he calls 'cut-up' and 'fold-in'.

No writer's work is more relevant to twentieth-century developments in music and the plastic arts than Stein's: I need only say 'atonal', 'Cage', 'cubism', 'abstract expressionism' to make my point, though many other words could be said as well.[7] Stein herself compares the 'successional' structure of her writing to the structure of film, defending her form by linking it to the representative genre of the twentieth century. And her notion of drama as static spectacle and as pure movement through time and space puts her at the centre of avant-garde theatre, and many of her plays and operas are, in fact, performed off-off-Broadway.

Why, if she is so central, is she so generally perceived as marginal? Why is she lucky, or are we lucky, when she is included in the mainstream modernist canon or syllabus at all, or even in the lesser pantheon of the American experimental tradition?[8] We know, thanks primarily to Catharine Stimpson, how much of the answer to that question is that Stein was a woman and a lesbian.[9] As a woman, Stein has been seen merely as the 'personality', the provider of social glue to hold together the glittering bohemian clan. That she herself took her work seriously may make her more interesting, charming, even quaint, but it need not make the guardians of the canon take her work seriously. However, if it were not for her writing, her reputation as a 'personality' would not have persisted as it has in the public mind. The myth of the interesting-woman-whose-work-can-be-ignored allows the notion that it is her life, and not her art, which supports her reputation. The world thinks of her as a personality, but it would not do so if she were not such an important writer.

Another, equally denigrating female stereotype, connected to

Stein's lesbianism, and the complement of the stereotype of the charming, unthreatening woman whose work can be ignored, has also been used to keep Stein out of the canon-formed and canon-forming syllabus. To some she is the domineering, overbearing witch who pushes her work on the men under her spell, compelling them to think they like it. We see this version of Stein in B. L. Reid's dismissive *Art by Subtraction*, for example, where he says that, charming as she was (and that is a loaded word), he is ultimately glad he did not know her because otherwise he would not be able to be so 'objective' about her work. He implies that male critics who admired Stein's work and were also her friends, such as Thornton Wilder, Sherwood Anderson, Carl Van Vechten and Donald Sutherland, were somehow under her spell, and incapable of arriving at his own 'objective', that is negative, judgement. As he says,

> Not to have known her is indeed in one sense a disqualification, since so much of her contemporary force has been that of her powerful presence. In another sense, not to have known her personally may be a positive qualification of some value; it was as a writer that she wanted to live, and doubtless it is easier, if duller, to focus on her printed page when one is not distracted by her ingratiating and forceful image.[10]

In *A Moveable Feast*,[11] perhaps the most vicious slander of Gertrude Stein in print, and one which has been the basis of all too many judgements of her, Hemingway manages to combine both these myths, and to reveal the deep male fear of lesbianism which is one basis of the second.

Beyond these demeaning female stereotypes are versions of Stein which do not have the same taint of sexism, but which are none the less affected by distortions or inadequacies in male perceptions of women. The two most important, comprehensive studies of Stein to date remain Donald Sutherland's *Gertrude Stein: A Biography of her Work* and Richard Bridgman's *Gertrude Stein in Pieces*.[12] Opposite and equally partial pictures of Stein emerge from these books. Sutherland's book, though full of brilliant analyses of particular works and syntheses of Stein's thought and writing, sees only a strong, confident Stein, the self-proclaimed 'genius'. He accepts her defensive self-aggrandisement unquestioningly. Accordingly, he echoes Stein's peculiar explanations of various developments in her work. He agrees with her, for example, that it is the special nature of the Spanish landscape that leads to the radical change in her style around 1911–12:

> All that being in the air, what precipitated the change for Gertrude Stein was a trip to Granada in 1911. She suddenly rediscovered the visible world. She had been to Spain before, to Granada, she had known Picasso for some time, and she had been looking at paintings intently for a very long while, but this visit was decisive because of the question in her mind about existence as both immediate and final, and because of the nature of the landscape of Spain, which is eminently both immediate and final.[13]

Although this analysis enters ingeniously and fully into Stein's own version of the shift in her style (see *The Autobiography of Alice B. Toklas*, ch. 2), it does not go very far toward a critical account of *Tender Buttons*.

Richard Bridgman, on the other hand, is correctly suspicious of Stein's aggressive insistence on her greatness, and looks behind it, finding much evidence of her insecurity and deep fear of failure: 'The emotional content of Gertrude Stein's apprentice writing deserves sympathetic attention, for it is in the process of taming and exorcising her demons that Gertrude Stein's stylistic course was irrevocably set.'[14] These very valuable insights lead, however, to some distortion. Bridgman puts too much emphasis on an insecure, fearful, self-hating Stein, seeing the strong Stein entirely as a defensive front. Accordingly, he locates the origin of many of her literary innovations exclusively in pathology, discounting the drive to reinvent literary language which propelled her career.

By assenting to Stein's self-aggrandisement and sometimes facile explanations of her work, Sutherland is drawn into some inflated or contorted defences and analyses, many of which make her sound ridiculous, subverting his intentions. Bridgman, on the other hand, often makes her appear a mere victim of neuroses, incapable of sustained purposiveness, whose literary experiments are frequently unintentional results of a pathological inability to write in the normal way. What we need instead of these two contradictory halves is a book-length whole woman: a synthesis that would show us the fear behind the power, the power behind the fear.

Bridgman's title, *Gertrude Stein **in Pieces***, reveals not only his vision of Stein's controlling psychopathology, but also the very condition of her centrality to twentieth-century culture which is, at the same time, the condition of her marginality. Because her *oeuvre* is so multiple, disjunct, important to so many *divergent* movements (as Kostelanetz says, 'her originality was so multifarious' – *YGS*, p. xxxi), she cannot be made to adhere to any single centre. But a centre is precisely, as she might say, what makes canon. Parts of her can fit fairly comfortably into mainstream modernist as well as avant-garde or revisionist canons. *Three Lives*, for example, is often taught, and sometimes even written about, as an atypical but *bona fide* work of impressionist or early modernist fiction. *Tender Buttons* is certainly written about, and sometimes even taught, as a central work in the experimental tradition. A number of Stein's works figure importantly in the growing, fluid body of texts under the rubric of the female tradition. But when we think of Stein whole, and not 'in pieces', we immediately see that she fits neatly nowhere.

If we then put that whole Stein next to any of the consensually accepted modernist (to take the 'central' twentieth-century canon) heroes – Conrad, Joyce, Lawrence, Faulkner, even Woolf; Yeats, Pound, Eliot, Stevens, even HD or Moore – the difference comes into sharper focus. The *oeuvre* of each of those writers can be organised into a hierarchy of great and not-so-great, primary and secondary, weighty and slight, mature and apprentice (like the List of Names itself, these hierarchies will vary in content from critic to critic, providing matter for endless printed and oratorical dispute). For Eliot, to consider (perhaps – none of this can be taken for granted) the clearest instance, 'Prufrock', *The Waste Land* and *Four Quartets* would be on anybody's list of major or great works, 'Ash Wednesday' and 'Gerontion' and perhaps 'Sweeney among the Nightingales' would come next, and the rest of the poems would trail off into the distance, with *Old Possum's Book of Practical Cats* barely visible on the horizon (though that is problematical too, now that the musical *Cats* has entered the culture). Joyce's career orders itself, for our everlasting convenience, into a steady upward progress from *Dubliners* to *Portrait of the Artist* to the culminating *Ulysses*, then over the precipice, for some, into *Finnegans Wake*. Woolf has *To the Lighthouse* and *Mrs Dalloway* for all, *The Waves* for the avant-garde, *A Room of One's Own*, *Three Guineas* and *Orlando* for feminists, and the rest of her writing for the Woolf industry. Critics of modernism read HD's imagist poems, feminists read *Helen in Egypt*. But whether or not their great works appeal to diverse factions of the critical industry, all these heroes have been assimilated as having a few heroic texts – *Lord Jim, Nostromo, Heart of Darkness; Absalom, Absalom!, The Sound and the Fury, Light in August* – followed by a body of lesser writing which we may love but which we do not revere in the same way. It is impossible to order Stein's *oeuvre* into such a hierarchy, not only because everything in her writing works to undermine hierarchy, but because there is no principle of 'the same' running through her writing, no spinal column along which her works could be arranged from head to bottom.

Those works, considered one by one, resist canonisation as well. If we were to try to incorporate her into some version of the mainstream modernist canon, which work(s) should we choose as her *Ulysses*, her *Waste Land*, her *Cantos*? *The Making of Americans* has the proper weightiness, but it is much too anomalous and unassimilable a text, more a *Finnegans Wake* than a *Ulysses*. *Three Lives* seems not to have the proper weightiness, although, in fact, it is a mordant, emotionally loaded, complex text, stylistically highly wrought, masquerading as simple, whimsical, even slight. Moreover – although this perhaps makes it more typical than atypical of heroic modernist texts – its politics of race and class are extremely troubling. *The Autobiography of Alice B. Toklas*, perhaps the best candidate, often seems to be mere gossip, and, as Stein said to Hemingway, remarks are not literature (of course it isn't 'mere' gossip at all, just as *Three Lives* isn't slight, but its complex uses of simplicity, and of anecdotal narrative, extremely fruitful material for feminist analysis, interfere, as women's works so often do, with standard canonisation practice).

Those three works are, however, far more canonisable (if there is no such word, I'm sure, alas, there will be) than the rest of Stein's great writings, which are either radically experimental or of indeterminate genre or both. Think of teaching *Tender Buttons, The Geographical History of America, Four Saints in Three Acts*, or *The Mother of Us All*, not to mention 'Patriarchal Poetry' or 'What Happened', on the same syllabus as *The Sun Also Rises* or *Mrs Dalloway* (I've done it – a great deal of special pleading is required, unless one opts simply to play the record of *Four Saints* and grin beatifically).

The most influential canonisers of modernism (apologies, again, to those who keep themselves lexicographically pure) have either left Stein out altogether, or might as well have,[15] or they have included her as 'personality' and influence first, writer second,[16] or, like Edmund Wilson, they have included her as an extreme point, a boundary which marks the limit of modernist discourse.[17] For Wilson, she is also a failure in her radical work, which he sees as a fruition of modernism's inherent corruption (it is very instructive to consider the female iconography involved in Wilson's use of Stein as a contradictory sign simultaneously of marginality – something eccentric to the modernist core – and of negative essence, embodying the rottenness of that core, which is otherwise more difficult to perceive).

My argument now seems to be pointing to the straightforward conclusion that Stein has been 'left out' by the powerful male canonisers and therefore, to the extent that her exclusion from major twentieth-century canons has been the result of patriarchal politics and not of her own intractable resistance to canonisation, she should in future be 'included in'. I intend, however, either to stop short of, or to go beyond, that satisfying but pat conclusion, because it distorts and glosses the double, contradictory nature of Stein's actual relation to canons: simultaneously inside and outside, at the centre and in the margin. Again, because Stein is central to so many divergent twentieth-century cultural phenomena, she inevitably becomes marginal or eccentric to any unified, coherent tradition.

Richard Kostelanetz's Introduction to *The Yale Gertrude Stein*[18] gives us an excellent objective correlative of Stein's double relationship to major twentieth-century canons. Throughout his essay, he alternates between what we might call canonising and anti-canonising gestures. He opens with a clear, strong anti-canonising gesture: 'The principal reason for such continued incomprehension [of Stein's works] is that her experiments in writing were conducted apart from the major developments in modern literature' (*YGS*, p. xiii). This statement is followed, however, by a series of equally clear, strong canonising gestures:

Stein's biggest book [*The Making of Americans*] also stands as an epitome of that colossal, uneven, digressive, excessive, eccentric masterpiece that every great American innovative artist seems to produce at least once. Its peers in this respect are Walt Whitman's *Leaves of Grass*, Ezra Pound's *Cantos*, Faulkner's *Absalom, Absalom!*, and Charles Ives's Fourth Symphony.   (p. xvii)

In this respect [structural flattening] in particular, Stein clearly precedes the formally uninflected, counter-hierarchical prose of, say, Samuel Beckett and Alain Robbe-Grillet.   (p. xviii)

Historically, we can see that the use of such forms placed her among the first imaginative writers to represent the modern awareness of discontinuous experience.   (pp. xviii–xix)

Though working apart from the French symbolists, she realized their theoretical ideal of a completely autonomous language – creating a verbal reality apart from extrinsic reality.   (p. xxii)

Stein also [as in modern music] recapitulated in literature the evolution of modernist painting.   (p. xxiii)

Stein foreshadowed the contemporary avant-garde principle of making art that is either much more *or* much less than before.
    Her essays also [like her plays] were unlike anything written in that genre before.   (p. xxvi)

These statements not only include Stein in the canon of the avant-garde, they place her at the origin of that canon.
    In his concluding paragraphs, Kostelanetz develops for Stein two contradictory relationships to the canonical centre of American literature: she is simultaneously, or in rapid alternation, a wrongfully neglected Great American Writer and a self-constituted Outsider (of course, Great American Writers are also self-constituted Outsiders,[19] but Kostelanetz is not invoking that paradigm here). On the one hand, Stein at fifty-nine was 'one of the most respected writers in the English language' (*YGS*, p. xxix), the 'excellences' of her poetry 'are still rarely acknowledged by poetry critics and anthologies' (ibid.), the 'special qualities' of her 'more extraordinary' works 'have never been exceeded', and, resoundingly, 'no other twentieth-century American author had as much influence as Stein; and none influenced his or her successors in as many ways' (p. xxx). On the other hand, and in the same pages, 'Largely because Stein's writings were so unconventional, even in terms of the developments of literary modernism, it took her long, far too long, to get them into public print' (p. xxix); and, resoundingly, 'most of her innovations went against the dominant grain of literary modernism' (p. xxxi; Kostelanetz might seem to be

distinguishing between modernism and the avant-garde here, an important distinction, which he writes about elsewhere, and which American critics often overlook;[20] however, he uses the terms loosely and somewhat interchangeably in this particular text).

Both of Kostelanetz's versions of Stein's relationship to canonisation are accurate. Stein occupies, has always occupied, and in fact constitutes precisely that middle ground between (male) canonical centre and (female) margin which deconstructs (puts into question, makes visible) the hierarchical–idealist duality of centre and margin itself, a middle ground that feminist critics such as Christine Froula invoke as a genuine non-separatist, non-self-excluding and therefore non-self-defeating) antidote to patriarchal cultural hegemony:

> But this 'pregnant' juxtaposition [of *Paradise Lost* and Isak Dinesen's 'The Blank Page'] points beyond static dichotomies to active rereadings of the texts that have shaped our traditions alongside those that have been repressed and toward questioning and reimagining the structures of authority for a world in which authority need no longer be 'male' and coercive nor silence 'female' and subversive, in which, in other words, speech and silence are no longer tied to an archetypal – and arbitrary – hierarchy of gender.[21]

Stein's *oeuvre* constitutes just such an 'active rereading', just such a 'questioning and reimagining', just such an unsynthesised dialectic of canonical and repressed, centre and margin, male and female, speech and silence, authority and subversion. Perhaps we are able to postulate this middle ground at the theoretical level precisely because it already exists, and has existed for half a century, in Stein's practice. If we insist either that she be squeezed into existing canons, or that she remain subversively outside them, we are wasting the opportunity she has given us to change our minds: to re-form not only literature itself, but also the politics of literature, as so many of us now know we must.

Notes

1. See Catharine R. Stimpson, 'The Mind, the Body, and Gertrude Stein', *Critical Inquiry*, 3, 3 (Spring 1977) 489–506; Elizabeth Fifer, 'Is Flesh Advisable? The Interior Theater of Gertrude Stein', *Signs*, 4, 3 (Spring 1979) 472–83; Carolyn Burke, 'Gertrude Stein, the Cone Sisters, and the Puzzle of Female Friendship', *Critical Inquiry*, 8, 3 (Spring 1982) 543–64; Gloria Orenstein, 'Natalie Barney's Parisian Salon: The Savoir Faire and Joie de Vivre of a Life of Love and Letters', *Moon*, 5, 1–2 (1980) 76–94; Cynthia Secor, 'Gertrude Stein: The Complex Force of her Femininity', in Kenneth W. Wheeler and Virginia Lee Lussier (eds), *Women, the Arts, and the 1920s in Paris and New York*, intro. Catharine R. Stimpson (New Brunswick, NJ: Transaction Books, 1982) pp. 27–35, and 'The Question of Gertrude Stein', in Fritz Fleischmann (ed.), *American Novelists Revisited: Essays in Feminist Criticism* (Boston, Mass.: G. K. Hall, 1982) pp. 299–310; Neil Schmitz, 'Portrait, Patriarchy, Mythos: The Revenge of Gertrude Stein', *Salmagundi*, 40 (Winter 1978) 69–91, and Marianne DeKoven, *A Different Language: Gertrude Stein's Experimental Writing* (Madison: University of Wisconsin Press, 1983).
2. See Wendy Steiner, *Exact Resemblance to Exact Resemblance: The Literary Portraiture of Gertrude Stein* (New Haven, Conn.: Yale University Press, 1978); Randa Dubnick, *The Structure of Obscurity: Gertrude Stein, Language, and Cubism* (Urbana and Chicago: University of Illinois Press, 1984); Marjorie Perloff, 'Poetry as Word-System: The Art of Gertrude Stein', in *The Poetics of Indeterminacy: Rimbaud to Cage* (Princeton, NJ: Princeton University Press, 1981) pp. 67–108; William Gass, 'Gertrude Stein and the Geography of the Sentence', *The World within the World* (Boston, Mass.: Nonpareil, 1979) pp. 63–123; Neil Schmitz, 'The Gaiety of Gertrude Stein' and 'The Genius of Gertrude Stein', in *Of Huck and Alice: Humorous Writing in American Literature* (Minneapolis: University of Minnesota Press, 1983) pp. 160–240; and again DeKoven, *A Different Language*.
3. See most recently the work of Perloff, Steiner, Dubnick, and Jayne Walker, *The Making of a Modernist: Gertrude Stein from 'Three Lives' to 'Tender Buttons'* (Amherst: University of Massachusetts Press, 1984).
4. Richard Kostelanetz, *Twenties in the Sixties: Previously Uncollected Critical Essays* (Westport, Conn.: Greenwood Press, 1979); Jerome Rothenberg, *Revolution of the Word* (New York: Seabury Press, 1974).
5. Allegra Stewart, *Gertrude Stein and the Present* (Cambridge, Mass.: Harvard University Press, 1967); Norman Weinstein, *Gertrude Stein and the Literature of Modern Consciousness* (New York: Frederick Ungar, 1970).
6. See particularly Schmitz's 'Gertrude Stein as Post-Modernist: The Rhetoric of *Tender Buttons*', *Journal of Modern Literature*, 3, 5 (July 1974) 1203–18.
7. Kostelanetz makes these points at greater length in his Introduction to *The Yale Gertrude Stein*.
8. Though Kostelanetz, in his Introduction, considers the 'default with Stein . . . an index of the more general failure of American criticism to acknowledge its native experimental tradition' (*YGS*, p. xxx), I find

Stein's relation to that tradition just as troubled as her relation to mainstream modernism.

9. See Stimpson, 'The Mind, the Body, and Gertrude Stein', *Critical Inquiry*, 3, 3.
10. B. L. Reid, *Art by Subtraction: A Dissenting Opinion of Gertrude Stein* (Norman: University of Oklahoma Press, 1958) p. x.
11. Ernest Hemingway, *A Moveable Feast* (New York: Charles Scribner's Sons, 1964).
12. Donald Sutherland, *Gertrude Stein: A Biography of her Work* (New Haven, Conn.: Yale University Press, 1951); Richard Bridgman, *Gertrude Stein in Pieces* (New York: Oxford University Press, 1970).
13. Sutherland, *Gertrude Stein: A Biography*, pp. 69–70.
14. Bridgman, *Gertrude Stein in Pieces*, p. 27.
15. I have in mind particularly Irving Howe, Hugh Kenner and Richard Ellmann.
16. Frederick J. Hoffman, *The Twenties: American Writing in the Postwar Decade* (New York: Free Press, 1949), and Roger Shattuck, *The Banquet Years* (New York: Vintage Books, 1955).
17. See Edmund Wilson, *Axel's Castle: A Study in the Imaginative Literature of 1870–1930* (New York: Charles Scribner's Sons, 1931), ch. 7.
18. An earlier version of this essay appeared in *The Hollins Critic*, XII, 3 (June 1975), titled 'Gertrude Stein: The New Literature'.
19. See Richard Poirier, *A World Elsewhere: The Place of Style in American Literature* (New York: Oxford University Press, 1966).
20. See Kostelanetz, *Twenties in the Sixties*; also Peter Bürger, *Theory of the Avant-Garde*, trs. Michael Shaw (Minneapolis: University of Minnesota Press, 1984).
21. Christine Froula, 'When Eve Reads Milton: Undoing the Canonical Economy', in Robert von Hallberg (ed.) *Canons* (Chicago: University of Chicago Press, 1984) p. 171. See also Rachel Blau duPlessis and Members of Workshop 9, 'For the Etruscans: Sexual Difference and Artistic Production – The Debate over a Female Aesthetic', in Hester Eisenstein and Alice Jardine (eds), *The Future of Difference* (Boston, Mass.: G. K. Hall, 1980) pp. 128–56; and Elaine Showalter, 'Feminist Criticism in the Wilderness', *Critical Inquiry*, 8, 2 (Winter 1981) 179–205.

3

The Artist's Model: American Art and the Question of Looking like Gertrude Stein

HENRY M. SAYRE

Everybody knows the story: how '[p]ractically every afternoon' (*ABT*, p. 60) during the fall, winter and spring of 1905–6 Gertrude Stein would cross Paris, usually on foot, to Picasso's littered studio in the Bateau Lavoir on the rue Ravignan, and there pose until evening, sitting in an old armchair with one of its arms missing, as Picasso ever so slowly progressed with his work on her likeness; how at first Picasso's mistress Fernande would read to Stein from the *Fables* of La Fontaine until Gertrude began to occupy herself with her own compositions; how, as she said, she 'meditated and made sentences' (*ABT*, p. 60), as she posed, writing in her mind the second story of *Three Lives*, 'Melanctha'; how she came, she said, 'to like posing, the long still hours followed by a long dark walk [which] intensified the concentration with which she was creating her sentences' (*ABT*, pp. 61–2), a kind of composition which she characterised in *The Autobiography of Alice B. Toklas* as distinguished by its 'exactitude, austerity, absence of variety in light and shade, . . . a symmetry which has a close analogy to the symmetry of the musical figure of Bach' (p. 62); how after some eighty or ninety sittings Picasso suddenly became irritated, painted out her head, and departed with Fernande for Gosol in Spain, leaving the painting to sit all summer in the Bateau Lavoir, its face a great blank; how, when he returned some months later, he completed it, this time without Stein to sit for him – she was with her brother Leo in Fiesole – her face taking on the character of a mask, perhaps Iberian; how this new face marked the outbreak of a new style in Picasso's art – 'In . . . the portrait of Gertrude Stein', Stein wrote, 'Picasso passed

21

from the Harlequin, the charming early italian period to the intensive struggle which was to end in cubism' (p. 66) – but this new style also made for a lack of coherence in the portrait which delighted Stein but offended her brother Leo, who felt Picasso should have reworked the rest of the picture to match the face; and how, finally, a year later, Alice B. Toklas told Picasso the first time she met him how much she liked his portrait of Gertrude Stein – 'Yes, he said, everybody says that she does not look like it but that does not make any difference, she will' (p. 14; see Plate 1).[1]

Like all such stories, this one is legend because it tells so much not only about the cultural milieu in which cubism was born, but also about the aesthetic basis of the movement itself. For the story embodies the shift, in Picasso's art, from a style of painting that had been primarily retinal to one that was becoming more and more cerebral, the actual Gertrude Stein disappearing in favour of Picasso's 'idea' of her.[2] And this new Gertrude Stein, moreover, her features reduced to such essential form that she resembles the archaic Iberian heads Picasso had seen that summer in Spain, seems to be a realisation of Cézanne's imperatives, everywhere current at the time, especially among the Bateau Lavoir crowd: 'All appearance is scattered,' he had said, 'nature is always the same'; or, even more to the point, 'Nature is more depth than surface, the colors are the expression on the surface of this depth, they rise up from the roots of the world.'[3] Picasso seemed to be tapping Stein's depth, detailing what Stein would call in *The Making of Americans* the 'bottom nature' of her being, a bottom nature she apparently shared with Picasso himself since during that prophetic fall of 1906 he painted his own self-portrait in the same style. Recalling this period in 'The Gradual Making of *The Making of Americans*' Stein would say,

> I began to get enormously interested in hearing how everybody said the same thing over and over again with infinite variations but over and over again until finally if you listened with great intensity you could hear it rise and fall and tell all that there was inside them, not so much by the actual words they said or the thoughts they had but the movement of their thoughts and words endlessly the same and endlessly different.   (*LIA*, p. 138)

It would be easy to extend Stein's thinking here to the example of Picasso and Braque – one needs only to substitute a rhetoric of 'seeing' and 'painting' for her 'hearing' and 'saying' – especially given the fact that Picasso and Braque were painting virtually the same things in these years. Such a rhetoric of sameness, the depiction of reality as a system of elemental likenesses repeated again and again, extends, in fact, from Cézanne's dictum, 'Deal with nature as cylinders, spheres, cones',[4] to Stein's own portrait of Picasso:

> This one was working and something was coming then, something was coming out of this one then. This one was one and always there was something coming out of this one and always there had been something coming out of this one. . . . This one was one who was working   (*P&P*, p. 18)

– with the phrase 'one who was working' repeated thirty-eight times in one form or another, 'one having something coming out of him' twenty-eight times, all in a matter of 900 words. Yet it is not, merely, the sameness of things which interested any of the Bateau Lavoir set – not Picasso, not Braque, and certainly not Gertrude Stein. It was, rather, that, though things might seem 'endlessly the same', they were, as well, 'endlessly different'. Recalling the time when she was composing 'Melanctha' as she posed for Picasso, Stein would say,

> The only thing that is different from one time to another is what is seen. . . . Nothing changes from generation to generation except the thing seen and that makes a composition. . . . Everything is the same except composition and as the composition is different and always going to be different everything is not the same.   (*CE*, pp. 6, 12–13)

In other words, composition is the site of difference, a difference epitomised by Picasso's willingness to paint a portrait of Stein that did not particularly look like her at all. It is this explosion of difference into the world of likenesses – into the realm, in fact, of representation – that I should like to explore here, for it is Stein's insistence on repetition as a system of differences that has been the most profoundly influential element of her work.

Let us begin, then, with what would appear to be as clear an example as there is in Stein of everything's being 'endlessly the same' and try to explain how it must be taken, instead, as the embodiment of endless difference: that is, with her motto, 'A rose is a rose is a rose is a rose'. In her *Lectures in America*, Stein explained the phrase in the following terms:

When I said.

A rose is a rose is a rose.

And then later made that into a ring I made poetry and what did
I do I caressed completely caressed and addressed a noun.

(*LIA*, p. 231).

Printed in a circle, as it would come to be on Stein's stationery and
linen, this seems to amount to little more than an overly insistent,
even wearisome tautology, and tautologies, we have learned from
Peirce, assume the status, like the proper name, of the index.[5] And,
yet, Stein's insistence that this motto is poetry forces us to address it
as something more. It is simple enough to undermine the indexical
function of 'a rose is a rose', in fact, by recognising, as Charles
Demuth did in his 1928 *Homage to Gertrude Stein* (Plate 2), that it is,
among other things, a pun: Eros is eros is eros / Love Love Love.
Such a pun, of course, undermines the referential certainty of
language, and the indexical character of the sign here collapses
under its weight. The sign becomes a kind of mask – as Demuth
depicts it – a surface reality behind or beneath which lurks
something entirely 'other', or perhaps (and in this Demuth captures
better than anyone else Stein's uncanny ability to 'dematerialise' her
subject even as she 'portrays' it) nothing at all.

A second, perhaps more important way to undermine the
seemingly indexical status of the tautology is to recognise that
anything *in the repetition of itself* necessarily changes. This was one of
the many lessons that Stein learned from William James, and its
importance to her writing has been nicely outlined by Randa
Dubnick in her *The Structure of Obscurity: Gertrude Stein, Language,
and Cubism.* According to James, 'Every thought we have of a given
fact is, strictly speaking, unique, and only bears a resemblance of
kind with our other thoughts of the same fact.'

Thus, my arm-chair is one of the things of which I have a
conception; I knew it yesterday and recognized it when I looked at
it. But if I think of it to-day as the same armchair which I looked at
yesterday, it is obvious that the very conception of it *as* the same
is an additional complication to the thought, whose inward
constitution must alter in consequence. In short, it is logically
impossible that the same thing should be *known as the same* by two
successive copies of the same thought.[6]

Such a mode of thinking has clear implications for phrases such as 'a rose is a rose', but it also possesses clear reverberations for the portrait process – the impossibility, for instance, of Picasso's ever knowing Stein *as the same* over the course of eighty-odd successive sittings. Stein's own verbal portraits are based upon the same principles. In *Lectures in America* she explained,

> Each time that I said the somebody whose portrait I was writing was something that something was just that much different from what I had just said that somebody was and little by little in this way a whole portrait came into being, a portrait that was not description and that was made by each time, and I did a great many times, say it, that somebody was something, each time there was a difference just a difference enough so that it could go on and be a present something.   (*LIA*, p. 177)

And in these terms Stein's famous description of the portrait process, in her second portrait of Picasso – 'Exact resemblance to exact resemblance the exact resemblance as exact as a resemblance, exactly as resembling, exactly resembling' (*P&P*, p. 22) – is more an oxymoron than an assertion of the indexical function of portraiture.[7] No 'resemblance' is ever an 'exact' replica of an 'original'. It is a reconstruction of the original, a *re*-presentation, a kind of difference.

Yet another way to approach the idea of difference in Stein's writing is in terms of structural linguistics, and particularly in terms of that ephemeral relationship between signifier and signified (S/s) in which the signifier is conceived as a *material* constituent of the sign and the signified as an immaterial idea or conceptual referent. Cubism's shift to a more 'cerebral' kind of painting, while, at the same time, it insisted on the materiality of the work itself by drawing attention, for instance, to the two-dimensional surface of the canvas, amounts to the first full-scale aesthetic manifestation of Saussure's more or less concurrent formulation of the operations of signification.[8] 'This opposition between the registers of the two halves of the sign', Rosalind Krauss has pointed out, 'stresses the status of the sign as substitutive, proxy, stand-in, for an absent referent. It insists, that is, on the literal meaning of the prefix /re/ in the word *representation*, drawing attention to the way the sign works away from, or in the aftermath of, the thing to which it refers.'[9]

Perhaps the clearest instance of such a 'dematerialisation' of the object and its reconstitution as *re*-presentation can be found in the cubist use of passage. In a drawing such as Picasso's 1910 *Figure*, or *Nude* (Plate 3), there is a sense that the figure, particularly on the right side, dissolves into the two-dimensional space of the picture's ground, creating a feeling of openness, dissemination and proliferation. At the same time, on its left side, the figure *seems* about to define itself, come into a rounded, material being. It is this give-and-take between two- and three-dimensionality, the realms of representation and 'reality', that defines *passage*. As Leo Steinberg has argued in a study of Cézanne's role in the advent of cubism,

> [the] *passage* of planes is . . . a working process that constantly starts and suspends materiality, regardless of whether the process occurs among the planes of one broken form or between things discrete. The definition articulates a structural principle that transcends individual objects and their constituent facets to involve larger pictorial continuities.[10]

The absence of the referent in Picasso's *Nude* is perhaps nowhere more apparent than in Alfred Stieglitz's name for it – after purchasing it early in the second decade of the century, he always called it 'The Fire Escape'.[11]

But Krauss sees this 'structural condition of absence' as playing a more important role in later cubist painting: it is, she insists, 'essential to the operations of the sign within [cubist] collage'.[12] Consider, for instance, a collage by Juan Gris, who, incidentally, had been sufficiently impressed by Picasso's *Gertrude Stein* to model his own 1912 *Portrait of Picasso* on it.[13] The delicate and very beautiful *Roses* (Plate 4) was purchased by Stein in July 1914, just before she left for London. It was the third painting by Gris that she had purchased – in June Kahnweiler had sold her *Glass and Bottle* and *Book and Glasses* – and, though these two did not mark Gris's first sale (Léonce Rosenberg had purchased one painting some months earlier), he surely understood the importance of the purchase.[14] It is possible that Gris conceived of *Roses* as a kind of homage to his new patron, or at least as a way to interest her in buying yet another painting at short notice. He was almost dead broke at the time, and, since he had lived at the Bateau Lavoir since 1906, he was surely in a position to know what Stein might like. Whether anybody knew, in 1914, of Stein's affection for roses is another question. She had coined the phrase 'Rose is a rose is a rose is a rose' the year before in

'Sacred Emily', but this piece was not published until 1922 in *Geography and Plays*, and the phrase does not reoccur in her writing until that year, when she employed it in both 'Objects Lie on a Table' and 'As Fine as Melanctha'. Her complete identification with the device came only after she used it in circular form on the cover of *The Autobiography of Alice B. Toklas*. Still, the repetition of the word 'rose' – and the wordplay it might generate – was on her mind in the years 1913–14. In her 1914 poem 'Oval', for instance, she writes,

> Rose
> Rose.
> Rose up.
> Rose.
> Rose.
> Rose up.
> Rose.
> Rose up.
> Able in stand.
> Able ink stand.
> Rose.
> Rose.
> Able in ink stand.
> Rose up.
>   (*BTV*, p. 130)

It is at least worth pointing out that the basic compositional device of Gris's *Roses* is the overlapping of two slightly askew *oval* mats on a table, upon which the roses stand, or, put another way, out of which they rise up. But even more to the point is the fact that, when Stein returned to a consideration of her writing of the 1913–14 era, in 'Objects Lie on a Table', which Richard Bridgman rightly sees as an attempt to elucidate hermetic writing such as *Tender Buttons* and 'Oval', she refers to compositions precisely like Gris's:

> Objects lie on a table.
> We live beside them and look at them and then they are on the table then.   (*O&P*, p. 105)
>
> Objects on the table meant to us an arrangement.   (p. 106).
>
> Do we suppose that all she knows is that a rose is a rose is a rose is a rose.   (p. 110)[15]

In other words, Stein is asserting here her recognition that the sign serves more than just an indexical function, that what matters in her art is not what a thing *refers* to, but the arrangement to which it lends itself. As John Malcolm Brinnin has noted in a comparison of Stein's writing of the *Tender Buttons* variety and Picasso's collage, 'These compositions represent a private ordering, rhythmic and visual, of materials one can recognise easily enough, but which serve to convey no programmatic meaning.'[16] *Roses* is no more a representation of roses than it is a representation of Stein, though it might *refer* to Stein just as it *refers* to flowers, both of which, whatever the case, are absent. Collage is essentially a device wherein one system of representation, in this case a magazine illustration of a bunch of roses, is introduced into – laid over – another system of representation, the painting proper, and, as Krauss argues, we are thus presented here with a literal *re-presentation of a representation*. Furthermore, the act of painting – a third level of representation, in which we tend to read the trace of the artist, the mark of the artist's expressive power and subjectivity – this reference to the creating ego, is itself lost, or at least problematised, literally hidden behind the façade of the 'found' collage element, masked as it were.[17]

I have developed Krauss's argument about the absent referent in collage here because her final point is ultimately the one I wish to make about Stein and her influence on contemporary art. 'We are standing now', she concludes her discussion,

> on the threshold of a postmodernist art, an art of a fully problematised view of representation, in which to name (represent) an object may not necessarily be to call it forth, for there may be no (original) object. For this postmodernist notion of the originless play of the signifier we could use the word *simulacrum*. But the whole structure of postmodernism has its proto-history in those investigations of the representational system of absence that we can only now recognize as the contemporaneous alternative to modernism. Picasso's collage was an extraordinary example of this proto-history . . . .[18]

And so, I am arguing, were Stein's portraits and plays. When she says at the start of the 'Rooms' section of *Tender Buttons*, 'Act so that there is no use in a centre' (*TB*, p. 63), she is in effect giving herself the authority to compose without direct reference, to free the activity of signifying from the necessity of representing the thing as if language were transparent, as if we could see behind its mask. Instead, when Stein names a thing – 'A Carafe', for instance, the first object in *Tender Buttons* – it is as if the thing were disappearing before our eyes:

A CARAFE, THAT IS A BLIND GLASS.

A kind in glass and a cousin, a spectacle and nothing strange a single hurt color and an arrangement in a system to pointing. All this and not ordinary, not unordered in not resembling. The difference is spreading.   (p. 9)

It is as if, in fact, the fabric of language is spreading out here across the carafe, masking the thing beneath its own concerns, stressing its difference from its absent referent. As Michael Davidson has said of this passage,

'The difference is spreading' not only foreshadows deconstructive thought; it recognises that between one term (a carafe) and a possible substitute (a blind glass) exists a barrier, not an equal sign, and it is this difference which supports all signification. Stein interrogates this barrier in order to break open the imperial Sign and leave 'a system to pointing', a language that no longer needs to contain the world in order to live in it.[19]

The precise nature of such a 'difference' can probably be clarified if we distinguish between two alternative theories of repetition, one of which we all probably still think of as the 'normative' one, while the other might best be characterised – since it has been most thoroughly articulated by the likes of Jacques Derrida, Gilles Deleuze, Jean Baudrillard and Guy de Bord – as postmodern. The first kind of repetition – I am quoting J. Hillis Miller's summary of the two positions in his 1982 *Fiction and Repetition* – 'is grounded in a solid archetypal model which is untouched by the effects of repetition. All the other examples are copies of this [original] model'. This notion of repetition is 'the reigning presupposition of realistic fiction and of its critics', who determine 'The validity of the mimetic copy . . . by its truth of correspondence to what it copies.' The other mode of repetition assumes, in contrast, that

Each thing . . . is unique, intrinsically different from every other thing. Similarity arises against the background of this 'disparité du fond'. It is a world not of copies but of . . . 'simulacra' or 'phantasms'. These are ungrounded doublings which arise from differential interrelations among elements which are all on the same plane. This lack of ground in some paradigm or archetype means that there is something ghostly about the effects of this second kind of repetition. It seems that X repeats Y, but in fact it does not, or at least not in the firmly anchored way of the first sort of repetition.[20]

In this second mode, the mode of both postmodernism and Stein, representation becomes a function of what Miller, like Benjamin, calls 'opaque similarity'; that is, 'opaque in the sense of riddling. How is a mother like a sock?'[21] How is a salad, to use the terms of *Tender Buttons*, like a 'winning cake', a cutlet like a 'blind agitation'?

Confronted by this opacity, the overwhelming tendency has been to read Stein's portraits and plays in terms of autobiography, either historical or psychological, which amounts to an urge to fix and limit the play of difference by determining – somehow – some referent or other behind the surface of her language. Initially, I suppose, in a poem such as 'Susie Asado' – 'Toasted susie is my ice cream' – Stein may have assumed something like the normative position in relation to her subject matter: if she isn't representing the Spanish dancer exactly, it might be that she is representing her own desire. But in her later work it is the structure of representation that interests Stein, not what is represented itself, be it the world or the mind. By concentrating on the presentation of language as a thing, she in fact attacks the valorisation of the individual psyche which sees its artistic productions as manifestations of its own spirit or soul – and in this she takes on the masculinist definition of individual creative production and undermines it, establishing once and for all the centrality of her work to the contemporary feminist project.

That is, in taking on what Michael Davidson calls the 'imperial Sign', Stein also takes on the imperial Author. The model for such an attack on the creating ego is, I am tempted to say, a writer who conceived of language in a manner diametrically opposed to Stein – that is, Balzac. But I am thinking of a Balzac slightly different from the one we habitually think of as the exemplary French realist. I have in mind, rather, the author of *Le Chef-d'oeuvre inconnu*, which Picasso illustrated first in 1931 for Vollard and then again, late in his career, in his *Suite 347*.[22] This Balzac is the creator of an artist named Frenhofer, the greatest painter of his age, at work on the ultimate masterpiece, a life-sized female nude modelled by the courtesan Catherine Lescault, which as he works he will let no one see, not even the promising young Poussin. But when his painting is finally revealed, at novel's end, all that Poussin can see is 'colours piled upon one another in confusion, and held in restraint by a multitude of curious lines which form a wall of painting . . . [a] chaos of colours, tones, vague nuances, a kind of mist without form'.[23] The next morning Frenhofer is found dead in his studio, having burned all his pictures the night before. Painting is defined here as an imperial venture, an ultimate effort to capture and contain its (female) object in its absolute essence. Yet, as opposed to the related Pygmalion myth – a story represented many times in nineteenth-century art – Frenhofer's attempt to capture the 'ideal' woman is frustrated. The imperial dream is denied, and its object escapes. *Le Chef-d'oeuvre inconnu* is in this sense a visionary novel. It is as if Balzac knew that the pressures of the realist imagination were about to erupt upon Western consciousness. And in Picasso, of course, they have: Frenhofer's madness is Picasso's truth, Frenhofer's tragedy Picasso's play, Frenhofer's loss Picasso's gain.

This ambiguous relation between the artist and his model – so thoroughly articulated in Balzac's Frenhofer – became Picasso's favourite subject in his later years. It was, on the one hand, a subject matter in which he could still assert his undeniably erotic frame of mind. But, in part because of this eroticism, it was also deeply problematised terrain, in which questions of representation were fully and openly implicated in questions of sexual politics, questions of power and control, mastery and desire. For clearly the female is the object of desire, submitted (as incidentally Stein had submitted herself) to the conceptual mastery of the artist figure. In fact, one of the real questions Stein's work raises – and one of the reasons she remains so influential – is what it means for the female artist to adopt what in effect has been set out in Western painting as the masculine position. The real effrontery of Manet's *Olympia* had rested in a reversal of position wherein the masculine (audience) found itself submitted to the feminine gaze, creating for modern painting a crisis of position. Stein fully understood this crisis, and it manifested itself not only in terms of her own sexual identity but also in such gestures as her assumption of the identity of Alice B. Toklas in order to write her 'autobiography'. In a certain real sense what Stein does is self-consciously adopt a masculine guise, like any number of other American women in Paris during those years – Jane Heap, Sylvia Beach, Janet Flanner, all of whom, for instance, can be seen dressed as men in various portraits by Berenice Abbott, who had been Man Ray's assistant from 1923 to 1926 until she struck out on her own. Abbott's portraits make clear that the masculine position is a kind of mask, a free-floating signifier laid upon something entirely other. The 'transvestite' look does not so much transform the feminine position as it does submit the masculine position, because of the very absence of what is signified, to the level of discourse. The transvestite look is, in fact, a sort of collage, the re-presentation of (sexual) representation. It is a mark of absence, which refuses literal figuration in order to foreground the discourse of sexual difference.[24]

I hope it is clear, then, that Stein's writing is by no means 'formalist' however preoccupied it seems to be with analysing and manipulating its medium in almost purely formalist ways, as if without concern for what lies beyond the page. Most fundamentally, Stein's writing is a direct and intentional undermining of writing itself – that is, the structure of power relations inherent in writing. As Stein herself put it in 1913 in her 'In the Grass (On Spain)': 'culture is power, Culture is power. Culture' (*G&P*, p. 75). Her writing is a systematic revelation of precisely this fact.

And it is, of course, Stein's ability to undermine the structures of representation which empower 'culture' that accounts for her considerable impact upon contemporary art. Like Picasso's, her work belongs to what Krauss has called the 'proto-history' of postmodernism, for she problematises representation, reveals that the word is but a simulacrum of its referent, and demonstrates that 'likeness' is itself a system of ungrounded relations constructed across a plane of *difference*. But as a result, Stein's influence upon the postmodern scene is itself problematised. She necessarily exists in the postmodern consciousness as a simulacrum of herself, as a phantasm, and her own 'continuous presence' becomes more and more difficult to trace.

Perhaps the best way to place Stein in the present is to look, briefly, at the larger avant-garde context which informed the enormously successful production, in 1967 at Judson Church in New York City, of the musical *In Circles*, based on Stein's writings and produced by Al Carmines, associate minister and supervisor of the arts programme at Judson since 1960. The church became active in the Greenwich Village avant-garde scene after its chief minister, Howard Moody, organised the Judson Gallery, a space which as early as 1959 exhibited works by pop artists such as Jim Dine, Tom Wesselman, Red Grooms and Claes Oldenburg and which sponsored a number of early Happenings as well. Carmines was hired by Moody to organise the Judson Poets' Theater, a group which performed, in October 1963, Gertrude Stein's play *What Happened. In Circles* was Carmines' idea, and it opened on 13 October 1967 to rave reviews. As Clive Barnes put it in the *New York Times*, 'I loved it'; 'What fun it would be if eventually Miss Stein . . . became more influential upon American drama than Arthur Miller, Tennessee Williams or . . . Edward Albee? What fun.'[25] Scored by Carmines, who also accompanied the play on the piano, *In Circles* ran for 222 performances in 1967, first at Judson and then at the Cherry Lane, won several off-Broadway awards, and reopened in June 1968 at the Gramercy Arts, to raves once again. It received, finally, its widest notice when segments of it were included in the Perry Adato documentary of Stein's Paris years, *When This You See Remember Me*.

If Stein's presence in the avant-garde activities which focused around Judson Church in the late fifties and early sixties is more or less highlighted and summarised by *In Circles*, that presence can be detected in any number of other ways as well. The Fluxus movement, for instance, whose members often participated in Judson activities, began to reissue, under the direction of Dick Higgins and his Something Else Press, much of Stein's harder-to-find writing, including *The Making of Americans*, *Lucy Church Amiably*, *G. M. P.*, *How To Write*, *Geography and Plays*, and *A Book Concluding with As a Wife Has a Cow: A Love Story*, with its illustrations by Juan Gris.[26] And it is hardly accidental that Fluxus was itself, to use Higgins' word, an 'intermedia' movement. The audience Higgins anticipated for the Stein books was hardly limited to the literary establishment – in fact, it hardly included the literary establishment at all. These books were meant for the avant-garde art scene – for the dancers at the Judson Dance Theater, for the painters who were their associates and the musicians who scored their performances. And it was Stein's sense of repetition and difference upon which all these various media drew.

It is, in fact, American avant-garde music which seems to have the most deep-seeded connection to Stein. Virgil Thomson is the important link. On New Year's Day 1926, he sent Stein a musical setting for 'Susie Asado', for which she thanked him instantly: 'I like its looks immensely and want to frame it and Miss Toklas who knows more than looks says the things in it please her a lot and when can I know a little other than its looks but I am completely satisfied with its looks.' Stein's delight with the surface of the score – the structure of its notation – is itself instructive, but Thomson's explanation of why he was interested in setting Stein to music is even more so:

> My theory was that if a text is set correctly for the sound of it, the meaning will take care of itself. And the Stein texts, for prosodizing this way, were manna. With meanings already abstracted, or absent, or so multiplied that choice among them was impossible, there was no temptation toward tonal illustration, say, of the birdie babbling by the brook or heavy heavy hangs my heart. You could make a setting for sound and syntax only.[27]

It is fair to say, I think, that out of just such a sense of text as sound an entire generation of 'text-sound' poets would be born, a poetic avant-garde whose roots, like Thomson's, can be traced to Stein.[28]

Thomson's scores for the two Stein operas *Four Saints in Three Acts* and *The Mother of Us All*, the first composed in 1928 and the second in 1947, have always been widely admired in avant-garde musical circles in New York. To celebrate the opening of his second one-man show at the Stable Gallery in 1964, for instance, the young painter Robert Indiana held a gallery concert of Thomson's collaborations with Stein, which Thomson attended, and Thomson in turn commissioned Indiana to design the sets and costumes for *The Mother of Us All* when it was performed at the Guthrie Theater in Minneapolis in January 1967. In an article which appeared in *Arts Magazine* just as the opera opened in Minneapolis, William Katz described Indiana's costumes in terms that should by now be familiar. There are over thirty characters in the opera, and Katz notes,

> An intentional ambiguity in Indiana's costumes occurs because of the progression of identities that takes place. As the women become more like men in having equal rights and gaining the vote they also begin to look more like men. They begin to wear straw

hats and ties like men and begin to wear men's styled shirts with high collars and cuffs. Some of them even wear pants. . . .

And the men. The men end by being sheathed in flags. Patriotic in their stars and stripes they look as if equality has made them more like women, less like men. Of course the language shows that Stein is concerned with this too. And Thomson's score keeps continually shifting tonalities as if to add the aural comment that everything still can sound the same even if it always sounds different.[29]

One of the people most intensely interested in Thomson during these years was the composer John Cage, who in the early fifties had accepted a commission to write a book on Thomson's music which finally appeared, after much unhappy haggling, in 1959. Cage shared Thomson's passion for Stein.[30] Asked to compile a list of the ten books having the greatest influence on his thought, he wrote, first, 'Gertrude Stein   Any title'.[31] Just as the 'look' of Thomson's setting for 'Susie Asado' interested Stein, the 'look' of musical notation has always interested Cage. But he has, even more importantly, adopted, in his more-or-less serial and minimalist compositions, Stein's sense of repetition and difference. There is probably no better, nor more extreme, an embodiment of the principle than Cage's 4'33", first performed by the pianist David Tudor at the Marverick Concert Hall in Woodstock, New York, in August 1952. The piece is simple enough: the pianist simply sits silently at the keyboard for 4 minutes and 33 seconds, flexing his arms three times to indicate that the piece has three 'different' movements, without ever playing a note. In such a context, time itself becomes repetitive, each movement – each passing second – agonisingly like the one which preceded it, and yet, as the audience begins to hear, at first with discomfort and then with more and more interest, the ambient noise of the performance space, each passing moment is indeed startlingly different from the last.

This is not the place to develop the many connections between Stein and Cage (and Marjorie Perloff has already begun to chart that ground in her *Poetics of Indeterminacy*),[32] but I do want to point out a sort of galaxy of influence that Stein asserts on contemporary art through him. Cage's collaborations, especially with Merce Cunningham and Robert Rauschenberg, connect him not only to the experimental music scene but to painting, dance and, through first Black Mountain and then the Judson Dance Theater and Judson

Poet's Workshop, to the Happening and performance art. At Black Mountain, both Cage and Rauschenberg had worked with Elaine and Willem de Kooning. Willem De Kooning's notorious *Woman* paintings of these years were directly inspired by Stein: 'When I was painting those figures, I was thinking about Gertrude Stein, as if they were ladies of Gertrude Stein', he said. And then he proceeds to describe his own paintings in terms which provide as good a definition as I know of the fate of the referent in Stein's writing: 'Then I could sustain this thing all the time because it could change all the time; she could get almost upside down, or not be there, or come back again, she could be any size. Because this content could take care of almost anything that could happen.'[33] Elaine de Kooning recalls reading Stein 'reverently but without understanding until the dance critic Edwin Denby read a page aloud to me a couple of years later, making its meaning clear in terms of its rhythms'.[34]

Stein's connection to dance had been recognised by Thomson, not only in his setting to 'Susie Asado', the Spanish dancer, but also in a setting called 'Lady Godiva's Waltzes' for eight poems dedicated to Stein by the French surrealist poet Georges Hugnet, including this one, quoted by Hoover and Cage in their book on Thomson: 'Nous ne savons plus danser, Gertrude, Gertrude. Nous avons perdu l'habitude. Gertrude, Gertrude, Gertrude, apprenez-nous à danser.'[35] Cage's own impact on the dance scene in New York has been outlined by Sally Banes in her invaluable book *Democracy's Body: Judson Dance Theater 1962–1964*.[36] Cage taught a seminar at the New School for Social Research in New York from 1956 to 1960 on 'The Composition of Experimental Music', which was attended by the Happening and Fluxus set (Dick Higgins, Jackson MacLow, George Brecht, and Allan Kaprow), a number of painters and sculptors (George Segal, Jim Dine and Larry Poons), and most importantly in terms of dance, Robert Dunn.[37] At Cage's invitation Dunn organised a class on choreography at Merce Cunningham's studio in fall 1960, which initially included Yvonne Rainer and Steve Paxton. By the time it had moved into the Judson Church in 1962, it included the likes of Trisha Brown, Alex Hay, Deborah Hay, Elaine Summers, Valda Setterfield and David Gordon, a virtual compendium of the contemporary avant-garde dance scene.

If Al Carmines helped to make clear the connection between Judson Church and Stein, the specific connections of its Dance Theater to Stein were somewhat less obvious. Still *Village Voice* dance critic Jill Johnston was quick to recognise them, especially in Yvonne Rainer's work, which was described by Rainer as 'unrelated, unthematic phrases, with some repetition', and which according to Johnston paralleled Stein's 'circular, repetitive style'.[38] Rainer's interest in repetition quickly led to her notorious *Word Words*, performed on 29 January 1963 at Judson. Consisting of a ten-minute sequence of repetitive movements, danced first by Rainer, then by Paxton, and then by both in unison as a duet, both dancers as nude as the limits of the law would then allow, it was an almost pure demonstration of how everything is endlessly the same and endlessly different. Of all the Judson dancers, however, perhaps Trisha Brown has most systematically explored the gestural dynamics of repetition and difference. A video made by Peter Campus for Boston public television station WGBH, entitled *Dancing on the Edge*, consists of Brown dancing before an overlay of Brown dancing the same dance. Consistently a little ahead of, then a little behind, her own image, her moves in the one dance a little different from the same moves in the other, her dance layered upon the image of her dance, the two viewed at times from different points of view, Brown's body becomes the articulation of difference. It defines dance itself as the difference within repetition.

Such issues continue to occupy Brown. Her most recent work calls attention to the idea of repetition and difference in its very title, *Set and Reset*. Thomas McEvilley has described the dance in terms that seem to me to capture, as well as anyone has succeeded in doing, the ebb and flow of presentation and re-presentation, the dynamics of repetition:

> Movements fragment and cross. Surprise catches abruptly terminate unmotivated leaps. Falls are caught by seemingly unrelated accidents. . . . Dancers run, leap, collide, dive, and drift with that loose flow of precisely reintegrated fragments of once recognizable gestures . . . like . . . intimations of ancient and even animal movements.[39]

This fabric of the half-recognisable, this intimation of likenesses, is complicated by Robert Rauschenberg's costumes and set. The costumes are silk-screened, black-and-white material which echoes three randomly edited black-and-white film strips that Rauschenberg has back-projected onto three scrim-stretched frames that float and hover above the stage. The total effect is that of an image continually about to come into focus but that is continually dissolving away.

Rauschenberg has, of course, been intimately connected with contemporary dance since his collaborations with Merce Cunningham began in 1954 (from 1954 to 1964, Rauschenberg worked on some twenty projects with Cunningham, many of them scored by Cage). He attended Robert Dunn's classes at Judson. *Word Words* was rehearsed in his loft. And in May 1963 he choreographed his own dance for Judson, *Pelican*, a work for two men on rollerskates and bicycle wheels with parachutes on their backs and one woman on pointe. This was followed by a series of works which seem half dance and half performance or theatre pieces – *Shot Put* and *Elgin Tie* in 1964, *Spring Training*, *Map Room I* and *Map Room II* in 1965, *Linoleum* and *Open Score* in 1966, and *Urban Round* in 1967.[40] But perhaps his debt to Stein is nowhere more obvious than in his painting. Asked in 1969 to design a poster for the Metropolitan Museum of Art's centennial, Rauschenberg gave Picasso's portrait of *Gertrude Stein* a prominent place in the collage (Plate 5). Layered over other images, the portrait hides as much as it reveals, rising up off the paper as the conscious trace of the original. Like the other masterpieces represented in the work, it embodies the power of the reproduction, and the difference of repetition.

This has, in a very real sense, always been Rauschenberg's theme. In the middle fifties he constructed two 'identical' collages, *Factum I* and *Factum II*, which are as different as they are the same. Even casual observation quickly reveals that each work is unique, that this is a sort of 'ungrounded doubling', a re-presentation of representation in which the referent – except on the plane of art itself, as one painting refers to the other – is emptied of value (and it is important to realise that the imagery Rauschenberg empties of value here is the imagery of the age itself – a 1954 calendar, a vacation landscape, and a picture of Eisenhower, itself featured twice in each collage). The famous *Rebus*, from the same period, invites us to read it, from left to right, but whatever its meaning – if there ever was one – it is masked by the collage elements of which it is composed. This is not discourse, but a simulacrum of discourse. And, as in Stein, *Rebus* overtly takes on the question of the power of discourse and representation, not only in the partial headline at its left ('THAT REPRE', it begins), but also by including within its frame a reproduction of a cultural 'masterpiece', Botticelli's *Birth of Venus*. At least implicitly, these same concerns govern his Metropolitan

Museum poster, even overtly in the reproduction of the Ingres *Grand Odalisque* in the lower right. In fact, the discourse of desire is a favourite Rauschenberg theme, probably nowhere more thoroughly investigated than in his own *Odalisque* (1955–8), the combine-box on a pillowed pedestal topped by a stuffed hen, which incorporates all manner of images of woman, including reproductions from fifties nudist magazines. Nevertheless, if the 'subject' of *Rebus* or *Odalisque* or the Metropolitan Museum poster is, perhaps, the relations between representation and power, as in so many of Stein's portraits, the works ultimately bear only an 'opaque similarity' to sense. And such opacity becomes the very subject of Rauschenberg's *Hoarfrost* series, combines draped with semi-transparent scrim which look forward to the half-recognisable likenesses of Trisha Brown's dance. As Rauschenberg puts it, the imagery of the work presents itself 'in the ambiguity of freezing into focus or melting from view'.[41] In Rauschenberg's poster, finally, Stein freezes into focus and threatens to melt away, participates in the same cultural hegemony which her example challenges. She is the very image of repetition, of what it means to look like Gertrude Stein.

Notes

1. There is an excellent summary of the events described here in James R. Mellow, *Charmed Circle: Gertrude Stein and Company* (New York: Praeger, 1974) pp. 90–3.
2. See, for instance, Paul Waldo Schwartz, *Cubism* (London: Thames and Hudson, 1971) pp. 21–2; and Albert Gleizes and Jean Metzinger, 'Cubism' ('Du Cubisme'), in *Modern Artists on Art: Ten Unabridged Essays*, ed. Robert L. Herbert (Englewood Cliffs, NJ: Prentice-Hall, 1964) pp. 6–7, 13.
3. Quoted in Werner Haftmann, *Painting in the Twentieth Century* (New York: Praeger, 1965), I, 33–4.
4. Letter to Emile Bernard, 15 Apr 1904, in *Paul Cézanne: Letters*, ed. John Rewald, tr. Seymour Hacker (New York: Hacker, 1984) p. 296.
5. Charles Sanders Peirce, *Collected Papers* (Cambridge, Mass.: Belknap, Harvard University Press, 1960), IV, 359–61.
6. William James, *Psychology* (briefer course) (New York: Henry Holt, 1892) pp. 156, 243. This passage is quoted by Randa Dubnick in *The Structure of Obscurity: Gertrude Stein, Language, and Cubism* (Chicago and Urbana: University of Illinois Press, 1984) p. 90.
7. I mean here to take issue with the thesis of Wendy Steiner's *Exact*

Resemblance to Exact Resemblance: The Literary Portraiture of Gertrude Stein (New Haven, Conn.: Yale University Press, 1978). Steiner bases her argument on the essentially indexical function of portraiture (pp. 6–7), assuming that reference to a subject is a defining characteristic of the genre. Thus, Stein's most hermetic portraits make sense to Steiner only in so far as they represent Stein's mind, in so far as they 'become a depiction of the author's thoughts' (p. 130), which are themselves inevitably isolated from us. Rather than seeing Stein's work as depending upon how things are the same – how a literary portrait is like a painted one, how a portrait is like either its subject or its author's mind – it seems to me more productive to view Stein's portraits as a systematic investigation of how representation differs from its object. This allows us to see Stein's project in terms other than some quasi-mystical desire to unify the object and its perceiver, and to conceive of her work instead as a kind of site in which the differences between the object and its representation can be realised. In so doing, one is able to avoid Steiner's sense that Stein's portraits are ultimately 'failed experiments' (p. 160).

8. Saussure delivered his lectures on linguistics from 1907 to 1911 as cubism itself developed. I am not arguing for any influence of either one upon the other, merely pointing out their contiguity.

9. Rosalind Krauss, 'In the Name of Picasso', *October*, 16 (Spring 1981) 15.

10. Leo Steinberg, 'Resisting Cézanne: The Polemical Part', *Art in America*, 67 (Mar–Apr 1979) 121.

11. Ibid.

12. Krauss, 'In the Name of Picasso', *October*, 16, p. 15.

13. The analogy between Gris's *Hommage à Picasso* and Picasso's *Gertrude Stein* is developed by Mark Rosenthal in his *Juan Gris* (New York: Abbeville Press, 1983) p. 24.

14. Rosenthal gives a 1913 date for Stein's purchase of these first two paintings (ibid., p. 153), but he is surely wrong. There is a letter from Kahnweiler to Stein dated 3 June 1914 in which Kahnweiler writes, 'I have today sent to you the two paintings by Gris and now enclose the bill for them. I am delighted that these paintings have been added to your collection' – quoted in Douglas Cooper, 'Gertrude Stein and Juan Gris', *Four Americans in Paris: The Collections of Gertrude Stein and her Family* (New York: Museum of Modern Art, 1970) p. 66.

15. Richard Bridgman's discussion of this work can be found in *Gertrude Stein in Pieces* (New York: Oxford University Press, 1970) pp. 165–6.

16. John Malcolm Brinnin, *The Third Rose: Gertrude Stein and her World* (New York: Grove Press, 1959) p. 162.

17. Not only is the idea of collage as the re-presentation of representation suggested by Krauss, but so is the notion of collage as a system of masking; see 'In the Name of Picasso', *October*, 16, pp. 19–20.

18. Ibid., pp. 20–1.

19. Michael Davidson, 'On Reading Stein', in Bruce Andrews and Charles Bernstein (eds), *The L=A=N=G=U=A=G=E Book* (Carbondale: Southern Illinois University Press, 1984) p. 197.

20. J. Hillis Miller, *Fiction and Repetition: Seven English Novels* (Cambridge, Mass.: Harvard University Press, 1982) pp. 5–6.
21. Ibid., p. 8.
22. The impact of Balzac's tale on modern art is the subject of Dore Ashton's *A Fable of Modern Art* (London: Thames and Hudson, 1980).
23. Translation by Ashton, ibid., p. 28.
24. For other examples of the 'transvestite' look in Paris, see [Gyula Halasz] Brassai, *The Secret Paris of the 30's*, tr. Richard Miller (New York: Pantheon, 1976). For more detailed discussion along similar lines see Sandra M. Gilbert's 'Costumes of the Mind: Transvestism as Metaphor in Modern Literature', *Critical Inquiry*, 7, 2 (Winter 1980) 391–417.
25. Clive Barnes, 'Theater: Gertrude Stein Words at the Judson Church', *New York Times*, 14 Oct 1967, p. 12.
26. For a history of these and related imprints see Peter Frank, *Something Else Press: An Annotated Bibliography* (New York: Documentext, McPherson, 1983).
27. Virgil Thomson, *Virgil Thomson* (London: Weidenfeld and Nicolson, 1967) p. 90.
28. See Richard Kostelanetz (ed.), *Text-Sound Texts* (New York: William Morrow, 1980), for an anthology of such texts. In his introductory essay, 'Text-Sound Art: A Survey', Kostelanetz outlines the tradition's debt to Stein.
29. William Katz, 'A Mother is a Mother', *Arts Magazine*, 41 (Dec 1966–Jan 1967) 47–8.
30. Kathleen Hoover and John Cage, *Virgil Thomson: His Life and Music* (New York and London: Thomas Yoseloff, 1959).
31. Quoted in Richard Kostelanetz (ed.), *John Cage* (New York: Praeger, 1970) p. 138.
32. Marjorie Perloff, *The Poetics of Indeterminacy: Rimbaud to Cage* (Princeton, NJ: Princeton University Press, 1981).
33. Quoted in Ellen H. Johnson (ed.), *American Artists on Art from 1940 to 1980* (New York: Harper and Row, 1982) p. 22.
34. Quoted in Eleanor Munro, *Originals: American Women Artists* (New York: Simon and Schuster, 1979) p. 251.
35. Hoover and Cage, *Virgil Thomson*, p. 152.
36. Sally Banes, *Democracy's Body: Judson Dance Theater 1962–1964* (Ann Arbor: University of Michigan Research Press, 1983).
37. Recollections of these classes by Cage, Higgins and Al Hansen can be found in Kostelanetz, *John Cage*, pp. 118–24.
38. Quoted in Banes, *Democracy's Body*, pp. 66, 32; see also p. 91.
39. Thomas McEvilley, 'Freeing Dance from the Web', *Artforum*, 22 (Jan 1984) 56.
40. For summaries and complete annotations of these works, see Nina Sundell, *Rauschenberg/Performance 1954–1984* (Cleveland: Cleveland Center for Contemporary Art, 1984).
41. Quoted in Lawrence Alloway, 'Rauschenberg's Development', in *Robert Rauschenberg* (Washington, DC: National Collection of Fine Arts, Smithsonian Institution, 1976) p. 22.

4

Gertrude Stein: Composition as Meditation

ULLA E. DYDO

Stein had discovered early that the only way she could come to terms with her experience was to write it. But writing was difficult. The love affair of 1901–3 told in her first novel, *Q. E. D.*, and the descriptions of acquaintances entered in her first notebooks record her struggle to comprehend her perceptions as her struggle to write them. Throughout the years, struggle characterised writing. The popular picture of Gertrude Stein working at her ample desk with easy concentration is part of the self-protective fiction created by *The Autobiography of Alice B. Toklas* and by its carefully chosen illustrations. It is far from the truth. Writing things as they were required stern discipline and created painful loneliness. The experience Stein tried to shape in words was sometimes depressing or frightening, which made it doubly difficult to overcome her resistance to seeing and saying it. Even when her perception was not painful, writing was a struggle.

In her early years Stein found that she could write what she knew if she freed her mind of all extraneous matters and concentrated on the patterns – the mathematics – of human being and human relations. Words and word patterns shaped themselves in her mind in the process of rigorous concentration that allowed no interference from outside. This process of realising perception is the Stein meditation. What Stein called a composition is the written process of meditation. Meditating does not precede composing but *is* composing. Reading Gertrude Stein is reading the 'written writing process'.

In an article published at the time of the International Exhibition of Modern Art (the 'Armory Show') of February 1913 in New York, Mabel Dodge described how Stein worked to 'extend consciousness' when she meditated:

Her habit of working is methodical and deliberate. She . . . brings all her willpower to bear upon the banishment of preconceived images. Concentrating upon the impression she has received and which she wishes to transmit, she suspends her selective faculty, waiting for the word or group of words that will perfectly interpret her meaning, to rise from her sub-consciousness to the surface of her mind.

Then and then only does she bring her reason to bear upon them, examining, weighing and gauging their ability to express meaning. . . . She does not go after words – she waits and lets them come to her, and they do.[1]

When Gertrude Stein saw in meditation she saw completely:

Eyes turn in in those not having wealth of experience or having no capacity for first-hand experience. Great thinkers eyes do not turn in, they get blank or turn out to keep themselves from being disturbed. It is only sentimentalists and unexperiencing thinkers whose eyes turn in. Those having wealth of experience turn out or are quiet in meditation or repose.

(Early Notebook N-1, YCAL)

The emphasis on looking out in meditation is central for Stein. It spells her conviction that artists receive their materials from the contemplation of the world, not from introspection, from emotion, or from invention. This conviction allowed her to insist that what she wrote was literally true. Stein may have invented literary methods, but she never invented subject matter. She looked at the world and she described literally what she saw. Her meditative literalism is the literalism of saints who contemplate in their exercises what is there to see. It is a dynamic form of contemplation that creates the movement of the perceiving mind but requires no activity and has no purpose. Here is the mind in movement: 'Now think a minute about no movement. I wish for no movement' ('How Are Fears', 1930; *PL*, p. 141).

Stein does not meditate *about* particular subjects but creates the verbal process of meditation. The result of meditation is not an insight that can be paraphrased but is a constructed meditation, a composition. In the course of the exercise that is a meditation, personality does away with itself and becomes pure perceiving consciousness, pure voice:

I am I not any longer when I see.
This sentence is at the bottom of all creative activity. It is just the
exact opposite of I am I because my little dog knows me.

(1933; *FIA*, p. 119)

What carries the meditation along is *voice*. It is not the personal
voice of Gertrude Stein talking to herself or to an identifiable
audience about an idea or event; rather it is the voice of words in the
process of becoming speech. What we hear in the meditations is the
process of consciousness constructing speech. There is of course a
persona or speaker in a meditation. But the meditating consciousness
that is perceiving in words is not the same as the social person with a
name. 'I am I not any longer . . . .' The meditating voice has a
quality that we associate with talk, but not with the talk that
accompanies daily life. When Stein uses personal pronouns in
Stanzas in Meditation, they are abstractions divested of identifiable
personal reference and are only 'personal' pronouns – which stand
for voices – moving about the piece.

That the 'I' she used so frequently has a connection with Gertrude
Stein is clear enough. But in the piece this connection is of entirely
minor importance. Rather than hunting for personal anecdotes
and annotating references, the reader hears the process of
consciousness in the voice of her words. It is a voice that must be
listened to but that requires no action or response. Quite unlike the
'I' and the 'she' of the *Autobiography*, which have public personalities
attached to them that exchange questions and answers audible in
every phrase, the pronouns and voices of *Stanzas* are stark and
abstract. They record no events and tell no stories. Or hardly any.
Tiny bits of stories can be found in the stanzas: there are fruits to
pick, peas and beans to collect, oxen to see, soup to eat (or drink). A
few people enter the stanzas, but they do not act and, with one
exception, have no names. There are the words, always the words
that lead us on in stark and abstract construction.

Writing for Stein was an affirmation of existence: 'was I I when I
had no written word inside me' (1934; *EA*, p. 64). Speech, like being,
is an unending process. The conclusion of the process of speech is
the end of being. Stein knew that she existed when she was able to
compose words. It was by making word constructions, not by
speaking about herself, by voicing opinions or by telling stories, that
Stein affirmed her own existence. What she describes is what she
sees, which always includes the process of seeing. And the process

of seeing is inseparable from the process of saying. Freed of personal life and personal subject matter, the words speak with a disembodied voice that is no longer the voice of Gertrude Stein but the voice of words becoming constructions. They speak their meaning by creating their own shapes. Throughout her life, Gertrude Stein looked for ways to concentrate in written words the movement of the speaking voice and the 'intensity of exactness' to which meditation opened the way. Her development as a writer reflects the changing solutions she found in the course of the years to the problem of how to compose exactitude, intensity ,and movement in words.

Stein's alternative title for *Stanzas in Meditation* is *Meditation in Stanzas*. The wordplay of the two titles makes stanzas, or poems, the same as meditations: the stanzas are composed in meditative concentration, or the act of meditation is the construction of stanzas. Both titles describe a *process*: for Stein, composing or meditating is the process of making patterns or shapes in words – what in *Q. E. D.* is described by Adele (Stein) as 'a bit of mathematics. Suddenly it does itself and you begin to see' (p. 67). The more troubled the process of perception, the greater the urgency to compose it, for composing it is making sense of it. Making sense of the world requires looking at it with clarity and concentration and not allowing feelings or preconceptions to colour the perception.

Stein learned how to look at the world while she was a student at Radcliffe College. The courses and seminars in psychology and the work at the Harvard Psychological Laboratory were all offered in the Department of Philosophy. The course Philosophy 3 bore the title 'Cosmology' and was offered by William James in 1894–5 with the following description: 'A study of the fundamental conceptions of Natural Science, with special reference to theories of Evolution and Materialism, Spencer's first Principles. Lectures and Theses.'[2] Stein learned scientific method in the same department where analytic philosophy was taught, even though the emphasis in the department was undoubtedly on scientific observation rather than on speculation and abstract logical reasoning. She must have discussed perception formally in classes and informally with friends, and she appears to have struggled over how to apprehend the world and how to form clear pictures of what she saw and judgements about it.

Leon Mendez Solomons (1873–1900), a friend from Berkeley with whom she had in early years roamed the hills behind San Francisco, worked at Harvard for his PhD and did some teaching in the Philosophy Department and research in the Psychological Laboratory in 1897 and 1898. It was with him that Stein undertook the investigations that led to their joint paper 'Normal Motor Automatism' in the *Psychological Review*.[3] On 27 February 1898, Solomons wrote to her from Berkeley in answer to what must have been a troubled letter:

> I don't think you need be alarmed at your change in character: it is a natural reaction and a perfectly healthy one. Your general view of things that you had before, was the generality and breadth of superficiality, as it always is in the case of the philosopher – don't breathe this heresy to anyone – ; that is it was obtained not by including details but by ignoring them. By and by you will attain the breath [*sic*] and intellectual perspective of the scientist, which includes details by systematizing them, but which never 'abstracts' from them as the philosopher does.   (YCAL)

The distinction between philosophers and scientists was meant to reassure Stein, who by 1898 was already at the Johns Hopkins Medical School, that she was on the way to becoming a serious and responsible scientist and was learning the attention to detail that medical training required. Solomons continued,

> Its correlation with a change in your automatic habits is not surprising to me though I do not think that I can make my theory clear to you in a few words. In a general way it is this. The speculative instinct is connected with the motor system, and its activity means the activity and therefore readiness to respond of the motor system. On the other hand the voluntary attention is I feel quite sure an outgrowth of the visual sense, and is connected with the instinct for observation. Its development means a strengthening of the attention and a corresponding loss of automatism.   (YCAL)

Solomons outlines the development of the visual sense and of consciousness as central for the scientist. His prediction for Stein's growth is shrewd and understanding. He appears to have comprehended instinctively what troubled Stein and to have encouraged her in every way. She never abandoned the conscious attention to detail that he describes in his letter. And the question of identity or character remained central to all her work.[4]

To meditate, for Stein, meant to concentrate all her attention upon what she saw immediately before her. Though not exclusively visual, this concentration is primarily visual. To meditate was to bring before her consciousness immediately and in detail all that she perceived. The process required full attention and the disciplined refusal of speculation and of sentiment. Her rejection of established modes of thought extended to her use of words. When she rejected what she called associative language, she was rejecting set forms of verbal expression, habitual phrases used in easy preference over first-hand observation in words that rendered exactly the unique characteristics she had perceived. Direct, conscious and detailed observation theoretically required as many different verbal forms as there were details observed. The only way to state the truth perceived was to state it in language as fresh as the perception itself. What was important was difference, not similarity.

Stein attempted the conscious contemplation of objects. In this process, all details required equal attention until they assumed shapes in words. 'Every little bit different', she said of details in *An Acquaintance with Description* (*AWD*, p. 3). And the different bits surely echo Cézanne's 'Le bon Dieu existe dans le détail.' Becoming conscious of what she saw required an act of words. To perceive a shape or design was a verbal form of seeing. It became a sacramental act: 'Devotion is determined by design' ('Vacation in Brittany', 1920; *RAB*, p. 78).

Stein said that she composed her verbal shapes (sentences or phrases presumably) in her mind before writing them down rather than composing them as she went along in the process of writing. In commenting on the fact that she did not revise (usually but not always true), she insisted that she wrote down only what she had completely composed in her mind. She also said that to change her wording by making revisions was to change the perception and to make a different composition from the one originally written – in short, to falsify it.

The process of meditation is as far from speculation as it is from automatic writing. Stein defended herself innumerable times against what she considered the charge of writing unconsciously, by association, as the surrealists did. To her such writing was uncontrolled and was not art. At the same time, she used the word *premeditated* to describe the opposite extreme, which she also rejected: the fitting of details into *a priori* categories. In the piece 'Sentences and Paragraphs' (elsewhere called 'Saving the Sentence Again'), composed early in 1930, a paragraph appears which presents a proposition followed by a commentary explaining the proposition. The explanation is emptily methodical.

> Premeditated meditation concerns analysis.
> Now this is a sentence but it might not be.
> Premeditated. That is meditated before meditation.
> Meditation. Means reserved the right to meditate.
> Concerns. This cannot be a word in a sentence.
> Because it is not of use in itself.
> Analysis is a womanly word. It means that they discover there are laws.   (*HTW*, p. 32)[5]

Stein paraphrases the meaning of the proposition word for word, as schoolchildren do, in an attempt to make sense of it. Premeditated is translated in the most literal, mechanical – and useless – manner by reference to *meditate*. To meditate before meditation makes no sense. We associate the word *premeditate* with criminal acts, but can the act of meditation be planned? If *premeditated* makes little sense, the word *unpremeditated*, Shelley's word describing the singing of the skylark,[6] which the passage probably echoes, makes interpretation even more confusing. To Stein, meditation is a conscious process rather than spontaneous song, as *unpremeditated* would suggest. Yet her compositions are not premeditated acts either. The explanation of *premeditated meditation* is unsuccessful. The words, pivoting on a single unexplained word, offer no clear meaning in Stein's would-be paraphrase. The proposition might not be a sentence.

About *concerns* she says that the word has no clear meaning by itself but merely connects one notion (*meditation*) with another (*analysis*) in an unclear way. The connection of the two is not explained by the word *concerns*, which is rejected as a useless word in a sentence.

Analysis is not usually thought of as a womanly word. Stein is poking fun at preconceived associations (such as male or female roles) with words. That analysis or analytic thinking have to do with the discovery or application of laws is clear enough. If premeditation has to do with logical thinking and with planning, Stein questions the use of such thought. Her interest is never in the discovery of laws but in the exact observation and description of that which is, all of it equally important, in order to discover what it is. The description of it tells what it is. In the long series of sentences that make up the two pieces about saving the sentence, where Stein considers by example whether there is such a thing as a sentence, she constructs both sentences that make sense and sentences that do not. By the time she finishes the meditations upon sentences, her answer is that there *is* such a thing as a sentence. She has in effect written two long odes upon the sentence.

The nature of meditative contemplation becomes particularly clear if we consider it, as Stein often did, as a landscape. Throughout *Stanzas*, the landscape of the Bugey that she saw from her house in Bilignin and that she explored on her walks is the scene in which the drama of perception takes place as it is also the occasion for perception. It is the landscape in which domestic living goes on – her own and that of friends and neighbours – and it is a landscape in which figures move. One might speak of a landscape in relation, a landscape of the mind as well as a landscape for the eye to see. In such a landscape everything that is is visible, moving and present. When Stein was in Bilignin, perception took place in the landscape in which she resided. Not until she settled in the Département de l'Ain, though before she found a house to rent on a long lease, did she experience with such power what a landscape was. What she saw in Bilignin entered virtually every composition she wrote there, quite unlike the Paris scene, which rarely entered her compositions.

A good example of a landscape in meditation is 'Scenery and George Washington', which composes both the scenery – the local landscape that Stein saw before her – and the figure of George Washington in relation to the scenery. The piece may be thought of as 'Landscape with Figure', though it must not be confused with a painting.

The scenery of the piece is the autumn scenery that Stein saw when she looked over the valley from her house.[7] Why George Washington? Washington was on Stein's mind for many reasons. One was his first name. Stein was interested in names and especially liked the name 'George'. Inevitably she had met many Georges. 'All the new young men were called George one year', said Virgil Thomson. 'Maybe it no longer mattered who was who or what was what – maybe all Georges were the same.'[8] Early in 1931, outdoing Thackeray's *The Four Georges*, Stein wrote a play which she called

The Five Georges. The Georges, who derive from friends, are differentiated in the text only by initial letters for their last names: *L* presumably derived from George Platt Lynes; *M* from Georges Maratier; *H* from Georges Hugnet (changed in the manuscript from the original *H* to *S*, presumably after the quarrel with Hugnet over the publication of Stein's 'translation' of his poem *Enfances*, in the late fall of 1931). Who the Georges are individually, however, does not appear to matter. The lines written following the various names carry few identifiable referential meanings and do not develop individual character. And on the cover of the manuscript notebook for the play Stein noted, 'I do not want individual character' (YCAL). Other Georges no doubt hovered in the background: George Eliot and George Sand must have contributed to Stein's awareness of the name George. 'Finally George: A Vocabulary of Thinking' (1928; *HTW*, pp. 271–382), one of the pieces on language and grammar, is also full of Georges of all kinds. It is even possible that the fact that Gertrude shared the initial *G* with the Georges added to their interest.

'George' is not the only name that interested Stein. She liked names of all kinds. She had met numerous Marcels (and Marcelles, whose name sounds the same) and in 1929 gave to a poem the title 'A Summer with Marcels' (*SIM*, pp. 246–7). The piece is a light-hearted, playful poem that has overtones of a counting game about three – or possibly four – Marcels. Neither the Georges nor the Marcels in these pieces interact as conventional characters might. 'Margite, Marguerite and Margherita' (1932; *SIM*, pp. 269–77) again plays with three 'identical' names in three different languages and with how the three are or are not the same. In this poem a great many carefully selected details allow identification of the three Marguerites, who take turns at talking their versions of being a Marguerite. Finally, the play *They Weighed Weighed-Layed* (1930; *O&P*, pp. 231–48) has a series of characters with first names such as Leon, Eugene, Maurice, Bernard and so on, all of them taken from acquaintances. Each of these appears in the play under Roman numerals from I to VII, so that Leon I is later replaced by Leon II and Leon III, who exchange words with Eugene II and III, and so on. All these pieces play upon the relation of person and name. Stein was preoccupied in the early thirties with character in relation to name. Such problems of identity are also the theme of *Four in America* (1933), the first major book after the *Autobiography* (which likewise raised serious questions of identity), and the book into which

'Scenery and George Washington' is incorporated. *Four in America* asks what Ulysses S. Grant (who changed his name), the Wright Brothers, Henry James and George Washington would have become had they not become the men we know: Grant is considered as a religious leader, the Wright Brothers as painters, James as a general and Washington as a novelist. 'Scenery and George Washington', written before Stein developed the thematic preoccupations of the book, does not consider Washington as what he might have been but introduces him directly, as a person, into the present scenery.

Why Washington, of all the possible Georges?

Bernard Faÿ, the French historian of American cultural history, had written a biography of Washington which appeared in French in 1932 and in English in 1931.[9] The English translation was prepared by Bravig Imbs, a young friend whom Faÿ had met through Stein and who needed money. Between July and August or September 1931, Stein herself checked the translation with care. In 1931 letters, Faÿ expresses profound gratitude for her interest. In a draft of an answer, Stein says that Faÿ's George Washington is 'a very typical George' (n.d., YCAL). The young professor of American history and the American writer must have discussed Washington at length while Faÿ was writing his book, just as earlier they discussed Franklin, of whom Faÿ had written a biography in 1924. Faÿ's biography of Washington is a study of a great man as maker of history. The volume is a portrait quite unlike Stein's portraits though no doubt influenced by her ideas of portraiture. In summer 1931, Faÿ visited Stein three times in the country, staying with her for several days each time: from 21 to 24 June, from 24 to 26 August, and from 14 to 17 September. Faÿ's preface to his biography is dated 'Paris, July 1931'. Washington – and a growing preoccupation with history – had wandered into Stein's life from Faÿ's pages and from prolonged discussions, which had no doubt reawakened what Stein had absorbed about Washington in her early years. Now she meditated upon him and prepared to compose her own Washington.

Finally, 1932 was the bicentennial year of Washington's birth. Faÿ had no doubt timed the publication of his book with care to coincide with the Washington Bicentennial. On 1 November 1931, Robert Carlton Brown told Stein in a letter that he had written a poem entitled 'G. W. Anniversary',[10] which Mencken had bought for publication for $150. Plainly George Washington was in everyone's mind. In fall 1931, before returning from the country to Paris, Stein meditated about Washington and composed her own portrait of him. Stein's subjects are never arbitrary or accidental. They always have a context which it is helpful to know.

When Stein meditates, she makes herself see in composition. In 'Scenery and George Washington' she composes the landscape of the Bugey and composes into it the figure of Washington. The figure is brought from the past into the landscape of autumn, of time passing and days shortening. As Washington enjoyed Mount Vernon, so Stein invites him to enjoy her country retreat:

> Autumn scenery is warm if the fog has lifted.
> And the moon has set in the day-time in what may be drifting clouds. It sets very quickly and this is when, anyone is watching and it is setting in the day-time when the sun is shining. Any sign is a good sign.   (*FIA*, p. 161)

The landscape is still but moving, as Stein always insisted landscapes were when she spoke of plays as landscapes. The scenery also becomes domestic rather than merely natural. 'Scenery if seen makes a home a home of their seeing how happily she may choose flowers. Will she feed him' (ibid.). Washington, the farmer and landowner, is welcomed into the French countryside and into the speaker's house. In a landscape one sees houses. Seen from inside, the houses become homes. The scenery is not merely 'background' for the figure of the American 'republican aristocrat', but it allows the gradual composition of George Washington in the scenery. The process of composing the two into one becomes a dramatic process. The piece that Stein produces is her own version of the Gilbert Stuart portrait of George Washington, which she must have known from childhood. Receiving Washington into her home, from memory into the present, from America to France, is the process of meditation which accounts for the fact that she calls the piece both a novel and a play.

The landscape makes possible an acquaintance with the famous American. It allows her to invite him and becomes the context for the acquaintance of the two representatives of America. 'George Washington is pleased to come' (*FIA*, p. 163). The landscape, she said in *Stanzas*, 'is what when they that is I / See and look . . .' (v.xxxiv). Seeing and looking allows her to perceive the figure entering the landscape or indeed to create the figure in the landscape.

Washington, at first merely remembered in the foggy autumn morning, becomes clear after the fog has lifted. Recollection, in meditation, becomes presence. Born in February, like Stein, he wanders into the land that she sees as hers. President of his country, he appears ready to rule. The encounter with him has a certain danger, for in her composition it is Stein who must rule, not the subject of her piece. She comments, 'Please do not let me wander' (*FIA*, p. 163). She must shape and control the composition of Washington and the scenery. After an interruption by a series of uncertain gestures she continues the composition. 'She is very sleepy' (ibid.) may be about Stein or about Alice Toklas. It may also be worry about the composition, translated into sleepy avoidance of the task of writing. But, whichever it is, it is a part of the meditation and is therefore stated rather than glossed over or eliminated as not pertinent. Into the picture now enters George Washington, 'famous as a nation' (ibid.), his claim to fame echoed by Stein's own or by her wish for fame. By 1931, when she wrote this piece, she was well aware of the conflicting claims upon her 'Of poetry. And friendship. And fame' ('Winning His Way', 1931; *SIM*, pp. 178, 194). Soon she was to speak of the conflict of God and Mammon.

Stein composes the portrait in a series of sections entitled 'Page 1', 'Page 2', and so on, as if each page were a chapter or a tableau in a series. The page units do not correspond to pages in the manuscript of the piece: she employs the designation simply as a variation from other numbered sections.

Time passes. By 'Page 9' the landscape, which opened in the morning, has turned dark, and the moon, again marking time, is full. Now 'They may be three to sing severally that George Washington may be seen to be beautifully with when they dwell then upon the beauty and autumn beauty of autumn scenery.' The landscape is composed of three. George Washington has become a part of it. 'One in two and one in three and one in one. And they may be not with some which may be that they are better with me. One and one. Or may be made a sun' (*FIA*, p. 164). Alone or together, one in one or two or three, George Washington is composed in the landscape, in the present of Stein's perception.

He enters the composition as an American, as a leader of his nation and a man of fame. The next day rain falls. The land is ploughed and planted. Washington is present as a farmer. By 'Page 12', Stein hints at the Bicentennial and the growth of America in two hundred years since George Washington, the father of his country, was born:

> And so George Washington is meant to be peopled.
> A play and an event.
> Also a story and their birth.   (*FIA*, p. 165)

The piece moves toward its completion with the hope for 'welfare in summer' (p. 166) after ploughing and planting and new growth.

The landscape is far more than a setting or background for Stein's meditations. It makes possible a way of composing and seeing. The enormous importance of the Bilignin countryside for Stein's life and work lies in the dramatic and visible shape that the landscape gives to her meditations.

But, if meditation is a highly dramatic process, it is never a process that requires an audience. The written meditation may be read *by* an audience, but it is never written *for* an audience. To Gertrude Stein, the word 'audience' spelled everything that was corrupt. It meant writing not for the sake of the composition but in order to please; not to shape a pattern of perception but to gain applause. Even in 1930 and 1931 – well before she wrote the *Autobiography* and became a best-selling author and a public personality – Stein began to worry about audience. Yet she always knew that in true meditation the author is present not as a personality but only as a perceiving, word-making consciousness. The exercises that are Stein's meditations are exercises of the mind, not exercises of a personality that displays itself. Throughout the *Stanzas*, which are filled with commonplace troubles and ordinary daily life, she attempts always to say what she sees, to state what is what and who is who in situations where everything is mixed up and where one is not always one but sometimes two and sometimes three and sometimes nothing. It is at times as if the stanzas hovered on the border of a no-man's-land where words become inaccessible and where identity dissolves and the visible world disappears from sight and from words. Disembodied and abstract kaleidoscopic patterns, her stanzas sometimes appear cut loose from the referential world. Yet these disembodied stanzas always begin with the events and objects of daily life. The process of meditation removes words from immediate referential connection with private experience only in order to make them speak their meaning more absolutely.

The commonplace and ordinary interested Stein far more than the extraordinary. Daily life in its most usual forms is the subject matter of all her work, and she constantly explored new ways to compose it accurately.

> She began at this time to describe landscape as if anything she saw was a natural phenomenon, a thing existent in itself. . . . I am trying to be as commonplace as I can be, she used to say to me. And then sometimes a little worried, it is not too commonplace. The last thing that she has finished, Stanzas of Meditation, and which I am now typewriting, she considers her real achievement of the commonplace.   (*ABT*, p. 276)

'It is not too commonplace' is not a question and requires no answer. Gertrude Stein knew that nothing was too commonplace for meditation and for composition. And meditation itself is simple and ordinary in the most serious sense of the word. 'In meditation. Florence Descotes. Is not resting. Nor indeed. Is she working. Nor preparing. And so they. Witness it' (*Civilization*, 1931; *O&P*, p. 133).[11]

When Florence Descotes meditates, the process is not dramatic and attracts no audience. Nor can it be called work or be measured by its results. Meditation is a disinterested, self-sufficient activity without measurable products and without preparation for anything beyond itself.

What Stein in 'An Elucidation' (1923) called 'an irregular commonplace' (*P&P*, p. 247), is that which is ordinary and particular, neither systematised nor regularised. The phenomena of nature are always irregular. Stein shows them in their everyday irregularity, which is also their singularity. In 'Sentences' (1928) she comments, after a lengthy discussion of one sentence, 'All this is an excellent example of a commonplace sentence which describes everything' (*HTW*, p. 168). She does not mean a vulgar sentence or a generalisation that applies to everything, although she is probably poking fun at sentences so vague that they apply to anything or nothing. She is speaking of an ordinary sentence for ordinary things – for anything. The word *commonplace*, for anyone born in the nineteenth century, also carries overtones of commonplace books, in which commonplaces or quotations – sentences worth preserving – are copied by the reader. Stein plays with all the many overtones of *commonplace*: the ordinary, the common, the vulgar, the trite, that which is interesting because it is irregular but overlooked because it is ordinary.

In *The Five Georges* it is said of two of the Georges

> That they were inclined
> To be mischievous
> Which makes it readily
> A commonplace
> Just as it is.
>   (*O&P*, p. 303)

The things that are at once typical and unique, as Sutherland has observed, are the things that are of interest. They are also the ones that not only provoke laughter but are the material of comedy. 'A festivity is a common place to-day' (*Madame Recamier*, 1930; *O&P*, p. 378). The commonplace makes for festivities and playfulness; it is never tragical. Hierarchies are serious matters; play is possible only among ordinary things. The opening-up of the word *commonplace* into *common* and *place* in the description of local festivities in Belley, familiar to Madame Récamier, creates a comic scene as a result of Stein's manipulation of the word.

In the world of Stein's writing the bonds that tie words to things are loosened and names split off from objects. Stein attempts to perceive everything fresh, as if she had never seen it before. She refuses to use words merely because they are associated with events or because grammatical habit prescribes their use in the construction of sentences. No class of words is more important than any other. Stein constructs with prepositions, pronouns and conjunctions as much as with nouns and verbs. There is no hierarchy of words or of usage. In 1927 she wrote a piece entitled 'Patriarchal Poetry', which implied that patriarchal poetry, along with other hierarchical systems, was dead and needed to be laid to rest.

> Patriarchal Poetry might be withstood.
> Patriarchal Poetry at peace.
> Patriarchal Poetry a piece.
> Patriarchal Poetry in peace.
> Patriarchal Poetry in pieces.

Patriarchal Poetry as peace to return to Patriarchal Poetry at
peace.

Patriarchal Poetry or peace to return to Patriarchal Poetry or
pieces of Patriarchal Poetry.   (*BTV*, p. 281)

She pays Patriarchal Poetry respect by capitalisation, but
capitalisation of something that is already in pieces becomes a
backhanded compliment.

Patriarchal organisation is vertical, hierarchical and fixed. The
landscape of Stein's world is horizontal, democratic and fluid. In it,
all things and all words are of equal value; nothing is more
important than anything else nor are words permanently attached
to things. To call hers a comic world means not that nothing is sacred
but that everything is sacred, from small to large, from near to far,
from word to word. Her meditations require slow reading, without
syntactical assumptions. The pleasure of reading Stein is the
pleasure of spreading out the words in a plentitude that creates not
uniformity but fullness of possibility.

The place where possibilities are unlimited, where new worlds
and identities are made and new relations are created, is the Forest
of Arden. Here the imagination rules that words are free, and
language breaks into song. *As You Like It* occupies a central position
in Stein's career. The epigraph to her early novel *Q. E. D.* is the
passage in which Sylvius responds to Phoebe's request to 'tell this
youth what 'tis to love' (v.ii.89). The early novel is an account of
Stein's own experience of love.

In the sixth stanza of part I of *Stanzas in Meditation* she returns to
the play, both in substance and language. A wedding day is
celebrated:

It is the day when we remember too.
We two remember two two who are theirs
Who are fat with glory too with two

The voice of these iambic lines rings of Shakespeare even though the
words are not a quotation. One phrase comes directly from 'Under
the Greenwood Tree':

This May in unison
All out of cloud. Come hither.[12]

In the Forest of Arden, where Jacques sings 'stanzos', identities change and names change. Women are the heroines of the play as they are of Stein's life. The play creates a world of words, and the words, disembodied and changeable, alter the course of lives. The pastoral forest allows no self-dramatisation, for serious workaday identities have been given up in comic detachment. Relationships change as names change, and words assume a life of their own. Gertrude Stein's saints would be comfortable meditating in Arden, where names and personalities move about like the glass pieces in a kaleidoscope, creating compositions.

Notes

Research for this essay, a part of a study of the work of Gertrude Stein from 1923 to 1932, was supported by a Fellowship for College Teachers from the National Endowment for the Humanities and by grant number 13220 from the PSC–CUNY Research Award Program of the City University of New York.

1. Mabel Dodge Luhan, 'Speculations or Post-Impressions in Prose', *Arts and Decorations*, 3 (1913) 172–4. It appears likely that Mabel Dodge relied at least in part on Gertrude Stein's own descriptions of her method. Since not all letters from Gertrude Stein are preserved, however, it is impossible to determine exactly what her statements may have been and how Mabel Dodge made use of them.
     Apparently Stein recommended her technique for achieving receptivity and concentration to others, who were not necessarily writers. On 27 December 1908, her friend Emily Dawson commented in a letter from London after her return from a visit to Paris, where she had seen Stein: 'I've tried – sometimes for quite 3 or 4 minutes – to sit, receptive and dumb, before the recollection of some of the Paris things you showed me! – There is no result except an intensifying of the wish to see it all again' (YCAL).
2. *Announcement of Courses of Instruction for 1894–1904*, Radcliffe College Archives.
3. Gertrude Stein and Leon Mendez Solomons, 'Normal Motor Automatism', *Psychological Review*, III, 5 (Sep 1896) 492–512.
4. More than twenty years after Stein's death, the theme of identity, which will be discussed in detail below, led to a finely written exchange between Virgil Thomson, who had collaborated with Stein, and Donald Sutherland, who had written about her work. In fall 1968, Sutherland, writing on board the SS *France*, thanked Thomson for the gift of two of his books and spoke of the pleasure they gave him. He continued,

The only bother is that there are certain turns of phrase or *clausalae* which I have used or might have used myself, as if I had cribbed them from you, but under God and Gertrude, we inevitably share, though so far apart, some movement or phrasing of the mind. I am, of course, more proud than anything else, to seem to resemble you when I do.

(Letter of 8 Oct 1968, Yale Music Library Archives)

Virgil Thomson answered Sutherland as eloquently as Sutherland had written to him. The rhetoric of their exchange must have delighted both the older and the younger man. It is a part of the larger context of Gertrude Stein's work that it is important to remember.

The turn of phrase identity we share with Maurice Grosser and Garrett Mattingly, both old Harvard friends. So maybe we all got it there, including Gertrude (except that you seem to be Princeton). Could it be Henry James via William? For Gertrude easily, for me possibly as a pupil of William's pupil Ralph Perry. The classical tinge won't work, since G. S. knew no Greek, no[r] do I. . . . But behind us all there is some Latinity and certainly the Macaulay that dominated American high schools. Anyway, I long ago noticed the consanguinity; and surely it is a good family we belong to.

5. The same passage is used again, introduced with the added subtitle 'Basic', in a piece written somewhat later in 1930, 'Absolutely as Bob Brown' (*PL*, p. 312).
6. Stein obviously knew Shelley's ode. The skylark recurs frequently in her writing of the 1920s and early 1930s. Here is one example, written in the country, which furnished the landscape central to Stein's perception from 1925 on: 'She says that skylarks should not be there. But says he cuckoos are there too. Not as pleasantly she said. She said not so pleasantly. Afterwards there was the arrangement that while some repeat all repeat two and two two and two four. Four and four four and four. Two' (1925–6; *NTY*, p. 28).
7. Autumn also dates the piece. The Haas–Gallup chronological listing attributes the piece to 1932. This date is the publication date rather than the composition date. The piece appeared in *Hound and Horn*, v, 4 (July–Sep 1932) 606–11. This issue of the magazine was distributed by early July 1932; the earliest review I have seen appeared in the *Boston Herald* on 13 July 1932 and was followed on 15 July by the *New York Times* review, others being printed later. The piece must have been written in autumn 1931. When Stein describes a particular season, it is safe to assume that she is describing what she sees, not what she remembers. See also Donald Gallup, 'A Note on the Manuscript', *FIA*, p. iv.
8. Virgil Thomson to Ulla Dydo, May 1981.
9. Bernard Faÿ, *Georges Washington Gentilhomme* (Paris: Editions Bernard Grasset, 1932), tr. as *George Washington: Republican Aristocrat* (Boston, Mass.: Houghton Mifflin, 1931).
10. Carlton's poem was published as 'National Festival: G. W., 1732–1932'

in *The American Mercury*, xxiv, 96 (Dec 1931) 402–8. The poem is an assemblage of innumerable details of popular culture, history, the movies, popular songs, cartoons, and so on. Not surprisingly, it also includes sections on contemporary writers, including many who were friends of Bob Brown: Sherwood Anderson, Ezra Pound, e e cummings, Gertrude Stein. This amusing poem is also a useful reminder of friendships among writers and of the ways in which they promoted and published each other. My account (forthcoming) of Stein's address at Cambridge and Oxford in 1926 (published as *Composition as Explanation*) tells in detail how one writer helped another who in turn promoted another. Mutual support is an important, though rarely discussed, part of literary history.

Here is the comment on Gertrude Stein from Brown's poem, which also reminds the reader that it was George Washington who had made Americans:

> Hold on a minute
> wait, wait
> begin again with Gertrude Stein in
> The Making of Americans.
> Begin again
> stop and don't stop
> with one foot in Heaven
> hay-foot, straw-foot
> belly full of bean-soup
> 　　(*American Mercury*, xxiv, 96, p. 404)

11. She is Florence Tanner, the elder sister of the pianist Allen Tanner. She married Georges Maratier at the beginning of September 1931. Stein gives her the name 'Descotes' in several pieces, for reasons that remain unclear to her brother also (letter from Allen Tanner to Ulla Dydo, 8 Sep 1981).

　　　The novelette 'Brim Beauvais' (1931), where she is called Florence, Florence Tanner or Florence Anna, is about her and Georges Maratier, who is given the name Brim Beauvais. A man of unclear identity and unsettled personality, he appears under a name other than his own; he has not yet come into his own. The Maratier–Tanner marriage was short-lived and ended in divorce.

12. The lines are quoted as they appear before revisions in the autograph manuscript text of *Stanzas*, which is different from the text in the Yale edition. The revisions are discussed in detail by Ulla E. Dydo, 'How to Read Gertrude Stein: The Manuscript of "Stanzas in Meditation" ', *Text: Transactions of the Society for Textual Scholarship*, ɪ (1981) 271–303.

5

(Im)Personating Gertrude Stein

MARJORIE PERLOFF

I

The Autobiography of Alice B. Toklas (1933) has always been considered Gertrude Stein's most 'readerly', her most 'transparent' text. In an important essay on *Stanzas in Meditation*, the difficult set of abstract poetic compositions written the very same summer as the autobiography, Ulla E. Dydo observes,

> The language of the *Autobiography* may surprise by its cleverness and felicity, but it never calls attention to itself by its difficulty. The life and times of Alice Toklas and Gertrude Stein make easy reading. The difficult language of *Stanzas*, on the other hand, demands a reader's full and equal attention to every single word as word. . . . The two books do not even sound as if they were by the same author. Gertrude Stein herself was quite clear about this difference. The *Autobiography* was the first of a series of books which she characterized as her 'open and public' books, or as 'audience writing'. . . . On the other hand, works like *Stanzas* – virtually everything Stein wrote up to 1932 and a good deal that she wrote after she became famous – she described as her 'real kind' of books: a literature of word compositions rather than a literature of subject matter.[1]

Compared to *Stanzas in Meditation*, the *Autobiography* is indeed an 'open and public' book, a book of 'subject matter' rather than of 'word compositions'. But, precisely because it does seem to be such 'easy reading', we tend to ignore its own very real difficulties. Both *The Autobiography of Alice B. Toklas* and the later *Everybody's Autobiography* (1937) are, in fact, anything but the straightforward,

61

anecdotal memoirs that readers, in search of good gossip about Picasso or Hemingway, take them to be.

A good example of the characteristic misreading to which the autobiographies are subjected may be found in Marty Martin's 'one-character play', *Gertrude Stein Gertrude Stein Gertrude Stein*, commissioned by the actress Pat Carroll, a play that has enjoyed extraordinary popularity since it opened at the Circle Repertory Theater in New York on 4 June 1979.[2] On the blurb of the Random House edition of the play we read,

> Here is the text of the one-woman play that has become for many the essence of Gertrude Stein. Set in 1938 in her famous apartment at 27 rue de Fleurus in Paris, from which she is being evicted, it is an imaginary monologue – in true Stein style – that covers her childhood in California, her studies at Harvard with William James, her decision to leave America and come to Paris with her brother Leo, her discovery of Alice B. Toklas (who, in the play, is asleep upstairs), her pleasure in that relationship, and her favorite reminiscences of the famous people they have entertained – Marie Laurencin, Bernard Berenson, Picasso, Matisse, Cézanne, Isadora and Raymond Duncan, Scott and Zelda Fitzgerald, the young Ernest Hemingway, and many more.[3]

The implication here is that 'true Stein style' is something that can be distilled from the actual Stein text by the mere retelling of the stories contained in the autobiographies. Indeed, in his Introduction to the play, Robert A. Wilson goes so far as to suggest that Martin's play captures the 'essence of Gertrude Stein' more fully than does Stein's own writing:

> In all the voluminous literature that has been written about Gertrude Stein, there is very little that gives us any clue as to what she was like in person. The preponderance of exegesis on her work, while in the main useful and helpful, has been pretty much one-sided. This unfortunate imbalance has been amply corrected by Marty Martin's *Gertrude Stein Gertrude Stein Gertrude Stein*. . . . It is an extraordinary work of art on many levels. It brings Stein to life so vividly that for many people the image of the real Gertrude has begun to fuse with that of Pat Carroll.[4]

The longing for 'the image of the real Gertrude' has bedevilled

Stein criticism almost from the beginning. On the one hand, there is the public persona, the legendary Gertrude of 'A rose is a rose is a rose is a rose' and the Picasso portrait. On the other, there are the non-representational, hermetic works such as *Tender Buttons* and *Stanzas in Meditation*. What mediates between these two would seem to be the 'open and public' *Autobiography of Alice B. Toklas*, but even this 'transparent' text has its curious evasions, the most obvious one being the avoidance of any overt reference to Stein's real relationship with Alice Toklas.[5] Hence the zeal, of which Martin's play is but one instance, to get 'behind' the matter-of-fact recounting of evenings on the rue de Fleurus and afternoons in Picasso's studio. In *Gertrude Stein Gertrude Stein Gertrude Stein*, Robert A. Wilson declares, 'Nothing is withheld. [Stein] shares with us her joys and sorrows, her dislikes and her enthusiasms, but above all her gusto and zest for life, communicated through mere words – words that were her lifelong passion and concern'.[6]

The assumption that 'mere words' constitute a vehicle by means of which a writer 'communicates' an already existing emotion such as 'joy' or 'sorrow' goes against the very essence of Stein's literary enterprise, whose purpose was precisely to demonstrate that language is not transparent, that it does not point innocently to a world of objects or ideas somewhere outside itself. Ironically, what the critics liked so much about Pat Carroll's 'Gertrude Stein' is that here the 'words' that ostensibly 'constituted her lifelong passion and concern' are, in fact, wholly subordinated to the stereotype of Gertrude the Eccentric, a woman memorable chiefly for her salon, her outrageous *bons mots* (such as 'A rose is a rose is a rose is a rose'), and her friendship with Picasso and other great artists. In the words of Walter Kerr for the *New York Times*, 'Miss Carroll . . . gives us the bizarre, close-cropped, richly robed woman who could be – and once was – mistaken for a bishop with a zest that is awesome.' In the *New York Post* Marilyn Stasio declared,

My dears, we were absolutely spellbound. Here is this woman, quite alone on the stage. . . . She sits like a monarch in a thronelike chair, her voluminous girth draped in brown, and she fixes us with a penetrating look. Then she takes a sip of iced tea, puffs on a thin cigar and begins to speak. Within minutes, she has us mesmerized . . . she is wonderful wonderful wonderful. . . . She talks to us of many fascinating things: of Picasso's views on Cubism and how she translated them into her poetry; of her

beloved brother Leo and their fierce aesthetic feud . . . . But best
of all she tells delightful stories.

'Wickedly funny' stories that cause Howard Kissel of *Women's Wear
Daily* to exclaim, 'Having always imagined Stein as a rather
foreboding woman, I found Carroll jollier than I would have
expected.' On the other hand, Don Nelsen, in the *Daily News*,
remarks that Pat Carroll succeeds in conveying 'much of the pain,
the loneliness that comes with being different. There is the touching
reference to her first lesbian encounter, which Carroll invests with
an aching nostalgia.' And Nelsen concludes, 'I have never thought
of Gertrude Stein as a particularly enchanting person but if she was
anything like Carroll's portrait, she must have been.'[7]

The *reductio ad absurdum* is perfect. Gertrude Stein sanitised, made
appropriately 'jolly' or 'touching', as the case may be, and filling our
hearts with an 'aching nostalgia' for *la belle époque* and its Parisian
aftermath – this is the feat evidently achieved by Carroll and Martin.
For those of us who care about Stein's work rather than her life, the
play would not be especially interesting, were it not that Martin's
vulgarised and trivialised pseudo-portrait of the artist is made up of
what are often only slight variations on Stein's own lexicon and
syntax. Indeed, many passages in the play are taken directly, almost
verbatim, from *The Autobiography of Alice B. Toklas*. Such passages
instruct us, negatively, as it were, about Stein's actual verbal and
syntactic habits. Again, since the two autobiographies are generally
held to be Stein's most accessible texts, texts that have none of the
difficulties or disjunctions of, say, *Stanzas in Meditation*, the Martin
adaptation can remind us that, even at its most seemingly
'transparent', Stein's language is itself what William Gass in his
Introduction to *The Geographical History of America* has called 'a
complete analogue of experience' (*GHA*, p. 25). 'I became', says
Stein in 'Portraits and Repetition' (1934), 'more and more excited
about how words which were the words that made whatever I
looked at look like itself were not the words that had in them any
quality of description' (*LIA*, p. 191). It is this resistance to
'description', even in the autobiographies, that I wish to discuss.

II

Like so many of Stein's early critics, Marty Martin seems to think that the famous Stein style depends upon the use of 'ordinary', everyday diction, simple declarative sentences, and, above all, verbal and phrasal repetition, often with complicated incremental patterning. Accordingly, *Gertrude Stein Gertrude Stein Gertrude Stein* opens with the sentence, 'It is   it always is   and it always most certainly is an inconvenience being evicted   I know   and we were.'[8] The childlike parataxis and additive repetition is calculated to appeal to an audience that vaguely knows of Stein's eccentric way of putting things, but it is actually wholly un-Steinian in its drive toward closure. Martin's is a suspended sentence that comes to rest in a tidy conclusion, the news of the eviction. The same pattern occurs at the beginning of the second paragraph, where we read, 'Before I came to be living here   I was going to be not living there   there is in America'. The repetition has an air of ingenuousness and bonhommie belied by the very tight logic beneath the surface: 'I came here because I was not going to live there.' It is a logic that contradicts Stein's insistence, in *Composition as Explanation* (1926), that 'Continuous present is one thing and beginning again is another thing. These are both things. And then there is using everything' (*CE*, pp. 31–2).

Critics regularly pay lip service to these Steinian principles but it is not always easy, especially in the case of *The Autobiography of Alice B. Toklas*, where repetition is not a prominent feature, to see what 'beginning again and again' and 'using everything' really means. In what sense, for that matter, is the *Autobiography* a 'continuous present'? 'So innocently discursive is the book's style', says Richard Bridgman, 'that it is regarded as gossip, pleasant to read but undeserving of serious critical attention'.[9]

The chief device of the *Autobiography* is, of course, the inversion of the autobiographical convention brought about by making Alice the narrator of Gertrude's story, what Stein herself called 'the inside as seen from the outside' (*ABT*, p. 192). The ambiguity created by this use of narrative voice cannot be duplicated in a dramatic monologue spoken by Stein herself, but there are other features of the *Autobiography* – its narrative structure, its pace, its syntax and word choice – that might have been left intact. What happens when a particular paragraph is rearranged or an adjective added is thus revealing.

Consider Martin's version of Stein's narrative portrait of Marie Laurencin, the proto-cubist painter who was, before the First World War, Apollinaire's mistress and whose graceful group portrait of herself, Apollinaire, Picasso and his mistress Fernande Olivier (Plate 6) Stein bought in 1908, thus signalling Laurencin's first sale. In the *Autobiography*, Marie Laurencin is introduced in the opening chapter, in which 'Alice' recalls the 'vernissage of the Independent', to which Gertrude had invited her shortly after her arrival in Paris:

> There was also there if my memory is correct a strange picture by the same douanier Rousseau, a sort of apotheosis of Guillaume Apollinaire with an aged Marie Laurencin behind him as a muse. That also I would not have recognised as a serious work of art. At that time of course I knew nothing about Marie Laurencin and Guillaume Apollinaire but there is a lot to tell about them later.
>
> (pp. 20–1, and see Plate 7)

Here Stein uses the naïve narrator, Alice, to set the stage for what is to come. Alice is soon dispatched by Gertrude to take French lessons from Fernande and, in the course of much idle chit-chat, '[Fernande] told me about a mysterious horrible woman called Marie Laurencin who made noises like an animal and annoyed Picasso. I thought of her as a horrible old woman and was delighted when I met the young chic Marie who looked like a Clouet' (p. 32).

Notice that both these preliminary versions of Marie Laurencin – the male painter's (Rousseau's) image of her as aged muse, and the gossipy dismissal, on the part of the bourgeois and vacuous Fernande, of Marie as a 'horrible woman' who 'annoys' a second man, this time the painter already established in the *Autobiography* as Stein's hero, Picasso – are cast in doubt by Alice's reference to 'the young chic Marie who looked like a Clouet'. In the larger structure of the autobiography, Marie Laurencin, an artist but not a literary artist and hence not a direct threat to Gertrude Stein, serves as one of the author's alter egos. There is a sympathy between the two women that, as we shall see, becomes overt in *Everybody's Autobiography*. But there is also a certain distance: Stein's complex response to Laurencin is presented most vividly in the comic scene in chapter 3 (a flashback to the pre-Toklas period in Stein's life) when the two women meet for the first time. This incident (Laurencin's first visit to the rue de Fleurus) is also prominent in Stein's monologue in Act I of *Gertrude Stein Gertrude Stein Gertrude Stein*. Compare the two openings:

Everybody   called   Gertrude   Stein   Gertrude,   or   at   most

Mademoiselle Gertrude, everybody called Picasso Pablo and
Fernande Fernande and everybody called Guillaume Apollinaire
Guillaume and Max Jacob Max but everybody called Marie
Laurencin Marie Laurencin.

The first time Gertrude Stein ever saw Marie Laurencin,
Guillaume Apollinaire brought her to the rue de Fleurus, not on a
Saturday evening, but another evening. She was very interesting.
They were an extraordinary pair. Marie Laurencin was terribly
near-sighted and of course she never wore eye-glasses, no french
woman and few frenchmen did in those days. She used a
lorgnette.   (*ABT*, p. 74)

Marie Laurencin and Apollinaire were lovers then and in
those days Fernande was *la belle* Fernande   Picasso
was   Pablo   I   was   Gertrude   or   Mademoiselle
Zhertrude   Max   was   Max   and   Apollinaire   was
Guillaume   but   Marie   Laurencin   was   always   Marie
Laurencin   she is still Marie Laurencin   Marie would
not do   it is not enough   it has to be the whole thing
always   with   her   and   so   she   was   always   Marie
Laurencin   and she still is.

She was a painter   Marie Laurencin   the only woman
painter in the movement and very strange. She did a portrait of
Picasso   Fernande   Apollinaire   and herself and
it was very strange   and I bought it from her   she had
never sold one before. Apollinaire was so pleased that he wrote a
little pamphlet about the movement in which he referred to it as
cubist   he was the first to call it that   and everybody
then   was   pleased   especially   Marie   Laurencin   who
was now being exhibited beside Picasso and Matisse.

Her first visit to the rue de Fleurus was an event   a real
one   it was not on a Saturday nor was it before
eleven   but she was so interesting and so we let her
in   what the hell.   The first thing she did was to
fall   she was terribly near-sighted and things got in her way
a lot   she did not wear eyeglasses   the French people
never do   she always used a lorgnette . . . .[10]

One can argue that the middle paragraph of the Martin passage is an essential addition, since the contemporary audience is not likely to know anything about Marie Laurencin, 'the only woman painter in the movement'. But the irony is that Stein's own prose, so much sparer and leaner than Martin's and quite devoid of Martin's pseudo-Steinian repetitions, tells it all anyway.

Why, to begin with, is Marie Laurencin called by her full name when everyone else is known by his or her Christian name? The poets and artists to whom Stein refers – Apollinaire, Jacob, Picasso – were close friends; to each other, they were quite naturally Guillaume, Max and Pablo. Fernande, as a mere appendage of Picasso's, was of course Fernande, whereas the Stein of the pre-war years was known chiefly for her salon and her paintings – hence she is 'Gertrude, or at most Mademoiselle Gertrude'. But the Picasso–Apollinaire cenacle did not quite know how to assimilate the woman painter in their midst. To call her 'Marie' would be to equate her with Fernande the mistress or Gertrude the hostess, and so she is called Marie Laurencin even as it is still customary today to talk of Joyce, Lawrence, and Virginia Woolf, or, for that matter, of Hemingway and Gertrude Stein.

Accordingly, Stein doesn't need to tell us that Laurencin was 'the only woman painter in the movement', that her style was cubist, or, indeed, that she and Apollinaire were lovers. But Martin's changes in the narrative of the visit itself are even more revealing. Stein has Alice tell us flatly, 'The first time Gertrude Stein ever saw Marie Laurencin, Guillaume Apollinaire brought her to the rue de Fleurus, not on a Saturday evening, but another evening. She was very interesting. They were an extraordinary pair.' Martin transforms this as follows: 'Her first visit to the rue de Fleurus was an event   a real one   it was not on a Saturday nor was it before eleven   but she was so interesting and so we let her in   what the hell.' Using everything: the invitation to come 'not on a Saturday evening, but another evening' is a sign of favour: the regulars were only invited on Saturdays. The narrator doesn't need to tell us that it 'was an event'. The adjectives 'interesting' and 'extraordinary' are characteristically Steinian in their inde-terminacy. Both can be spoken in different voices, interpreted in different ways. 'Interesting' in what sense? What made Apollinaire and Laurencin 'an extraordinary pair'? Stein lets the question hang. The notion in the Martin text that Laurencin was allowed in the door *because* she was 'so interesting' makes a travesty of the codes that governed the Stein salon: it implies that Marie

Laurencin had to make a particular impression in order to be
admitted, that she all but forced her way into the salon, whereas in
the *Autobiography* she comes there quite naturally as Apollinaire's
mistress. The false note of these lines reaches its climax in the
curiously un-Steinian 'what the hell'.

By now we can begin to see that Stein's strategy in the
Autobiography is to be absolutely precise about person (Apollinaire
and Marie Laurencin), place (the rue de Fleurus) and time ('The first
time', 'not on a Saturday evening, but another evening'), even as
she implies that her characters can never be fully knowable. There
are certain things, the text implies, that can be known and others
that cannot be; the despised adjective ('the first thing', says Stein in
'Poetry and Grammar' [1934], 'that anybody takes out of anybody's
writing are the adjectives' – *LIA*, p. 211) cannot, in any case, directly
describe human behaviour. Rather, the writer, like the cubist painter,
digresses metonymically from actor to action: 'Marie Laurencin was
terribly near-sighted and of course she never wore eye-glasses, no
french woman and few frenchmen did in those days. She used a
lorgnette.' This has the ring of ordinary conversation, wholly
'natural'. Doesn't everybody write this way? Not Marty Martin: 'The
first thing she did was to fall   she was terribly near-sighted
and things got in her way a lot   she did not wear
eyeglasses   the French people never do   she always used
a lorgnette.' Again, the Martin passage adds gratuitous clauses
(obviously, if Laurencin was near-sighted, things got in her way and
she was prone to fall), even as it misconstrues the import of Stein's
sentences. The 'of course' refers to the treatment of women 'in those
days', a phrase that is essential to Stein's meaning because she is
characterising, from the vantage point of the early 1930s, the first
decade of the century, when cubism and its cognates were born.
Martin's switch to the present tense – 'French people never do' –
thus distorts an important social reality, the *belle époque* etiquette
which demanded that a woman be as pretty and as perfectly turned
out as possible, even if she might literally not see what was in front
of her – surely a terrible fate for a painter. The rule 'in those days'
applied to men as well, but, the text suggests, there were already 'a
few frenchmen' who were willing to break it. When we remember
how the Stein who wrote *The Autobiography of Alice B. Toklas* violated
'normal' dress, coiffure, and make-up codes, we realise that the
account of Laurencin's myopia is not mere anecdote.

The portrait of the lady with the lorgnette now comes to life, both in the *Autobiography* and in *Gertrude Stein Gertrude Stein Gertrude Stein*: Here is Stein's own account as reported by Alice:

> She looked at each picture carefully that is, every picture on the line, bringing her eye close and moving over the whole of it with her lorgnette, an inch at a time. The pictures out of reach she ignored. Finally she remarked, as for myself, I prefer portraits and that is of course quite natural, as I myself am a Clouet. And it was perfectly true, she was a Clouet. She had the square thin build of the mediaeval french women in the french primitives. She spoke in a high pitched beautifully modulated voice. She sat down beside Gertrude Stein on the couch and she recounted the story of her life, told that her mother who had always had it in her nature to dislike men had been for many years the mistress of an important personage, had borne her, Marie Laurencin. I have never, she added, dared let her know Guillaume although of course he is so sweet that she could not refuse to like him but better not. Some day you will see her.
>
> And later on Gertrude Stein saw the mother and by that time I was in Paris and I was taken along.
>
> Marie Laurencin, leading her strange life and making her strange art, lived with her mother, who was a very quiet, very pleasant, very dignified woman, as if the two were living in a convent. The small apartment was filled with needlework which the mother had executed after the designs of Marie Laurencin. Marie and her mother acted toward each other exactly as a young nun with an older one. It was all very strange. Later just before the war the mother fell ill and died. Then the mother did see Guillaume Apollinaire and liked him.
>
> After the mother's death Marie Laurencin lost all sense of stability. She and Guillaume no longer saw each other. A relation that had existed as long as the mother lived without the mother's knowledge now that the mother was dead and had seen and liked Guillaume could no longer endure. Marie against the advice of all her friends married a german. When her friends remonstrated with her she said, but he is the only one who can give me a feeling of my mother.   (*ABT*, pp. 74–6)

Martin renders this passage as follows:

> the next thing she did was to examine every picture within reach going over them one inch at a time with the lorgnette.

I prefer portraits   she finally said   being one
myself   I am a Clouet   you know   and she was a
perfect Clouet. We sat down together and she told me her life
history   and how in all the years that she and Guillaume had
been lovers   her mother   with whom she lived
alone   had never known. She did not care much for
men   her mother   and their apartment was rather like
a convent but then the mother died and it did not seem to matter
to Marie Laurencin anymore   and so she and Guillaume
stopped seeing one another   the mystery was gone.
Anyway   after that   she married a German   who
reminded her of her mother and her friends were
grieved   but it did not last and before long she was back to
the rue de Fleurus   but with Eric Satie now.

*   *   *

New lovers were like jewelry to women then   and they
always wore their new lovers whenever they went out   or
took the air as they would say.[11]

In Stein's own 'continuous present', Marie Laurencin is defined in
the act of looking at the pictures: the syntax of the opening sentences
mimes the narrator's perception of the action – 'She looked at each
picture carefully', to which is added the qualification 'that is, every
picture on the line', and finally the specification 'an inch at a time'.
In recording Laurencin's words, Stein imitates, as she does
throughout the *Autobiography*, the actual French syntax Laurencin
would have used: 'Quant à moi [as for myself], je préfère les
portraits . . . .' Her 'I myself am a Clouet' is followed by the
narrator's ironic comment, 'And it was perfectly true, she was a
Clouet' – ironic in that this confident assertion cannot really be
Alice's; it is only the masked 'I' of Gertrude who knows it to be the
case. Martin turns the opening sentence around – 'going over them
one inch at a time with the lorgnette' – so that what Stein calls in
'Poetry and Grammar' 'the balance of a space completely not filled
but created by something moving' is destroyed (*LIA*, p. 225).[12] More
important, she has Marie say 'I prefer portraits . . . being one
myself   I am a Clouet', rather than, in Stein's words, 'I prefer
portraits and that is of course quite natural, as I myself am a Clouet'.
To say 'I am a Clouet' is to specify, to define oneself as having a

particular look, an aura. To say, 'I prefer portraits being one myself' is merely foolish, the sort of thing no artist would say since any person is potentially the subject of a portrait. Even more telling is the transferred epithet in the next sentence. Stein writes, 'And it was perfectly true, she was a Clouet'; Martin: 'and she was a perfect Clouet'. But the phrase 'a perfect Clouet' would have made no sense whatever to Stein, according to whose poetic the subject either is or is not a Clouet. For what would an 'imperfect Clouet' be?

To understand Stein's concept of the sentence, we must study precisely the omission of such lazy modifiers. 'She was a perfect Clouet' is a sentence one might read in *Vogue*; one would never find it in Stein's work. On the other hand, it makes sense to say that a given statement – for instance Marie's 'I am a Clouet' – is 'perfectly true'. 'Using everything' means knowing when not to use something.

The same principle governs Stein's account of Marie Laurencin's relationship with her mother. The paradox of the mother 'who had always had it in her nature to dislike men' and yet 'had been for many years the mistress of an important personage' (the unnamed personage being Marie's father) is flattened out in Martin's version: 'She did not care much for men   her mother   and their apartment was rather like a convent'. Notice that Stein says no such thing. It is the mode of living, not merely the physical space of the apartment, that calls to mind a convent. And that mode of living is characterised by the typically Steinian adjective, 'strange', used three times:

> Marie Laurencin, leading her strange life and making her strange art, lived with her mother, who was a very quiet, very pleasant, very dignified woman, as if the two were living in a convent. The small apartment was filled with needlework which the mother had executed after the designs of Marie Laurencin. Marie and her mother acted toward each other exactly as a young nun with an older one. It was all very strange.

It is important to know that Laurencin's mother was 'very quiet, very pleasant, very dignified', because it is precisely her pleasantness, her dignity, her use of Marie's designs as models for needlework that evidently creates the conflict in Marie's life. The details of the mother–daughter relationship matter less than the irony that Marie's is the life of 'a young nun with an older one', imposed on the sensibility of an artist who frequents the Bateau Lavoir.

The irony of Marie Laurencin's portrait, as it is presented to us in the *Autobiography*, is that she is capable only of living this double life. 'Later', reports Alice Toklas with a touch of malice, 'just before the war the mother fell ill and died. Then the mother did see Guillaume Apollinaire and liked him.' But there can be no freedom from a needed double-bind. Stein now presents us with a paragraph built on the permutations of the words 'mother' and 'longer' and on the opposition of the words 'knowledge' and 'feeling':

> After her *mother's* death Marie Laurencin lost all sense of stability. She and Guillaume no *longer* saw each other. A relation that had existed as *long* as the *mother* lived without the *mother's knowledge* now that the *mother* was dead and had seen and liked Guillaume could no *longer* endure. Marie against the advice of all her friends married a german. When her friends remonstrated with her she said, but he is the only one who can give me a *feeling* of my mother.

The mother must not 'know' about Apollinaire (or indeed about her daughter's life as an artist) but the daughter needs (again the syntax is based on the French) 'the feeling of my mother' ('le sentiment de ma mère'). The anonymous 'german' can meet this need only as long as he is the enemy. Inevitably, then, when the war ends, so does this particular marriage.

The poignant irony of Laurencin's situation becomes, in Martin's text, no more than a crude joke: 'then the mother died and it did not seem to matter to Marie Laurencin anymore   and so she and Guillaume stopped seeing one another   the mystery was gone'. 'The mystery was gone' is a sort of soap-opera summary of what really happened; equally reductive is the reference, in the next sentence, to the German (note the capital 'G' here) 'who reminded her of her mother'. 'He is the only one who can give me   a feeling of my mother' means 'the only kind of husband I can rebel against even as I rebelled against my mother'. It has nothing to do with actual resemblance or substitution.

As her version of what the reviewers have considered a 'delicious anecdote' about Marie Laurencin reaches its climax, Martin gives it a final twist, designed for the off-Broadway, which is to say the Broadway, audience:

before long she was back to the rue de Fleurus   but with Eric
Satie now.

*   *   *

New lovers were like jewelry to women then   and they
always wore their new lovers whenever they went out   or
took the air as they would say. Fernande disapproved of such
behavior. . . .

Anyway. In the midst of all that   there was
Picasso   always totally Picasso   listening and watching
and thinking Spanish thoughts. He was busily creating the
twentieth century in those days . . . .[13]

Ah, *la belle époque* when women wore their lovers like new jewelry!
How charming! A sea of lovely women, Maries or Fernandes as the
case may be, in the midst of which there is Picasso, 'always totally
Picasso', singlehandedly 'creating the twentieth century'. And what
thoughts could the exotic Picasso have but 'Spanish thoughts'?

But of course by this time the 'real' Gertrude Stein, if by 'real' we
mean the author inscribed in the text of *The Autobiography of Alice B.
Toklas*, has evaporated. For the 'Gertrude Stein' of the *Autobiography*
is, as Neil Schmitz has so convincingly shown,[14] the antagonist as
well as the close friend of Picasso. 'The risk of becoming Picasso's
Gertrude' is, indeed, the animating force that informs the narrative,
involving, as it does, the crucial question of Stein's identity both as
woman and as writer. In the world of *Gertrude Stein Gertrude Stein
Gertrude Stein*, however, Picasso, Apollinaire, and Marie Laurencin
became mere grist for the anecdotal mill. When, for example, Martin
adapts Stein's account of the famous 'Rousseau Banquet' (*ABT*,
ch. 5: '1907–1914'), comic pathos gives way to smart sarcasm. In the
Autobiography, we are told that Marie Laurencin, who, in the
absence of Apollinaire, 'has been taking too many preliminary
apéritifs', is led up the steep Montmartre streets to the Bateau
Lavoir, 'supported on the one side by Gertrude Stein and on the
other by Gertrude Stein's brother and . . . falling first into one pair
of arms and then into another, her voice always high and sweet and
her arms always thin graceful and long' (*ABT*, p. 128). In Act II of the
play, the reference is to 'Marie Laurencin [who] was up and
dancing   drunk of course', and Gertrude then recalls how

'Marie Laurencin . . . had lost all sense of direction   so Leo and I exchanged her back and forth   until we got to the top'.[15] The qualification introduced in the Stein sentence by the references to the 'voice always high and sweet' and the 'arms always thin graceful and long' is erased, even as 'falling' is portentously made to symbolize the '[loss] of all sense of direction'. Laurencin becomes, in short, a stock comedy character, the likable but nutty artist. But, since Martin's Gertrude is herself such a 'character', we respond to this and related anecdotes as all part of what Robert A. Wilson calls 'the exquisite pleasure of getting to know Gertrude Stein herself'.[16]

Stein the writer had little use for such exquisite pleasures. In *Everybody's Autobiography*, Marie Laurencin reappears as one of the painters (the others are Braque and Matisse) who are angry at Gertrude Stein for portraying them in a less than flattering light in *Alice B. Toklas*. The two women, the narrator tells us, had not seen each other for a long time when they met in the salon of Marie Louise Bousquet in the mid-thirties. Here is Stein's account, now presented not as the discourse of 'Alice' but as that of Gertrude herself, a discourse written in Stein's characteristic mode of repetition which Marty Martin so painstakingly imitates in her play:

> Marie Laurencin had been in Paris ever since the war was over, and sometimes everything went well with her and sometimes everything did not go so well but she always went on pretty well. She was not one of the painters who made an extraordinarily large amount of money during the period that was called the epoch roughly from twenty-three to thirty-three she made less then than any of them and finally she took to teaching and all her pupils found her very amusing. She had grown stout by then but not too stout to be amusing. The French women always used to say a woman's silhouette should change every ten years. It should not grow less it should grow more and mostly it does. Marie Laurencin's had but it made her just that more pleasing. She used to play the harmonium and René Crevel and all the others described her doing so and it was very pleasing. Her pupils later were pleased that when they could not draw a foot she would tell them that she herself when she could not do anything always did it in profile, that was an easier way to do everything. (*EA*, pp. 33–4)

'A sentence', said Gertrude Stein, 'should never think.' And further, 'Remember a sentence should not have a name. A name is familiar. A sentence should not be familiar. . . . If there is a name in a sentence a name which is familiar makes a data and therefor there is no equilibrium' (*HTW*, pp. 166–7).[17] Like most of Stein's prescriptions for literature, this one is puzzling, but in comparing Stein's own sentences to Marty Martin's we can see what Stein means by 'equilibrium'.

To speak of Picasso 'thinking Spanish thoughts', of Marie Laurencin as a 'perfect Clouet', of Leo Stein as being a 'quattrocento art enthusiast'[18] and of Ambroise Vollard as 'a collector *extraordinaire*'[19] is to introduce what Stein calls 'a name which is familiar' and hence 'makes a data'. Sentences should not centre on such nouns and adjectives, for these are tags that leave nothing to the reader's imagination. Value judgements, moreover, are at best tentative. Martin's Gertrude says, 'My mother was very nice and very dull';[20] in *The Autobiography of Alice B. Toklas* we read 'Gertrude Stein's mother as she describes her in The Making of Americans, a gentle pleasant little woman with a quick temper, flatly refused to see her sister-in-law again' (*ABT*, p. 92). Martin's Leo tells Gertrude, 'I like the term publish   Gertrude   for me it holds a certain dignity   and you like the term publicity'.[21] 'Publicity' is what Stein calls a 'name', mere data. In *Everybody's Autobiography*, on which this passage in the play draws, names (nouns) give way to pronouns ('Pronouns', says Stein, 'are not as bad as nouns because . . . they cannot have adjectives go with them' – *LIA*, p. 213), and the repetitive grammatical constructions produce the desired 'equilibrium': 'He said it was not it it was I. If I was not there to be there with what I did then what I did would not be what it was. In other words if no one knew me actually then the things I did would not be what they were' (*EA*, pp. 76–7).

Which brings us back to the portrait of Marie Laurencin, who 'had been in Paris ever since the war was over, and sometimes everything went well with her and sometimes everything did not go so well but she always went on pretty well'. By the time we reach the end of this sentence, we know that 'pretty well' is much less than 'well'. The next sentence bears this out: Laurencin 'was not one of the painters who made an extraordinarily large amount of money' during the twenties; 'she made less then than any of them'. Nowhere does Stein say that this lack of success has anything to do with Laurencin's being not like 'any of them' in that she is a woman, but it is implicit in what follows. Marie Laurencin becomes a teacher and all her pupils find her 'very amusing' – an equivocal epithet. Is Marie 'amusing' in the sense of 'entertaining' or 'amusing' in the sense of 'to be laughed at'? The next sentence, 'She had grown stout by then but not too stout to be amusing' compounds the issue. Laurencin is judged to be not brilliant or exciting or even interesting, but merely 'pleasing'. 'Pleasing' in her stoutness. 'Very pleasing' in her playing of the harmonium for René Crevel. And, further, 'Her pupils later were pleased that when they could not draw a foot she would tell them that she herself when she could not do anything always did it in profile, that was an easier way to do everything.'

But since when should art be the domain of the 'pretty well', the 'amusing', the 'pleasing', and the 'easier way'? The stout Marie Laurencin who now is 'pleased' to see Gertrude but 'not . . . pleased that I had spoken of all of them and of the old days', and who declares that 'no painter could be pleased' by *The Autobiography of Alice B. Toklas* because 'the past of a painter was not a past because a painter lived in what he saw and he could not see his past' (*EA*, p. 34) is a woman who, so the text implies, cannot see her past, cannot see, in other words, that she has given up her art for the 'easier way to do everything'. The unstated comparison is that between the stout Marie and the equally stout Gertrude, who has fulfilled her potential as an artist.

But this comparison is never pressed. 'A sentence should never think', it should 'not have a name . . . a name which is familiar makes a data and therefor there is no equilibrium'. In *Everybody's Autobiography*, the portrait of Marie Laurencin is not contaminated by such data as 'drunk as usual', or 'quattrocento' or 'the extraordinary world of the struggling artists and poets who lived in the Latin Quarter in Paris'.[22] In Stein's world, there are no such facile judgements; there is only a continuous present. 'Everything went well with her and sometimes everything did not go so well but she always went on pretty well.' 'Pretty well' – 'teaching' – 'amusing' – 'stout' – 'pleasing' – 'very pleasing' – 'an easier way to do everything': this chain of equivocal adjectives, gerunds and noun phrases gives us the measure of Marie Laurencin, as the narrator sees her.

The portrait of Marie Laurencin, as it appears in *Everybody's Autobiography*, can thus be neither summarised nor 'translated' into a more accessible, clear-cut version. Hence the difficulty, indeed the impossibility, of impersonating Gertrude Stein. It is a question of distorting, not fact, as Robert A. Wilson fears,[23] but inflection.

Stein's conclusion that 'Marie Laurencin said it and she saw it and it has to be seen' (*EA*, p. 35) might profitably be applied to the text itself, which also has to be seen, or rather read. To ventriloquise such a text is all but impossible, for its 'equilibrium' depends upon the most minute adjustment of word and syntax, on its refusal to discriminate between the 'more' and 'less' important and to tell us what to think of Picasso or Laurencin or, for that matter, of Stein herself.

'In the *Autobiography*', writes Ulla E. Dydo, '[Stein] renders the appearance and the public image, with the sort of peace-loving statements an audience likes to hear. In the [*Stanzas in Meditation*] she depicts the war, in all its disparate pieces.'[24] It is true that what the 'audience likes to hear' in the *Autobiography* is a pleasant, 'peace-loving' statement such as the following description of the 'Rousseau Banquet': 'The ceremonies began. Guillaume Apollinaire got up and made a solemn eulogy. I do not remember at all what he said but it ended up with a poem he had written and which he half chanted and in which everybody joined in the refrain, La peinture de ce Rousseau' (*ABT*, p. 128). If this is not the 'war' of *Stanzas* (and Dydo is referring to the sexual tension between Stein and Toklas in summer 1932), neither is it as pretty as it seems on a first reading. 'I do not remember at all what he said but it ended with a poem he had written and which he half chanted' – the implication of Alice's disclaimer is that Apollinaire's poem, sloppily incorporated into the eulogy, is not worth remembering; it is, in any case, one of those familiar lyric poems that rely on conventional refrain rather than on the repetition of which Stein herself was the master. A quick shift into French, 'La peinture de ce Rousseau', serves to mock the rival poet. And what did Stein herself recite at the Rousseau banquet? What toast did she make to the Douanier? As Alice recalls it, 'Guillaume Apollinaire solemnly approached myself and my friend and asked us to sing some of the native songs of the red indians. We did not either of us feel up to that to the great regret of Guillaume Apollinaire' (*ABT*, p. 129).

And, it would seem, to the great regret of Stein's own audience, which is troubled by her austerity, by the absence, as it were, of song in her work. Soon, no doubt, someone will write a play or make a film in which Gertrude and Alice will appear in Harry's Bar, singing the native songs of the red indians.

Notes

1. Ulla E. Dydo, *'Stanzas in Meditation:* The Other Autobiography', *Chicago Review*, 35 (Winter 1985) 4. Cf. Marianne DeKoven, *A Different Language: Gertrude Stein's Experimental Writing* (Madison: University of Wisconsin Press, 1983), which rules out discussion of the autobiographies as not part of the canon of Stein's 'experimental writing'.
   There are two excellent studies of narrative in Stein's autobiographies: S. C. Neuman's *Gertrude Stein: Autobiography and the Problem of Narration*, English Literary Studies, 18 (Victoria, BC: University of Victoria, 1979); and Neil Schmitz, *Of Huck and Alice: Humorous Writing in American Literature* (Minneapolis: University of Minnesota Press, 1982). Neither of these is especially concerned with questions of style, syntax and vocabulary.
2. In October 1979 the play moved to the Provincetown Playhouse and had a two-year run before going on a nationwide tour. I myself saw *Gertrude Stein Gertrude Stein Gertrude Stein* at the Westwood Playhouse in Los Angeles in 1983.
3. Marty Martin, *Gertrude Stein Gertrude Stein Gertrude Stein* (New York: Random House, 1980). The text of the monologue is printed as a series of phrasal or clausal units with space (three or four characters) between units. I reproduce this format here.
4. Robert A. Wilson, Introduction to Martin, *Gertrude Stein Gertrude Stein Gertrude Stein*, p. xi.
5. As Ulla E. Dydo shows in *'Stanzas in Meditation'*, *Chicago Review*, 35, pp. 4–20, Stein's 'other autobiography', *Stanzas in Meditation*, is the story, highly coded and intentionally private, of the troubled sexual relationship between the two women in 1932.
6. Wilson, Introduction to Martin, *Gertrude Stein Gertrude Stein Gertrude Stein*, p. xiii.
7. Walter Kerr, *New York Times*, 31 Oct 1979; Marilyn Stasio, *New York Post*, 5 Sep 1979; Howard Kissel, *Women's Wear Daily*, 5 June 1979; Don Nelsen, *Daily News*, 3 July 1979.
8. Martin, *Gertrude Stein Gertrude Stein Gertrude Stein*, p. 5.
9. Richard Bridgman, *Gertrude Stein in Pieces* (New York: Oxford University Press, 1970), p. 218.
10. Martin, *Gertrude Stein Gertrude Stein Gertrude Stein*, pp. 19–20.
11. Ibid., pp. 20–1.
12. The discussion of the sentence on pp. 223–30 in this, the last of Stein's *Lectures in America*, is seminal.
13. Martin, *Gertrude Stein Gertrude Stein Gertrude Stein*, p. 21.
14. See Schmitz, *Of Huck and Alice*, pp. 206–11.
15. Ibid., pp. 33–4.
16. Wilson, Introduction, Martin, *Gertrude Stein Gertrude Stein Gertrude Stein*, p. xii.
17. Cf. Jacques Roubaud's important essay 'Gertrude Stein Grammaticus', in *Gertrude Stein, Encore*, ed. Jacques Darras, *In 'Hui*, supplement 0 (1983) 45–59, esp. p. 54.
18. Martin, *Gertrude Stein Gertrude Stein Gertrude Stein*, p. 6.

19. Ibid., p. 37.
20. Ibid., p. 9.
21. Ibid., p. 45.
22. Ibid., p. 17.
23. Wilson, Introduction, ibid., p. xii.
24. Dydo, *'Stanzas in Meditation'*, *Chicago Review*, 35, p. 18.

6

Gertrude Stein and Henry James

IRA B. NADEL

I wish every one knew exactly how to feel, about Henry James.
(Gertrude Stein, 'Henry James', *FIA*, p. 152)

In *The Autobiography of Alice B. Toklas*, Gertrude Stein emphatically denied the influence of Henry James on her writing, although she recognised his importance for the development of twentieth-century literature (*ABT*, p. 96). This ambivalent attitude toward James persisted throughout her career: on the one hand she rejected his direct importance to her writing, but on the other she praised his formative role in fashioning the style of American literature. In her 1935 lectures entitled *Narration*, for example, Stein celebrated James as one of the characteristic American writers for whom words were 'moving', deriving their energy from their detachment from 'the solidity of anything' (*N*, p. 10). When she wrote *Four in America* in 1932–3, Stein chose James to accompany General Grant, Wilbur Wright and George Washington: 'Henry James nobody has forgotten Henry James even if I have but I have not', she declared (*FIA*, p. 128).

But Stein persistently failed to acknowledge the influence of James on her work despite his role in her stylistic development and literary identity. Why? And why did it remain the task of Alice B. Toklas to document the actual interest of Stein in James's fiction as she did in her 1947 letters to Donald Sutherland?[1] This essay provides some answers suggested by the theory of *tessera*, the completing link. Essentially the enlargement of a precursor's work by a follower, *tessera* is actually the completion of a style, habit or attitude initiated by the predecessor.[2] Stein, in other words, extends and expands the work of James but, in order to maintain her own integrity, denies his influence. He becomes, rather, one of a series of innovative writers whom she soon absorbs and supersedes. In

James, Stein recognised how language could re-create the immediacy of mental consciousness and individual experience, but her identification with him as an American and expatriate and his experiments with form made her acknowledgement of him as her predecessor alternately difficult and welcomed.

Henry James entered Stein's consciousness at several critical periods. The first was from 1897 to 1902, before Stein composed *Q. E. D.* in 1903. That period was one of personal growth and literary transformation for Stein who had recently ended a tumultuous love affair with May Bookstaver (who was herself entangled with the protective Mabel Haynes and hence the triangle in *Q. E. D.* of Helen [May], Mabel [Mabel Haynes] and Adele [Stein]) when she sailed to Europe in spring 1902. In February 1903, on a return trip to America, Stein again saw May Bookstaver (it was an unhappy reunion), began *The Making of Americans*, wrote *Q. E. D.* in New York and then sailed to Europe in the spring. 'Fernhurst', later integrated with *The Making of Americans*, followed in 1904, then *Three Lives* in spring 1905 and *The Making of Americans* in 1906, although early draft notes exist from 1903. Integrated with these compositions was an appreciation of Henry James, whom she probably first read, if we accept Toklas's statement, at Johns Hopkins. In 1947 Alice B. Toklas told Donald Sutherland that 'it must have been when she was at Johns Hopkins that she read [James's] last two long novels'. Toklas also reported that in 1907, when she and Stein met, 'we subscribed to the N. Y. Scribners' edition of H. J.', adding that Stein 'always liked to use his word – *the precursor* – in speaking of him'.[3]

But Toklas's comments, some forty years after the fact, are unclear as to exactly which James novels Stein read. Does the reference to 'the last two long novels' in her letter include *The Sacred Fount*, published in February 1901? Does it also imply that Stein read *In the Cage* (Sep 1898), *The Two Magics* (Oct 1898, containing *The Turn of the Screw*) and *The Soft Side* (Sep 1900), a collection of twelve short stories? If Toklas is exact in stating that Stein read James at Hopkins, that would mean between the fall of 1897 and the summer of 1901, when, having failed an exam, Stein declined an opportunity to make up the work in summer school, preferring to join her brother Leo in Perugia. The major James novels published then were *What Maisie Knew* (1898), *The Awkward Age* (1899) and *The Sacred Fount* (1901). Toklas's comment suggests that it was probably the two novels dealing with young women, *What Maisie Knew* and *The Awkward Age* (the latter having prompted Toklas to write to James to propose a stage version!), that Stein knew.

A number of features in *The Awkward Age* in particular make that novel valuable in understanding Stein's early writing, especially her first novel, *Q. E. D.* The narrative of Mrs Brookenham and her eighteen-year-old, liberally educated daughter, Nanda, caught between the provocative world of London and the protective world of Mr Longdon, displays a series of features Stein enlarged in her own early work. These include an emphasis on dialogue over description, the focus on a limited point of view (often tentative and self-conscious), the themes of friendship and the dilemmas of adolescence, the admiration of 'free talk' (Stein actually uses the phrase in *Q. E. D.*, p. 128), and the dramatisation of unresolved issues (cf. the condition of Nanda at the end of the novel with that of Adele's 'dead-lock' described on the final page of *Q. E. D.*).

There is, furthermore, the triangular love plot (Mrs Brookenham and Nanda vying for Vanderbank) in *The Awkward Age* and the similar triangle in *Q. E. D.*, plus the disguised, often off-stage and even puritanical presence of sex in both novels. Tone, style and syntax are also remarkably similar between the two works. Vanderbank in *The Awkward Age*, remarking on the verbal world of the novel, says that 'It's impossible to say too much – it's impossible to say enough',[4] while Adele tells Helen in *Q. E. D.* that 'I have talked too much but you on the other hand have not talked enough' (p. 132). Language becomes the subject of both novels as 'the atmosphere of the unasked question', to quote Stein (p. 86), characterises both. The topic demonstrates an important principle shared by James and Stein which James expresses when he declares that 'All life . . . comes back to the question of our speech. . . . The more it suggests and expresses the more we live by it . . . .'[5] Speech, as the primary element of relations, is a Jamesian concept Stein will elaborate in a series of later essays and talks.

By late August 1902, the month Constable published the first English edition of *The Wings of the Dove*, Leo and Gertrude Stein were both in London and it is most likely that Stein read the novel at this time. Her interest in James and the public attention paid to his work would have made it difficult to escape the enthusiasm in England for his writing, and *The Wings of the Dove*, with its English and Italian settings, would have naturally appealed to her, since she had recently returned from Italy to England. During the fall she began her eclectic reading programme at the British Museum, filling notebooks with phrases and passages that pleased her. By February 1903 Stein was again in America, writing *Q. E. D.*

Following her 1907 meeting with Alice B. Toklas, Stein renewed her admiration for James, continuing to read and appreciate him through their subscription to the New York Edition of his novels. (This of course included his important Prefaces, a source, I would propose, for several of her later critical ideas presented in her American lectures of 1934–5.) Seven years later, in 1914, Stein's appreciation of James took physical form when the American expatriate photographer Alvin Langdon Coburn, who provided the photo frontispieces for James's New York Edition (1907–9), tried to arrange a meeting between Stein and James in July at Lamb House, Rye. James declined, outwardly because of ill health, inwardly because he was unsympathetic to new acquaintances. None the less, Stein saved the cable James sent to Coburn rejecting the meeting with the young American writer. In the twenties Stein continued to refer to James as a literary source, telling T. S. Eliot at a Paris party in 1924, for example, that her authority for the consistent use of the split infinitive was no less than James; and in the subsequent year she announced to Robert McAlmon that 'nobody has done anything to develop the English language since Shakespeare, except myself, and Henry James perhaps a little'.[6]

A critical comparison between Stein and James partially justifies this declaration, underscored by their parallel careers as playwrights and their similar aesthetic. James spent nearly five unsuccessful years, from 1890 to 1895, adapting and creating works for the English stage. His earliest such effort actually occurred in 1869 at the age of twenty-six, when he published a short dialogue, 'Pyramus and Thisbe', set in a New York rooming house. His only dramatic success, however, was *The American* (1890), a four-act dramatisation of his 1877 novel, written at the urging of Edward Compton of the Compton Comedy Company. After touring the English provinces, the play ran for seventy nights in London, partly aided by a visit from the Prince of Wales, whose attendance increased public curiosity in the play. But among his fifteen plays, plus monologues, James had no other box-office success. *Guy Domville* (1895), in fact, was publicly condemned on opening night when James was humiliated by catcalls and boos as he appeared on stage at the final curtain. None the less, the theatre continued to fascinate him and he persisted in writing plays and monologues up to 1913.

As a young boy, James was enthralled by productions he saw in New York; as a young man, he became a serious drama critic; as a successful novelist in middle age, he became an ambitious playwright. But James's interest in the theatre in the 1890s was as much financial as it was literary. While seeking public acceptance as a popular writer, he also hoped for a substantial income so that he could comfortably 'retire' from London to write further novels. While unable to meet the demands of the stage – the need for dramatic action, the required economy of scene, the helpfulness of emotional dialogue – James none the less learned from playwriting. In its scenic alternation, retrospective action, analysis of motive, and limited use of dramatic action, the later fiction of James exhibits the advantages of the dramatist's techniques, while a return to the novel allowed him to luxuriate in the expansiveness of prose to elaborate thought. *The Tragic Muse* (1889–90), a novel about the classic theatre, which precedes his experiences with the stage, romanticises its illusory successes; *The Sacred Fount* (1901), written after his unhappy attempts at drama, summarises much of what James realistically learned from it. But to dramatise became his principle of composition, since every idea 'must resolve itself into a little action, and the little action into the *essential* drama'.[7] Being booed off the stage on the opening night of *Guy Domville* did not cancel his commitment to what, at sixty-seven, he called 'the dramatic way'.[8]

Gertrude Stein was similarly attracted to the theatre, writing over seventy-seven plays, operas and ballets between 1913 and 1946. But like those of James, they met with indifferent success. Only *Four Saints in Three Acts* (1927), with music by Virgil Thomson, and *The Mother of Us All* (1945–6) roused any critical or commercial interest. Like James's, her playwriting, difficult, obscure, undramatic in the traditional sense, was little appreciated or understood. What role, then, did playwriting have in Stein's work and aesthetic? This question is only now being given adequate study but one can provide some tentative responses.[9] Drama allowed Stein to innovate and to demonstrate through structure and action the physicality of language on the stage. It also allowed her to emphasise the functions of language and to develop a concept of time close to the conception of space which she believed was the essence of American experience and its literature; this in turn led to a new appreciation of James.

In such works as 'I Like It to Be a Play', 'Capital Capitals', or 'Say It with Flowers', Stein found new forms that expanded earlier experiments such as *Tender Buttons* (1914). Theatre allowed her to explore the moment, to use what she called 'a continuous present' (*CE*, p. 24), just as it allowed James to develop what in his late fiction he called 'the dramatic way'. What Stein learned from the theatre – I am of course condensing here – is parallel to what James discovered in his theatrical experiences; that discovery points to a quintessential American feature: 'It is singularly a sense for combination within a conception of the existence of a given space of time that makes the American thing the American thing, and the sense of this space of time must be within the whole thing as well as in the completed whole thing' (*LIA*, p. 160). Individual units that at the same time establish a whole is the essence of Stein's discovery that tension, movement and balance exist between separate words and a sentence. Words are, for Stein, concentrations – complex, demanding, challenging terms that require the attention of readers. James recognised this same concept when composing the stage version of 'The Covering End', as he explained to the American actress Elizabeth Robins: 'the *real* difficulty in the whole thing is *compression* – to play in an hour; for the action is already so close and tightly logical'.[10] To establish the 'space of time' is the challenge for James as well as for Stein.

The 'space of time' and individuality within a whole, the 'sense of combination', generates the 'continuous present' of Stein and leads to her assertion that 'the business of Art . . . is to live in the actual present, that is the complete actual present, and to completely express that complete actual present' (*LIA*, pp. 104–5). In her view of history, this becomes the idea that 'Events had got so continuous that the fact that events were taking place no longer stimulated anybody. . . . People are interested in existence' (*HWW*, pp. 157–8). Henry James anticipates this and other ideas in Stein's aesthetic in the Prefaces (which Stein is likely to have read) to the New York Edition of his work.

In the Prefaces of James, collected and published in 1934 as *The Art of the Novel* (did Stein in America that year read a copy, repeating her earlier experience of reading the New York Edition?), James articulates numerous concepts Stein enlarged as her own poetic, as the following passages illustrate:

Really, universally, relations stop nowhere, and the exquisite problem of the artist is eternally but to draw, by a geometry of his own, the circle within which they shall happily *appear* to do so. He is in the perpetual predicament that the continuity of things is the whole matter . . . that this continuity is never, by the space of an instant or an inch, broken . . . .

(James, Preface to *Roderick Hudson*[11])

There should not be a sense of time, but an existence suspended in time. (Stein, *TI*, p. 20)

To name a place, in fiction, is to pretend in some degree to represent it . . . . (James, Preface to *Roderick Hudson*[12])

I used to take objects on a table, like a tumbler or any kind of object and try to get the picture of it clear and separate in my mind and create a word relationship between the word and the things seen. (Stein, *TI*, p. 25)

. . . I would rather, I think, have too little architecture than too much – when there's danger of its interfering with my measure of the truth. (James, Preface to *The Portrait of a Lady*[13])

I try to call to the eye the way it appears by suggestion the way a painter can do it. . . . I want to indicate it without calling in other things. (Stein, *TI*, p. 25)

What a man thinks and what he feels are the history and the character of what he does; on all of which things the logic of intensity rests. Without intensity where is vividness, and without vividness where is presentability?

(James, Preface to *The Princess Casamassima*[14])

I had to find out inside every one what was in them that was intrinsically exciting and I had to find out not by what they said not by what they did not by how much or how little they resembled any other one but I had to find it out by the intensity of movement that there was inside in any one of them.

(Stein, *LIA*, p. 183)

Art deals with what we see, it must first contribute full-handed that ingredient. . . . But it has no sooner done this than it has to take account of a process . . . .
(James, Preface to The Ambassadors[15])

After all, human beings are interested in two things. They are interested in the reality and interested in telling about it.
(Stein, TI, p. 18)

What James in the Preface to *The Ambassadors* calls 'the terrible *fluidity* of self-revelation'[16] is fundamental for Stein and her artistic processes; it impels her forward creatively. On the final page of the Preface to *The Golden Bowl*, James praises the artist's inability to disavow his work and his responsibility 'not to break with his values, not to "give away" his importances'. In a Steinian sentence James writes, 'Thus if he is always doing he can scarce, by his own measure, ever have done.' '[C]onduct with a vengeance' is James's plea and Stein, possibly knowing this passage, embraced its call to artistic commitment and action: 'care [is] nothing if not active, finish [is] nothing if not consistent'.[17] This aesthetic of commitment never altered in James or in Stein.

Further linking Stein and James are their conceptions of time and scene. Stein's idea of the 'continuous present' and the Jamesian moment or centre of consciousness, where the character transcends time, are parallel. These moments (Joyce's epiphanies are variations of this durational time) are what Stein meant when she explained in 'A Transatlantic Interview' that 'there should not be a sense of time, but an existence suspended in time' (*TI*, p. 20) or that, stylistically, James's paragraphs appear to float upward: 'that is the thing to notice, his whole paragraph was detached what it said from what it did, what it was from what it held, and over it all something floated not floated away but just floated, floated up there' (*LIA*, p. 53). American writing, Stein noted, is 'an existing without the necessary feeling feeling of one thing succeeding another thing of anything having a beginning and a middle and an ending' (*N*, p. 25). The exemplar of this writing is Henry James.

A passage from *The Golden Bowl* illustrates these features. It describes a Jamesian moment of consciousness for Maggie Verver as she analyses the quality of her relationship with her father and what they share:

Plate 1   Pablo Picasso, *Gertrude Stein* (1906). The Metropolitan Museum of Art, bequest of Gertrude Stein, 1946 (47.106).

Plate 2   Charles Demuth, *Poster Portrait: Love, Love, Love (Homage to Gertrude Stein)* (c. 1928). Collection unknown.

Plate 3   Pablo Picasso, *Nude*, charcoal (1910). The
Metropolitan Museum of Art, Alfred Stieglitz Collection,
1949 (49.70.34).

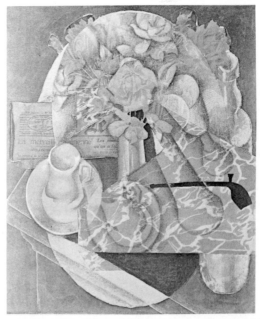

Plate 4   Juan Gris, *Roses* (1914). Private collection, New
York.

Plate 5   Robert Rauschenberg, *Centennial Certificate,
MMA,* colour lithograph (1969). The Metropolitan
Museum of Art, Florence and Joseph Singer Collection,
1969 (69.630).

Plate 6   Marie Laurencin, *Group d'artistes* (1908).
Baltimore Museum of Art, Cone Collection
(BMA 1950.215).

Plate 7   Henri Rousseau, *La Muse inspirant le poète*
(1909). Kunstmuseum, Basel.

The equilibrium, the precious condition, lasted in spite of rearrangement; there had been a fresh distribution of the different weights, but the balance persisted and triumphed: all of which was just the reason why she was forbidden, face to face with the companion of her adventure, the experiment of a test. If they balanced they balanced – she had to take that; it deprived her of every pretext for arriving, by however covert a process, at what he thought.[18]

Several pages earlier we have been told that 'their equilibrium was everything, and that it was practically precarious, a matter of hair's breadth for the loss of the balance'.[19] But, as she reviews the actions of Charlotte Stant and the Prince concerning their disruption of the balance between herself and her father, Maggie also realises 'that there might be but a deeper treachery in recoveries and reassurances'.[20] The thought and style of this section of the novel underscore the similarities between language and idea in James and Stein which a later sentence in the novel confirms: 'It had operated within her now to the last intensity, her glimpse of the precious truth that by her helping him, helping him to help himself, as it were, she should help him to help *her*.'[21] The passage refers to Maggie Verver's thoughts about Amerigo after the golden bowl has been smashed and she has discovered its true meaning. The combination of the Steinian 'continuous present', generated by the character's complexly unravelling her thought, with the repetitive syntax and the seemingly confused meaning vividly anticipates the style and technique of Stein.

An even later James work, *The Sense of the Past*, develops time in the Steinian manner. This unfinished philosophic fantasy of time, begun by James in 1900 and picked up again in 1914, is an experiment in transposition as a young American and amateur historian is transported back to 1820 from 1910. He then exchanges identity with a relative from 1820 who is to emerge in the twentieth century. This is a structural and historical exploration of the 'continuous present' which is not, as Stein makes clear, repetition 'because naturally each time the emphasis is different' (*LIA*, p. 179). It is rather a suspension from time past and future as James develops it in his story. Stein condenses James's sense of the past, transforming what he records in his novel into shorter, more concentrated forms of intensely abstract and obscure expression.

But the emerging ambiguities and abstractions borrow strongly from James, who in *The Sacred Fount* focused exclusively on ambiguity, in *The Golden Bowl* on abstractions and in *The Sense of the Past* on ahistorical time. And simultaneous with these developments was James's emphasis on scene.

Stein was fascinated with scene and its ability to concentrate action through language. Drama for her was exclusively scene: 'What is a play. / A play is scenery' (*GHA*, p. 202), she writes in *The Geographical History of America*, and in 'Scenes. Actions and Disposition of Relations and Positions' (*G&P*, pp. 97–121), she develops a variety of examples to demonstrate the essential patterning of scenes. *Tender Buttons* is itself a set of scenes with objects rather than characters at the centre. The first piece written by Stein after *The Autobiography of Alice B. Toklas* was called 'Scenery and George Washington, A Novel or a Play' (1932). She announced the tension between the two genres in the text: 'A play and an event. / Also a story and their birth. / Possibly the men and their arrival. / May be they will' (*FIA*, p. 165).

For James the scenic principle came to control much of his fiction, especially after his experiences in the theatre; its function is to make perceptible inward and outward aspects of action. As James himself noted, *What Maisie Knew*, 'The Pupil', and *In the Cage* 'demean themselves . . . as little constituted dramas . . . founded on the logic of the "scene", the unit of the scene, the general scenic consistency'.[22] The formula of the scene is 'Action which is never dialogue and dialogue which is always action'.[23] Stein will refine these ideas into her concentrated moments of verbal intensity:

RED ROSES.

A cool red rose and a pink cut pink, a collapse and a sold hole, a little less hot.   (*TB*, p. 24)

What James and Stein recognised in their different but related ways is the 'law of successive Aspects', a phrase from *The Ivory Tower*, [24] another unfinished novel by James. This is the scene-by-scene accumulation of contrasting, paratactic views of interpersonal relations whose comprehension by participant and observer is gradual and in which each entity is individual:

You see I tried to convey the idea of each part of a composition being as important as the whole. It was the first time in any language that anyone had used that idea of composition in literature. Henry James had a slight inkling of it and was in some senses a forerunner. . . . You see he made it sort of like an atmosphere, and it was not solely the realism of the characters but the realism of the composition which was the important thing, the realism of the composition of my thoughts.   (*TI*, pp. 15–16)

Stein saw in the work of James possibilities for prose which her radical experiments confirmed, with terms such as 'continuous present' and 'entity' substituting for James's 'center of consciousness' and 'intensity'.

In the 1930s the presence of James asserted itself more directly as he became a personal model as well as a literary source for Stein. The crucial event around which James hovers is Stein's visit to the United States from October 1934 to May 1935, her first since she settled in France in 1903. James's introductory appearance at this stage of Stein's development is in *The Autobiography of Alice B. Toklas*, published in 1933, where Stein misleadingly suggests she had never read him (*ABT*, p. 97). But in *Four in America*, written at about the same time, she provides a more detailed assessment of James, studying his quality as a writer and importance as a leader in American literature. His triumph as a 'general' in that work is not only on a military but also on a literary battlefield. And, during her actual trip to America, she comes close to identifying with James's own experiences and attitudes toward both the country and its language. Indeed, Stein's entire experience in the States parallels James's 1904 trip to America, his first after a twenty-year absence. Furthermore, the presence of James in essays such as 'What is English Literature?', 'Poetry and Grammar' and *Narration*, all written for Stein's American lecture tour, further illustrates the central position of James in Stein's concept of literary history and critical theory.

The interpretation of James in *Four in America* may give us a clearer understanding of his importance to Stein at that time. The lengthy portrait examines several topics: the question of accident and coincidence in writing, the significance of style – 'It is not clarity that is desirable but force' (*FIA*, p. 127), she declares – and what James would have done if he had been a general. This discussion is as close as Stein could come to paying tribute to James and his influence on her work. But her acknowledgement is indirect and impersonal, through the genre or the medium rather than the personality or character of the man. She furthermore absorbs James into her own power when she argues that she has undertaken to expand what he initiated in prose style. The thrust of her comments is her perpetual concern with language and writing, concentrated in the dilemma of 'How can you state what you wish to say. That is the question' (p. 142). James becomes a vehicle for investigating the formal qualities of language, expression and the distance between them, the space that cannot be duplicated by what we think in words that have meaning. In this essay James becomes not 'the precursor' but the model of one who stopped, looked and responded to the changes in language as Stein herself was doing and was about to do.

A measure of the affinity between Stein and James in the essay, and possibly the closest acknowledgement by Stein of their likeness, occurs in her discovery of the two ways of writing found in her discussion of translation. Commenting on *Before the Flowers of Friendship Faded Friendship Faded*, initially a translation of poems by her friend Georges Hugnet, Stein notes that they became the poems he 'would have written' (*FIA*, p. 129) if he had written them. She then identifies two ways of writing, one where words have a literal meaning, what they say on the page, the other a 'meaning [that] had to be meant as something [that] had been learnt' (p. 135). This may be condensed, perhaps, to meaning as product and meaning as process. The two ways of writing are 'writing as it is written [and] writing as it is going to be written' (ibid.). Stein asserts that she herself uses the 'two ways as one way' (p. 123), as does James. Analogous with the subject of writing method is the question of audience, an issue James constantly explored in his Prefaces, novels and notebooks. As Stein remarks, 'When you are writing who hears what you are writing. / That is the question' (p. 121). The problematics of audience puzzle and fascinate both writers, often masking anxiety over which of the two ways of writing best relates to readers.

For Stein, James unequivocally combines 'the two ways of writing and that makes him a general' (p. 137). Shakespeare similarly used two ways of writing but this, she asserts, is the difference between Shakespeare's plays and sonnets: the plays were 'written as they were written. Shakespeare's sonnets were written as they were going to be written' (p. 120). James becomes a general, however, because he combines both methods and, being a general, he is capable of doing both – that is, he can do what he has to do in a prepared situation *and* respond to the unexpected brought on by the prepared situation. In terms of audience, this means that James's writing satisfies his preconceptions of what his story should be when finished, as well as satisfies someone else's. This ability to combine form and freedom, intention and execution, original and developed meaning makes James an authentic general who can command and triumph in every aesthetic engagement. '[A]ny general', Stein emphasises, 'has selected both [methods of writing] otherwise he is not a general and Henry James is a general' (p. 138). James was for Stein both the creator and audience of his work as Stein was for hers. She discovered this in Hugnet and Shakespeare but found it epitomised in James.

In America, both James and Stein decided to lecture on language, both written and spoken. James made this the subject of his keynote address at Bryn Mawr College in June 1905, the very location of the events that shaped Stein's first work, 'Fernhurst'. *The Question of our Speech* was his title. Anticipating such later essays as 'The Speech of American Women' and 'The Manners of American Women',[25] James reasserts the primacy of speech for communication and civilisation in his talk. He also stresses the parallel between its richness and that of a culture, anticipating a number of Stein's later views on language expressed throughout *Lectures in America*. A new flexibility of language and reliance on repetition characterises the style of James, as this passage illustrates:

> The possibility, the preferability, of people's speaking as people speak when their speech has had for them a signal importance, is a matter to be kept sharply present; from that comes support, comes example, comes authority. . . . You don't speak soundly and agreeably, you don't speak neatly and consistently, unless you *know* how you speak, how you may, how you should, how you shall speak, unless you have discriminated, unless you have noticed differences and suffered from violations and vulgarities.[26]

The modifying repetitive clauses, circuitous development and informal tone anticipate Stein; or, to reverse the statement, Stein, in a variety of texts from her Amerian visit, echoes James both in this late style and subject matter.

Like James's, one of Stein's principal subjects in her lecture series

Narration is talking and the speech of Americans. And in the first chapter of *Everybody's Autobiography* Stein highlights the problem of a written versus a spoken language. She argues, in fact, that 'the spoken language is no longer interesting and so gradually the written language says something and says it differently than the spoken language' (*EA*, p. 13). Later, she explains the distinction between writing and speaking (p. 264), extending James's argument that speech must be improved as a necessary step in cultural elevation. In his own account of his 1904–5 visit to the States, *The American Scene*, published in 1907, James recorded that his ear taught him that a European connection still existed in American speech in the 'proper intimate idiom and accent: a dialect as much its very own, even in drawing-rooms and libraries, as the Venetian is that of Venice'. But the 'free vernacular' of American speech 'candidly, consistently, sometimes almost contagiously'[27] entertains the visitor. Anticipating an idea Stein pursued throughout her American lectures, James suggests that language even *constitutes* a society and with Stein he shares a similar quest: 'We scour the surface of American life in vain for the semblance or the echo of a plot.'[28] The identity between James and Stein is remarkable, not just in subject matter but in tone and attitude. 'Do? The question isn't of your doing, but simply of your being',[29] wrote James in 1917, summarising in a general way his and Stein's attitude toward language, the major subject of their addresses in America.

In her evaluation of the evolution of American prose style, Stein places James at the centre. Accentuating the move to phrasing in 'What is English Literature?' she cites James as its culmination and notes that he saw beyond emphasis on the phrase to the need for paragraphing (*LIA*, pp. 52–3). With phrases no longer able to contain emotion or meaning, the paragraph became the natural extension of prose and 'Henry James being an American knew best what he was doing when he did this thing' (p. 53). Stein sees herself in that same tradition and, after closing with the Jamesian epithet, 'And so there we are', continues in two paragraphs to explain that she 'had to do more with the paragraph than ever had been done' (p. 54). Stein once more cites James in her lecture 'Poetry and Grammar' (p. 225) and, in her lecture series *Narration*, with Emerson, Whitman, Hawthorne, Twain and Stein, he joins a group that 'got the words to express moving' and got the American vocabulary to detach itself 'from the solidity of anything' (*N*, pp. 9–10). In the lectures, parallel to James's Prefaces in their concern about style, point of view and narrative technique, Stein outlines a number of Jamesian issues: audience, narration, language and character. Modernising James's own pronouncements, she declares that 'What makes writing writing is hearing what an audience is . . .' (p. 56).

Inverting the normal order of influence, Alice B. Toklas said in 1947, 'There are some pure Gertrude phrases in *The Wings of the Dove*',[30] suggesting to many what should be apparent – that James's tone, manner of phrasing, attitude toward language and perception of the paragraph infiltrated Stein's method. Whether it is in such echoes as the concluding line of *The Wings of the Dove*, 'we shall never be again as we were!', and the concluding scene of *The Mother of Us All*, when Susan B. Anthony announces, 'we cannot retrace our steps, retrace our steps', or in parallels found in such works as *The American Scene* and *Everybody's Autobiography* (cf. also *The Ivory Tower* or 'A Round of Visits' with *The Mother of Us All*), James and Stein remain inextricably linked. It is ironic but appropriate, then, that they should have a final moment of coalescence. During his visit to New York in October 1904, James told a reporter that 'Life leaves with you a question – it asks you questions.' At her death, Stein's supposed last words were not 'What is the answer?' but, in the manner of James, 'What is the question?'[31]

Notes

1. Alice B. Toklas, *Staying on Alone: Letters of Alice B. Toklas*, ed. Edward Burns (New York: Liveright, 1973) pp. 84–96.

I do not propose to study the parallels between *Q. E. D.* and *The Wings of the Dove*. This has been treated by Michael J. Hoffman in *The Development of Abstractionism in the Writings of Gertrude Stein* (Philadelphia: University of Pennsylvania Press, 1965) pp. 34–5; and by Carolyn Faunce Copeland in *Language and Time and Gertrude Stein* (Iowa City: University of Iowa Press, 1975) pp. 10–12. For useful discussions of James, Stein, and language, however, see Richard Bridgman, *The Colloquial Style in America* (New York: Oxford University Press, 1966) pp. 165–74, 177–8, 193–4; and Sharon Shaw, 'Gertrude Stein and Henry James: The Difference between Accidence and Coincidence', *Pembroke Magazine*, 5 (1974) 95–101. On James and Stein as expatriates see Martha Banta, 'James and Stein on "Being American" and "Having France"', *French–American Review*, III, 3 (Fall 1979) 63–84. See also Charles Caramello, 'Reading Gertrude Stein Reading Henry James: Eros is Eros is Eros is Eros', *Henry James Review*, 6, 3 (Spring 1985).

2. Harold Bloom, in *The Anxiety of Influence: A Theory of Poetry* (New York: Oxford University Press, 1973) pp 66–8, discusses the idea of *tessera*, adding 'that British poets swerve from their precursors, while American poets labor rather to "complete" their fathers' (p. 68). This may be true for American prose writers as well.

3. Toklas, *Staying on Alone*, p. 86.

4. Henry James, *The Awkward Age*, ed. Vivien Jones (Oxford: Oxford University Press, 1984) p. 13.

5. Henry James, *The Question of our Speech* (Boston, Mass.: Houghton, Mifflin, 1905) p. 10. For a useful discussion of language in *The Awkward Age*, see Tzvetan Todorov, 'The Verbal Age', tr. Patricia Martin Gibby, *Critical Inquiry*, 4, 2 (Winter 1977) 351–71.

6. James R. Mellow, *Charmed Circle: Gertrude Stein and Company* (New York: Praeger, 1974) pp. 212, 287, 290.

7. Henry James, *Notebooks*, ed. F. O. Matthiessen and Kenneth B. Murdock (New York: Oxford University Press, 1947) p. 198.

8. James, quoted in Leon Edel, 'Henry James: The Dramatic Years', *The Complete Plays of Henry James*, ed. Leon Edel (Philadelphia and New York: Lippincott, 1949) p. 19.

9. On Stein and the theatre see Wilfred Leach, 'Gertrude Stein and the Modern Theatre' (PhD dissertation, University of Illinois, 1956); and Betsy Alayne Ryan, *Gertrude Stein's Theatre of the Absolute* (Ann Arbor: University of Michigan Research Press, 1984).

10. Henry James to Elizabeth Robins in Robins, *Theatre and Friendship: Some Henry James Letters* (New York: G. P. Putnam's Sons, 1932) pp. 209–10.

11. Henry James, *The Art of the Novel*, intro. Richard P. Blackmur (New York: Charles Scribner's Sons, 1934) p. 5.

12. Ibid., p. 8.

13. Ibid., p. 43.

14. Ibid., p. 66.

15. Ibid., p. 312.

16. Ibid., p. 321.

17. Ibid., p. 348.

18. Henry James, *The Golden Bowl* (1904; Harmondsworth, Middx: Penguin, 1966) p. 349.

19. Ibid., p. 311.

20. Ibid., p. 350.

21. Ibid., p. 427.

22. James, Preface to *What Maisie Knew*, *The Art of the Novel*, p. 157.

23. James, *Notebooks*, p. 102.

24. Henry James, *The Ivory Tower*, ed. Percy Lubbock (1917; New York: Charles Scribner's Sons, 1945) p. 268.

25. Published in *Harper's Bazaar*, XL–XLI (Nov 1906–Feb 1907) and XLI (Apr–July 1907), respectively.

26. James, *The Question of our Speech*, p. 15.

27. Henry James, *The American Scene*, ed. Leon Edel (1907; Bloomington: Indiana University Press, 1968) pp. 286, 287.

28. Henry James, 'The Speech of American Women', *French Writers and*

American Women, Essays, ed. Peter Buitenhuis (Branford, Conn.: Compass, 1960) p. 40.

29. James, *The Ivory Tower,* p. 112. Cf. Stein: 'I like anything that a word can do. And words do do all they do and then they can do what they never do do' (*EA,* p. 317).
30. Toklas, *Staying on Alone,* p. 86.
31. Henry James, *New York Herald,* 2 Oct 1904, quoted in *The American Scene,* p. 468; Stein, quoted in John Malcolm Brinnin, *The Third Rose: Gertrude Stein and her World* (New York: Grove Press, 1959) pp. 403–4.

7

The Allure of Multiplicity: Metaphor and Metonymy in Cubism and Gertrude Stein

STEPHEN SCOBIE

In setting up comparisons or analogies between different arts, one fundamental technique is to use words which are established and well-defined in the critical discourse of one art form and to apply them to another.[1] Thus, taking our examples from painting and literature, we may proceed either by beginning with an art-historical term such as 'cubism', which has a (more or less) clearly defined meaning in painting, and attempting to apply it to literature – saying, for instance, that Gertrude Stein is 'a cubist writer' – or *vice versa*. Among the literary terms which have recently been extended beyond their traditional bounds, none has received greater play than 'metonymy', especially when it is distinguished from, yet held in a complementary relation with, 'metaphor'. The purpose of this essay is to examine some of the recent uses of 'metonymy', especially in relation to cubist painting, to Gertrude Stein and to the description of Stein as 'a cubist writer'.

In the simplest definitions of metaphor and metonymy, as they are seen within the context of the traditional rhetoric of figures of speech (and using here the definitions in *The Oxford English Dictionary*), both are concerned with *substituting one noun for another*. Metaphor is the 'figure of speech in which a name or descriptive term is transferred to some object different from, but analogous to, that to which it is properly applicable'; metonymy is a 'figure of speech which consists in substituting for the name of a thing the name of an attribute of it or of something closely related'. The essence of metaphor is *difference*; the essence of metonymy is *contiguity*. Although both figures suggest a connection between their two terms, metaphor will initially foreground the apparent distance between them, while metonymy will focus attention on their apparent relationship. Since that relationship is very often that of the part for the whole, the commonest form of metonymy is synecdoche; synecdoche may indeed be seen as a sub-species of metonymy.

These traditional definitions have been recast by Roman Jakobson, and it has been Jakobson's reformulation which has most deeply influenced the contemporary use of the term 'metonymy' by such writers as David Lodge in *The Modes of Modern Writing: Metaphor, Metonymy, and the Typology of Modern Literature.*[2] Jakobson's distinction arose out of his discussion 'Two Aspects of Language and Two Types of Aphasic Disturbances',[3] and it projects metaphor and metonymy onto the structuralist schema of language as deployed along two axes: a vertical axis of selection by substitution and a horizontal axis of combination by contiguity. Jakobson places metaphor on the vertical axis, working by similarity, and metonymy on the horizontal axis, working by contiguity. The two figures of speech are then compared to two types of aphasia. 'Similarity disorder' involves a 'major deficiency . . . in selection and substitution, with relative stability of combination and contexture'; specific nouns tend to be replaced by generalising ones, or else to disappear altogether; 'words syntactically subordinated by grammatical agreement or government are more tenacious, whereas the main subordinating agent of the sentence, namely the subject, tends to be omitted'.[4] All this is seen as an extreme instance of metonymy, in which 'The relation of similarity is suppressed'.[5] Conversely, 'Contiguity disorder', which is seen as an extreme instance of metaphor, produces a state in which 'The syntactical rules organizing words into higher units are lost; this loss, called *agrammatism*, causes the degeneration of the sentence into a mere "word heap" . . . words endowed with purely grammatical functions, like conjunctions, prepositions, pronouns, and articles, disappear first',[6] leaving the discourse dominated by nouns, and by nouns used in a metaphoric way.

One effect of Jakobson's formulation has been to shift the whole metaphor–metonymy distinction itself away from the axis of selection and onto the axis of combination. I previously noted that the traditional definitions of metaphor and metonymy saw *both* of them as ways of substituting one noun for another; in Jakobson's formulation, this remains the major function of metaphor, even or especially in the aphasic 'word heap', but it has been drastically diminished as a function of metonymy, which is now seen as the *suppression* of nouns. The traditional definitions saw metaphor and metonymy as two different operations on the axis of selection, i.e. vocabulary; Jakobson sees them both as operations on the axis of combination, i.e. syntax. Metaphor survives this shift better, since it is still essentially conceived as a process of naming; but metonymy has become muddled, divided between a vocabulary choice which still involves nouns and a syntactic deferral which suppresses them. This muddle in the use of 'metonymy' has bedevilled recent attempts to apply it both to cubism and to Gertrude Stein.

A second effect of this redefinition has been to align metaphor–metonymy with other paired terms: modernism and post-modernism, structuralism and poststructuralism. Metaphor, on its static vertical axis, may be used to describe the modernism of such writers as Eliot and Joyce, and the structuralism of Lévi-Strauss, or of schematic narratologists such as Greimas. Metonymy, on its dynamic horizontal axis, leads to the postmodernism of such writers as (in the Canadian context) Robert Kroetsch and bpNichol, and to the poststructuralism of Derrida's 'dissemination' and 'grammatology'.[7] Kroetsch especially has stressed the use of the metaphor–metonymy pair as a key to explaining forms of experimental writing which have rebelled against the tight, closed, hierarchic structures of metaphor in the name of the open-ended, disseminative accumulations of metonymy. 'To go from metaphor to metonymy', he has said, 'is to go from the temptation of the single to the allure of multiplicity.'[8] If metonymy, in Jakobson's words, suppresses 'the main subordinating agent of the sentence, namely the subject', then the term may be especially useful for describing writing which puts into question the whole concept of subordination to a single subject, whether grammatical, philosophical, or sexual: writing which is 'incoherent, open-ended, anarchic, irreducibly multiple . . . indeterminate, anti-patriarchal (anti-logocentric, anti-phallogocentric, presymbolic, pluridimensional)'. The adjectives are all offered by Marianne DeKoven as descriptions of the 'experimental writing' of Gertrude Stein.[9]

However, before we wholeheartedly adopt the metaphor–metonymy distinction, and before we attempt to situate Gertrude Stein on either side of it, two caveats need to be made. The first is that this very fondness for classification by binary pairs is itself a characteristic of structuralism, an operation on the vertical axis, an instance of metaphor. The kind of radical multiplicity toward which metonymy seems to lead should itself prevent us from using metaphor–metonymy as a rigid conceptual grid into which any given writer can be neatly slotted. Anticipating a later stage in the argument, I should like to point here to the difficulties encountered by Jane Gallop in her chapter 'Metaphor and Metonymy' in *Reading Lacan*. Gallop notes that 'In both Jakobson and Lacan, a shadow of femininity haunts the juncture of metonymy and realism. It is not that either of them defines realism or metonymy as feminine (that would be a metaphoric, symbolic gesture), but that by contiguity, by metonymy, a certain femininity is suggested.'[10] The idea that 'metonymic interpretation might be called feminine reading'[11] is clearly important for any reading of Gertrude Stein (and I will later suggest that metonymy is a key to Stein's textual 'naming' of the absent Alice), but Gallop is rightly wary of accepting such a 'metaphoric' reading of metonymy itself. Searching for what would be 'more properly a metonymic reading of metonymy', she comes up against the uneasy ubiquity of Lacan's concept of the phallus:

> A metonymic reading construes metonymy as phallic whereas a metaphoric interpretation attributes the phallus to metaphor. Each sort of reading inevitably locates the phallus in its own narcissistic reflection in the text . . . as I struggle with this portion of my reading/writing, . . . a nausea, a paralysis creeps over me, a difficulty in going further, an aphasia on the level of metalanguage.[12]

Pushed far enough, the metaphor–metonymy distinction, and the attempt to give a metonymic reading to a metaphoric distinction, disappear into their own *mise en abyme*, reflecting each other in endless recession.

Secondly, even if we do persist in using these terms (as I shall be doing in most of this essay, albeit with a Derridean 'erasure' understood to hover over them), it is by no means certain that Stein can be usefully situated within the limits of either category exclusively. Much of Stein's writing transgresses both the traditional and the Jakobsonian definitions. In so far as both metaphor and metonymy are types of *naming*, they fail to account for Stein's *un*naming, or *dis*naming: her dislocations of the naming process itself. Furthermore, Stein refuses to sit easily in either the modernist or the postmodernist camp. While DeKoven's title, with its emphasis on 'different' and 'experimental', inclines to one side of the dichotomy, another title – that of Jayne L. Walker's study, which is by far the best of the recent books on Stein – is equally 'one-sided' in its emphasis on 'The Making of a *Modernist*'.[13] In fact, most of the attempts to apply the metaphor–metonymy distinction to Stein have concluded that both figures are to be found in her work; what is at issue is the distribution and balance between them, and it is into that discussion that I propose to enter.

In doing so, I will be using the common distinction between two styles in Stein's writing of the period between 1906 (the completion of *Three Lives*) and 1914 (the publication of *Tender Buttons*). The first style – that of lengthy, convoluted repetitions in highly generalised language – is exemplified by *The Making of Americans*; the second – that of briefer, more lyrical sentences, sometimes in a fractured syntax, and using a much more vivid, concrete vocabulary – by *Tender Buttons*. There are, of course, several mixed or transitional texts, notably *A Long Gay Book* (1909–12), in which the change can be quite dramatically seen in progress.[14] In this essay, while I have taken some of my quotations from the 'exemplary' texts, I have chosen to concentrate on *A Long Gay Book*: partly because *The Making of Americans* and *Tender Buttons* are so fully treated elsewhere, and partly as a continuing reminder that even this initial gesture of distinguishing betwen the two styles is not quite as unproblematic as it might seem.

The application of the metaphor–metonymy distinction to the works of Gertrude Stein may be seen in representative form in David Lodge, who describes the first style as metonymic, the second as metaphoric. He cites the three techniques which Stein later described as 'using everything', 'beginning again and again', and 'the continuous present', and sees them all as 'experiments along the metonymic axis of discourse'.[15] Using Jakobson's formulations, he points to the stress on connectives and on non-specific forms of speech: Jakobson had noted that in the metonymic 'Similarity disorder' of aphasia, 'A specific noun . . . is replaced by a very general one', while 'Words with an inherent reference to the context, like pronouns and pronominal adverbs, . . . connectives and auxiliaries, are particularly prone to survive.'[16] This does indeed seem like a fair description of the style of *The Making of Americans* and of the early stages of *A Long Gay Book*:

Any one being started in doing something is going on completely doing that thing, a little doing that thing, doing something that is that thing. Any one not knowing anything of any one being one starting that one in doing that thing is one doing that thing completing doing that thing and being then one living in some such thing. (*LGB*, p. 18)

Coming to be anything is something. Not coming to be anything is something. Loving is something. Not loving is something. Loving is loving. Something is something. Anything is something. (p. 21)

Conversely, Lodge argues that with *Tender Buttons* Stein moved 'from length to brevity, from verbs to nouns, from prose to poetry and (in our terms) from metonymic to metaphoric experiment'.[17] The vocabulary of *Tender Buttons*, replete with specific terms, 'is clearly a type of metaphorical writing based on radical substitution (or replacement) of referential nouns', while its syntax moves toward Jakobson's 'Contiguity disorder', toward the state 'where grammar has disintegrated to the point where "word heap" seems an appropriate description'.[18] Before examining the adequacy of this argument, let us look at its further extension into the analogy between Stein's writing and cubist painting.

Lodge is content to accept Jakobson's identification of 'the manifestly metonymical orientation of cubism', as opposed to the 'patently metaphorical attitude' of surrealism.[19] Thus, having described *Tender Buttons* as metaphorical, Lodge also has to argue that it is not, as has so often been claimed, 'the literary equivalent of cubism', but is 'in fact much closer to surrealism'.[20] Randa Dubnick[21] attempts to reclaim *Tender Buttons* for cubism, while still classifying it under metaphor, by inserting the metaphor–metonymy distinction into cubism itself, along the classical lines of the division between analytical and synthetic cubism. If it were successful, this tactic would produce a very neat dichotomy, with metonymy, analytic cubism and *The Making of Americans* on the one side, and metaphor, synthetic cubism and *Tender Buttons* on the other.

Dubnick attempts to argue that analytic cubism is metonymic because it constricts the pictorial vocabulary and emphasises the connectives: 'most lines and planes in cubist paintings', she writes, 'refer only to spatial relationships (a concern with contiguity and therefore with the horizontal axis of language)'. 'In analytic cubism, contiguity is emphasized, as the spatial configuration of the subject extends over the ground of the painting and the lines delineating the object are extended and realigned into segments that form small, overlapping planes which repeat similar configurations.'[22] Conversely, in synthetic cubism, 'the vocabulary of signifying elements . . . is extended', while spatial syntax 'is suppressed . . . by a use of the picture plane that emphasizes its flat surface more than its traditional illusion of depth'.[23]

That last comment is indicative of one of the major weaknesses in Dubnick's argument. What are put forward as characteristics distinguishing synthetic from analytic cubism are often, in fact, elements common to both, which distinguish *all* cubist painting from more traditional forms. It is absurd to suggest, as that comment seems to do, that analytic cubism did not emphasise the flat surface, or that it gave a 'traditional illusion of depth'. Or take this passage: 'Lines do not clarify spatial relationships by providing perspective. Depth becomes ambiguous as relationships of *in front of*, *behind*, *forward*, and *back* become impossible to read. . . . We are looking at an opaque surface, not through a window on the world.'[24] Again, this is offered as a description of synthetic cubism *as opposed to* analytic; and, again, it is nothing of the kind. It is an accurate-enough description of synthetic cubist 'syntax' (see the analysis of the Braque collage, below), but it would apply equally well to most analytic works. Dubnick's analysis collapses on the sheer wrong-headedness of her descriptions of cubism.[25] Of synthetic cubism, she claims, 'The color is applied arbitrarily or decoratively rather than descriptively. Textures also are used to provide interest rather than to describe objects.'[26] This is a travesty of the subtle and complex relationships between colour, texture and the description of objects in synthetic cubism – but then, since these relationships are mostly metonymic, Dubnick obviously cannot afford to admit them into her argument.

Dubnick's argument fails, because of her insensitivity to the painting, and because of her overeagerness to squeeze everything into a neatly dichotomised pattern. Jayne L. Walker, however, presents the case in a much more careful and sophisticated way. Walker repeats the argument, out of Jakobson, for the metonymic nature of the syntax in both analytic cubism and *The Making of Americans* – that is, that in both the 'compositions are dominated by connective signs'[27] – and also argues for the metaphoric nature of the syntax in synthetic cubism and in *Tender Buttons*. The signs in cubist collage, she writes, 'are simply juxtaposed to one another or overlaid . . . [producing a] stark "asyntactical" arrangement of iconic signs on a rigorously flat plane'.[28] However, Walker recognises that in synthetic cubism (and also in Stein) the *individual signs continue to be metonymic*. Pointing to the fundamental disparity which Jakobson introduced by treating metonymy both as syntax and as vocabulary, Walker writes that Jakobson 'never deals with the fact that characteristics of the two polar extremes sometimes coexist, at different levels of analysis, in the same structures. In cubist collage, the individual signs are metonymic, but the syntax is close to the metaphoric pole.'[29]

This view, while considerably more accurate than Dubnick's, still seems to me to oversimplify the 'syntax' of synthetic cubism. It is true that the paintings and collages of this later period reduce or eliminate much of the 'armature' of analytic cubism, its delicate grid of connective lines and shifting spatial indicators, but they are still very far from 'simple' juxtaposition, or from any valid analogy to an agrammatical 'word heap'. By freeing both colour and texture from the contours of the represented object, synthetic cubism, collage, and *papiers collés* opened up possibilities of spatial depiction and ambiguity which rely more than ever on subtle forms of contiguity: that is, of metonymy. Consider, for example, Braque's *La Guitare*, a *papier collé* of 1912.[30] Three separate 'objects' are depicted, each by a different form of metonymy. The guitar is suggested by synecdoche, part for the whole: a few sketched lines give the shape of its body, the sound hole, and the pegs; a newspaper is represented by its name, again partially, JOU and an obscured R; the table on which the two lie[31] is a collage element of *papier faux bois*. The spatial relationships between these objects, however, far from being 'simply juxtaposed', 'asyntactical', or 'flat', are highly complex and multivalent. Common sense would suppose that the guitar and newspaper must be on top of the wood surface; yet the *papier faux bois* is pasted *over* the drawn outlines. One corner of the newspaper is clearly *under* the guitar; but its top line disappears *into* the sound hole. The wooden texture of the (assumed) table *might* also belong to the guitar, and decorative lines in the *faux bois* effect could also be 'read' as signs for the guitar's strings. Far from being used merely 'to provide interest', as Dubnick claims, the texture is here used to intensify the indeterminacy of the spatial relationships.

These relationships are, however, still based on contiguity (guitar, newspaper and table would very naturally be found next to one another), not on any far-fetched metaphorical identity. In synthetic as in analytic cubism, the concern is not the metaphorical suppression of syntax but its metonymic dissemination. Or, to put it another way, deconstruction – in, precisely, the Derridean sense of the word: neither the negation nor the simple reversal of a structure, but rather a putting into question of the terms of that structure *at the same time as* working within it. Even in its starkest and most minimal forms, synthetic cubism is never 'simple' juxtaposition; it is always working with the re-representation of space. In syntax as in vocabulary, cubism is consistently metonymic through *all* its phases.

One argument for 'metaphoric' technique in cubism concerns what Walker calls 'complex visual and verbal puns [which] create relationships of equivalence'[32] – or what Juan Gris, and most of his critics after him, have called 'rhymes'. 'Rather like rhymes in a poem', writes Daniel-Henry Kahnweiler in his definitive book on Gris, 'two forms, generally of different sizes, are repeated'.[33] Thus, the curved line of a guitar is 'rhymed' in the curve of a bottle, or of a pear. It could be argued that, as 'relations of equivalence', these rhymes are, in Jakobson's terms, metaphor – and Kahnweiler does use that word, describing them as 'plastic metaphors to reveal to the beholder certain hidden relationships, similarities between two apparently different objects'.[34] However, Kahnweiler is equally insistent that Gris's rhymes are *not symbols*:

> they never have a dual identity. . . . They *are* the objects which they represent, with all the emotive value attaching to them; but they never signify anything outside of these objects. . . . These 'rhymes', like every other rhyme, are a form of repetition: the repetition of two forms, each of which retains its own unique identity.[35]

Even at the level of the syntax, the counter-argument (as I suggested above, in my discussion of the Braque collage) would be that cubist 'rhymes' have as much to do with metonymic contiguity as with metaphor equivalence: guitar, pear, bottle are all naturally present in the same scene (a café, for instance) alongside each other.[36] But Kahnweiler's point leads to the more fundamental argument, at the level of vocabulary, against the notion of cubism as metaphor.

The *signs* of cubism are overwhelmingly metonymic. From at least as early as Braque's *trompe-l'oeil* nail in 1909, or Picasso's 'piercing of the closed form' in 1910, cubism retained its stubborn grip on the outside world, its representational refusal of abstraction, by means of synecdoche. Scattered across the complex grids of analytic cubism, or reduced to a few lines or collaged elements in synthetic, the parts of objects stood for the whole – or, more accurately, *the sign of* the part stood for *the sign of* the whole. A single curve could evoke a guitar; five strings stood for six; two or three letters implied a complete word; the decorative fringe of a tablecloth stood in for the whole cloth, and then, by metonymic extension, for the table on which the cloth was spread, for the café in which the table was situated, for the life and atmosphere of the café and its clientele. But none of this was metaphor: for metaphor implies *difference*, a jump from one area of signification to another (from 'wind' to 'change', for example), across a gap which cannot be encompassed within the normal associations of contiguity. Very occasionally, cubist signs do function like this, usually as sexual symbols. A guitar's curves may be read as metaphoric for a woman's body, and Picasso could never resist the *double entendre* of a key in a lock. But these are exceptions which, precisely, prove the rule. Cubism is *about* guitars and bottles and café tables: all these representational elements are linked to each other in an intricate pattern of metonymy, but they do not stand for, as metaphors, anything outside themselves.

I have argued, then, that the attempt made by Dubnick and, in a more modified form, by Walker, to divide cubism into metonymic and metaphoric phases corresponding to the traditional division of the analytic and synthetic periods, is not a convincing one. While there are undoubtedly some metaphoric aspects to cubism, its dominant mode is that of metonymy, both at the rhetorical level of its vocabulary and at the Jakobsonian level of its syntax. It is time now to return to Stein. It will be recalled that Dubnick introduced metaphor into cubism in order to preserve the alleged analogy between cubism and Stein's *Tender Buttons* style, which Lodge had described as 'clearly a type of metaphorical writing'. If cubism is not, in this sense, metaphorical, then can the analogy hold? Or, conversely, can the argument supporting the metonymic nature of cubism also be used to describe Stein? That is, can we not classify Stein's writing also as being metonymic rather than metaphoric in *all* its phases (still bearing in mind, of course, the earlier caveats against the rigid use of such binary classification)?

Certainly, as we have earlier seen, Jakobson's descriptions of the metonymic pole of 'Similarity Disorder' do apply, at least superficially, to the prose style of *The Making of Americans* and the early sections of *A Long Gay Book*. That is, there is an evident avoidance of specific nouns (to the point of almost total indeterminacy – 'anything is something'), and a concomitant emphasis on connectives, auxiliaries, undifferentiated pronouns. The novel's expansiveness, its continual adding on of instances in the attempt to define a character's 'bottom nature', may also be seen as an exemplary process of metonymic *naming* along the horizontal axis. Talking about metonymy in *Labyrinths of Voice*, Robert Kroetsch says,

> I guess I have the absurd hope that if I provide twenty names, then somewhere I will reach a point where they all connect and become more realized and identifiable . . . one just moves on and around, and there are further namings and renamings. I trust that process. I trust the *discreteness* of those naming acts.[37]

The question arises, however, of just how 'discrete' the acts of naming are in Stein. For all its great length, *The Making of Americans* is concerned with a strictly limited number of characters, and its avowed intention is to reveal their unified 'bottom nature'. Repetition is not here aimed at 'discreteness', singularity or difference, but at the eventual discovery and emphasis of what is the same. In her chapter on *The Making of Americans*, Walker provides a fine analysis of how this ambition breaks down, how the attempt to realise 'paradigms based on identities' runs up against Stein's growing 'desire for comprehensive factual data',[38] how repetition as identity is contaminated by repetition as pure difference. In Stein's own terms, the structural model for the writing moves from the *diagram* to the *list*.

Walker's discussion of the diagram[39] is interesting for the parallels it draws to cubist theory (which, however, is frequently misleading and reductive in comparison to cubist practice: only the minor cubists, such as Gleizes and Metzinger, actually painted by diagrams). Walker cites Stein's use of the word 'diagram' in her notebooks, and in *The Making of Americans*. Whereas early in the novel Stein's ambition was to 'make a kind of diagram' (*MOA*, p. 225), later on the diagram has to be supplemented by the list: 'It would be a very complete thing in my feeling to be having complete lists of every body ever living and to be realising each one and to be making diagrams and lists of them' (p. 594). While there are, as Walker points out, proliferating lists toward the end of the novel, it is in *A Long Gay Book* that the list really takes over from the diagram; and the very process of the takeover is enacted in the following paragraph:

> There can be lists and lists of kinds of them. There can be very many lists of kinds of them. There can be diagrams of kinds of them, there can be diagrams showing kinds of them and other kinds of them looking a little like another kind of them. There can be lists and diagrams, some diagrams and many lists. There can be lists and diagrams. There can be lists. (*LGB*, p. 23)

The diagram is a form of metaphor, and the list a form of metonymy. While both *The Making of Americans* and *A Long Gay Book* appear metonymic in style, according to Jakobson's description, the deeper structural intentions of the two books move from metaphor toward metonymy, from the diagram toward the list, from repetition as identity toward repetition as difference. The acts of naming in *The Making of Americans* are not in fact totally 'discrete'; they accumulate toward a totalising definition of characters, and those characters are conceived of as *representative* (of, for instance, 'dependent independent being'). The acts of naming in *A Long Gay Book*, however, are 'discrete' – Sloan, Gibbons, Johnson, Hobart, Carmine, Watts, Arthurs, Vrais, Jane Sands, Larr, Mrs. Gaston, George Clifton, and so on – never connecting, never consolidating into any stable sense of identity. These are *non*-characters, representative of nothing except the impossibility of being representative. Even when a name is repeated on several occasions – Clellan, for example – the different appearances do not coalesce or reinforce each other. Specific names ought, in Jakobson's terms, to be metaphoric, standing for unified identities; but, as I have insisted, metonymy is also a naming process, *substitute* naming, *deferred* naming. The 'proper' names of *A Long Gay Book* are in fact quite improper. They name no one; they can be used as title to no one's property.

A Long Gay Book is a 'transitional' text not only in the obvious sense that the prose style changes so dramatically but also in the sense that even its initial project, to give 'short sketches of innumerable ones' (*LGB*, p. 17), is already a shift away from the metaphoric diagram to the metonymic list. One may suspect, then, that the whole text is more continuous with itself than the surface appearance would suggest, and that the metonymic impulse, in one form or another, continues into the last twenty pages of *A Long Gay Book*, and so into *Tender Buttons*. At this point, however, we return to the orthodox Lodge argument that the style of *Tender Buttons* is, in Jakobson's terms, metaphoric.

At the level of syntax, Lodge himself admits that 'The analogy is not exact', and that much of the word order in *Tender Buttons* is 'still basically regular'.[40] Certainly the writing has moved away from connectives, indeterminate pronouns such as 'some' and 'any', and verbs in the continuous present; there is a far greater stress on nouns, and on short, enigmatic sentences. But the enigma is more often produced by semantic than by syntactic dislocation; indeed, a sentence such as 'A dirty bath is so clean that there is eyesight' (*LGB*, p. 106) *depends upon* its syntactic regularity to produce its semantic puzzle. There are some agrammatical 'word heaps' in *A Long Gay Book* ('No no, not it a line not it tailing, tailing in, not it in' – p. 115) and they appear somewhat more frequently in *Tender Buttons* ('Please could, please could, jam it not plus more sit in when' – *TB*, p. 26) but they remain, as Walker says, 'rare'.[41] They do not *dominate* the syntax in the way that the 'metonymic' patterns of the earlier style did. Frequently, also, the 'word heap' is in fact a list, whose items are added to each other not by metaphoric equation but by metonymic association – as in 'Pale pet, red pet, pink pet, blue pet, white pet, dark pet, real pet, fresh pet' (*LGB*, p. 97). Stein is working here with what Walker, citing Derrida, describes as 'the unlimited freeplay of association'[42] – and, indeed, the notion of 'play' will go further to account for this writing than any strict application of either metaphor or metonymy. (Metonymy, however, by its open-ended, horizontally accumulative nature, is more amenable to notions of play than metaphor is.)

The same holds true at the level of vocabulary. Lodge and Dubnick both see the nouns of *Tender Buttons* as metaphor – for Lodge, 'The very title *Tender Buttons* is a surrealist metaphor'[43] – but Walker argues that 'this is clearly not the case', since 'the nouns that are linked together in this text are not semantically equivalent; their relationship is what Jakobson describes as metonymic, not metaphoric. In a figural sense, they are all synecdoches, naming contiguous "pieces of any day".'[44] Just like the objects depicted in cubist painting, the objects described in *Tender Buttons* do not refer, metaphorically, to anything outside themselves; rather, as Walker says, the work 'describes a female world (circa 1912) of domestic objects and rituals – a world of dresses and hats, tables and curtains, mealtimes and bedtimes, cleanliness and dirt'.[45]

This range of association and imagery is evident very early in the 'new' style. Within a page of the first sentence in *A Long Gay Book* which announces the new vocabulary ('A tiny violent noise is a yellow happy thing' – *LGB*, p. 82), and before the new syntax is established, we find the following paragraph:

> A little way is longer than waiting to bow. Not bowing is longer than waiting longer. It would sadly distress some powder if looking out was continual and sitting first was happening and leaving first was persisting. It would not change the color, it would not harmonise with yellow, it would not necessitate reddening, it would not destroy smiling, it would not enlarge stepping, it would not widen a chair or arrange a cup or conclude a sailing, it would not disappoint a brown or a pink or a golden anticipation, it would not deter a third one from looking, it would not help a second one to fasten a straighter collar or a first one to dress with less decision, it would not distress Emma or stop her from temperately waiting, it would not bring reasoning to have less meaning, it would not make telling more exciting, it would not make leaving necessitate losing what would be missing, it would though always mean that three and one are not always all that remain if ten remain and eight are coming.   (pp. 83–4)

The links through this paragraph are formed partly by association of sound (a topic I shall discuss in more detail later), but all these associations lead into the domestic world, and thus form a metonymic chain of associations. 'Bow' suggests 'powder' by rhyme, while the alternative pronunciation plays on 'bows' with ribbons. The string of 'colors' leads to a 'collar' which must be straightened, and perhaps to the callers who are enumerated at the end. Domestic visits are also suggested by 'bowing' itself, by the 'little way' that has to be gone, by the distressing (dressing) prospect of 'looking out' being 'continual', by the social graces of blushing and smiling, and by the arrangement of chairs and cups. Such a reading does not, of course, account for everything in the passage – right from the start, Stein's dislocations are too radical to be entirely recuperated – but it is just specific enough to indicate the sphere of association within which, for the most part, the language plays.

The centre of this 'iconography of domestic life'[46] is of course Alice B. Toklas: and metonymy is the key to understanding both Alice's presence in the text and her absence from it. For if Alice is the centre (of the text, and of the domestic life itself), she is so only as a displaced one. 'Act', wrote Gertrude in *Tender Buttons*, 'so that there is no use in a centre. . . . If the centre has the place then there is distribution' (*TB*, p. 63). But, if the centre is displaced, orderly distribution is itself distributed into metonymic disorder. Alice is so distributed throughout the text – its 'dresses and hats, tables and curtains, mealtimes and bedtimes' – so that she is both everywhere and nowhere.

There is an obvious danger in a kind of reductive interpretation of Stein's writing which sees all its obscurities as disguised erotic references and which 'solves' them like crossword-puzzle clues. A degree of displacement and deferral should be preserved in the reading as much as in the writing. Nevertheless, the erotic tone of many passages is unmistakable, even if the details remain unspecified. The change of style in *A Long Gay Book* is immediately accompanied by repeated assertions of the writer's pleasure:

> If there are two and there is one there and another in the other direction then slightly being pleased is to be happy.   (*LGB*, p. 93)

> If the little that is not bigger has gone away it has not been there. That is the way to complete pleasure. It is alright.   (p. 98)

> The union is perfect and the border is expressing kissing.
> (p. 100)

At times the erotic content is totally explicit: 'A lovely love is sitting and she sits there now she is in bed, she is in bed. A lovely love is cleaner when she is so clean, she is so clean, she is all mine' (p. 101).

But Stein's urge to celebrate her love for Toklas was balanced by her need to conceal, disguise or displace it. We should examine here an extended passage from the end of *A Long Gay Book*:

> Beef yet, beef and beef and beef. Beef yet, beef yet.
> Water crowd and sugar paint, water and the paint.

Wet weather, wet pen, a black old tiger skin, a shut in shout and a negro coin and the best behind and the sun to shine.

A whole cow and a little piece of cheese, a whole cow openly.

A cousin to a cow, a real cow has wheels, it has turns it has eruptions, it has the place to sit.

A wedding glance is satisfactory. Was the little thing a goat.

A, open, Open.

Leaves of hair which pretty prune makes a plate of care which sees seas leave perfect set. A politeness.

Call me ellis, call me it in little speech and never say it is all polled, do not say so.

Does it does it weigh. Ten and then. Leave off grass. A little butter closer. Hopes hat.

Listen to say that tooth which narrow and lean makes it so best that dainty is delicate and least mouth is in between, what, sue sense.

Little beef, little beef sticking, hair please, hair please.

No but no but butter.

Coo cow, coo coo coo.

Coo cow leaves of grips nicely.

It is no change. It is ordinary. Not yesterday. Needless, needless to call extra. Coo Coo Coo Cow.

Leave love, leave love let.

No no, not it a line not it tailing, tailing in, not it in.

Hear it, hear it, hear it.

Notes. Notes change hay, change hey day. Notes change a least apt apple, apt hill, all hill, a screen table, sofa, sophia.

(pp. 114–15)

This passage illustrates the many different levels of Stein's evocation of Toklas. First, there is the metonymic suggestion of her presence distributed, as I have indicated, in the domestic imagery: beef, water, sugar, cheese, wedding, hair, prune, place, butter, hat, dainty, delicate, needles(s), apple, table, sofa. Secondly, there is a direct naming of Alice through a pun: 'Call me ellis'. (In *Tender Buttons*, she appears as 'ale less' – *TB*, p. 26.) Other women's names also appear in punned form: 'Sophia' from 'sofa' and Susan from 'sue sense'. Thirdly, as Neil Schmitz points out, there is the literary evocation of Walt Whitman ('Leaves of hair,' 'Leave off grass', 'leaves of grips'), who had also 'addressed the issue of "forbidden voices" in his poetry . . . [and] spoke openly (a paradox Gertrude Stein might well have appreciated) about his encoded discourse'.[47] And, fourthly, there is the central word in that 'encoded discourse' or 'little speech', Stein's private vocabulary for her erotic experience: 'cow'. Elizabeth Fifer summarises the meanings attached to this term:

> If, as Richard Bridgman suggests, it is involved in both the nurturing aspect of Alice and some sort of birth, it is also the orgasm, even the potential for it. . . . ['Cow'] alternately bears the feeling of sexuality, the organ itself, food, protection, or the mythical idea of lesbian birth. It is both a derogatory female symbol (in the beast's placidity, stupidity) and a positive symbol of mothering and unselfishness, of pure animal sensuality and nurture in an Edenic world of simplicity and warmth.[48]

The first of these four modes is clearly metonymic – Alice is evoked by the repeated mention of the domestic objects which surround her – but the others, it might be argued, are closer to metaphor. In the use of terms such as 'cow', the distance between tenor and vehicle is more characteristic of metaphor than of metonymy; there is no intention of evoking an *actual*, contiguously present cow, except at one remove, through *its* metonymies (beef, butter). Public symbols (such as the key sticking in a keyhole in Picasso's paintings) do operate metaphorically, but a private symbol (such as Stein's 'cow') is less easy to pin down to a single determinate meaning. Picasso's keyholes are all too obvious, too crude (they represent that level of sniggering adolescence in him which Stein herself, it must be admitted, enjoyed and indulged); in its very privacy, 'cow' expresses the depth and the desperation of Stein's need for concealment.

The rhymes on Alice's name raise the wider question of the status of transitions by homophony in Stein's writing: 'Hear it', she insists, 'hear it, hear it.'[49] Rhymes, puns and all links based on sound rely upon Jakobson's *vertical* axis: *similarity* of the signifier, if not of the signified, renders them metaphoric. The structure is that of equivalence, not of contiguity. It will be recalled that a similar argument was made for the visual 'rhymes' in cubist painting, especially Juan Gris's. I argued then that most of the 'rhymed' objects in cubist painting are in fact contiguous to each other – for instance, in the café setting; the same argument cannot be used for

Stein, whose linguistic 'rhymes' range wide and free. But I also argued that cubist rhymes did not imply identity, that each object stood only for itself, not for a metaphoric equivalence. In Stein, the *difference* of each object is so absolute that frequently it defies not only metaphor but *any* appropriation into a context of meaning wider than the individual word. The 'apple/apt hill' transition is neither metaphor (there is no implied identity or semantic similarity between the two terms) nor metonymy (there is no contiguity either): it is sheer play, an attempt, if you like, to 'sue sense'.

It may be noted here that the systematic use of homophony is described by Gregory L. Ulmer as a central characteristic of Jacques Derrida's 'grammatological' writing. Derrida, writes Ulmer, 'adopts as an operational device the exploitation of the pun', creating 'a homonymic procedure . . . allowing terms to circulate and interbreed in a festival of equivocality'.[50] Such a writing would surely be not unlike *Tender Buttons*. Ulmer refers to Derrida's essay 'Fors' (which is an introduction to Abraham and Torok's commentary on the language of Freud's Wolf Man), where Derrida notes that 'the allosemic pathways in this strange relay race pass through non-semantic associations, purely phonetic contaminations', with the result that Abraham and Torok 'are hesitant to speak of metonymic displacement here, or even to trust themselves to a catalogue of rhetorical figures'.[51] In other words, 'phonetic contamination' is seen as a *limit* to metonymy, to metaphor, indeed to all rhetorical figures.

In the same way, the substitution of 'ale less' for 'Alice' implies neither Alice's similarity to a smaller quantity of beer nor the contiguous presence of such liquid. A further pun, however – 'ail less' – might indicate a metonymic relationship, Alice being invoked by her association with the decrease in Gertrude's suffering. Again, when Alice is referred to as 'Ada' and then as 'aider' (*TB*, p. 29), it is clear that Alice's function as a helper is one of her metonymic attributes. Thus, while the process of homophony may be seen either as metaphoric (in Jakobson's terms) or as a phonetic contamination beyond rhetoric (in Derrida's), the terms produced by that process may frequently be referred back to the 'distributed' centre of the discourse by the familiar links of metonymy. Such is the curious suggestion which lurks in 'Call me ellis'. Although the major literary reference of the passage is Whitman (and such references, in a literary household, are themselves domestic metonymies), the form of this phrase ('Call me xxxx', plus the simple reversal of the *is* and *el* syllables) surely recalls Melville. Alice is here invoked as Ishmael to Gertrude's Ahab – and indeed, twenty years later, 'Alice' was to fulfil the role of narrator of Gertrude's epic quest. 'Call me ellis' is what Genette would call an *amorce* (bait of a trap, primer of an explosive charge, foreshadowing, germ of an idea) for *The Autobiography of Alice B. Toklas*.

I have indicated, then, some of the ways (and the limits of these ways) in which metonymy may be useful in explaining Alice's presence in Stein's text; but I have also claimed that metonymy is a key to her absence from it. Metonymy is a way of naming Alice when Alice herself cannot be named. The major reason for this is of course the social and moral taboo which prevented the open acknowledgement of a lesbian relationship, the unspoken censorship which necessitated linguistic disguise. But 'what does man find in metonymy', asks Jacques Lacan, 'if not the power to circumvent the obstacles of social censure?'[52]

The reason that Alice cannot be named is that the object of desire can *never* be fully or adequately named. Desire is always for the Other, for something *else* ('Call me ellis'). As Terry Eagleton writes, expounding Lacan, 'All desire springs from a lack, which it strives continually to fill. Human language works by such lack. . . . To enter language . . . is to become a prey to desire.'[53] The operation of desire in language is, according to Lacan, metonymy: that is, the *displacement*, analogous to the Freudian 'dreamwork', of signifier to signifier. 'Along this metonymic chain of signifiers, meanings, or signifieds, will be produced; but no object or person can ever be fully "present" in this chain. . . . This potentially endless movement from one signifier to another is what Lacan means by desire.'[54] And 'desire *is* a metonymy', writes Lacan;[55] the 'enigmas' which it poses 'amount to no other derangement of instinct than that of being caught in the rails – eternally stretching forth towards the *desire for something else* – of metonymy'.[56]

As the language of desire, metonymy breaks out of the logocentric, patriarchal world of 'presence', the imposed 'identities' of metaphor; along the horizontal axis of combination, it offers the unlimited freeplay of dissemination; by offering a multiplicity of alternative names, it denies the authority of the single name, le Nom du Père, the Name which says No. Any book embarked along such an axis must of necessity be both long and gay.

Notes

1. This essay is a revised and extended version of a paper initially presented to the Twentieth Century Literature Conference at the University of Louisville, Kentucky, in February 1986.
2. David Lodge, *The Modes of Modern Writing: Metaphor, Metonymy, and the Typology of Modern Literature* (Ithaca, NY: Cornell University Press, 1977).
3. Originally written in 1954, and published in 1956; included in Roman Jakobson, *Selected Writings*, II: *Word and Language* (The Hague: Mouton, 1971) pp. 239–59.
4. Ibid., p. 245.
5. Ibid., p. 254.
6. Ibid., p. 251.
7. I am thinking here especially of the sense of 'grammatology' explored in Gregory L. Ulmer, *Applied Grammatology: Post(e) Pedagogy from Jacques Derrida to Joseph Beuys* (Baltimore: Johns Hopkins University Press, 1985).
8. Shirley Neuman and Robert Wilson, *Labyrinths of Voice: Conversations with Robert Kroetsch* (Edmonton, Alta: NeWest Press, 1982) p. 117.
9. Marianne DeKoven, *A Different Language: Gertrude Stein's Experimental Writing* (Madison: University of Wisconsin Press, 1983) pp. xiii, xvii.
10. Jane Gallop, *Reading Lacan* (Ithaca, NY: Cornell University Press, 1985) p. 126.
11. Ibid., p. 129.
12. Ibid., p. 131.
13. Jayne L. Walker, *The Making of a Modernist: Gertrude Stein from 'Three Lives' to 'Tender Buttons'* (Amherst: University of Massachusetts Press, 1984).
14. It is interesting to note that Stein herself, though clearly aware of a change in style, persisted in regarding *A Long Gay Book* as a single text. DeKoven's decision not to respect Stein's division of her own work is perhaps premature; her acceptance of the 'closed' definition of 'a work' as 'a coherent literary unit, separate and distinguishable from any other' is symptomatic of the conservatism of her critical practice, if not her theory. If Stein's 'experimental' writing 'disrupts . . . orderly, closed, hierarchical, sensible, coherent' modes, why should it not also disrupt the idea of 'the book'? See DeKoven, *A Different Language*, pp. xv, xiii.
15. Lodge, *The Modes of Modern Writing*, p. 147.
16. Jakobson, *Selected Writings*, II, 245–6.
17. Lodge, *The Modes of Modern Writing*, pp. 151–2.
18. Ibid., p. 153.
19. Jakobson, *Selected Writings*, II, 256.
20. Lodge, *The Modes of Modern Writing*, p. 152.
21. Randa Dubnick, *The Structure of Obscurity: Gertrude Stein, Language, and Cubism* (Chicago and Urbana: University of Illinois Press, 1984).
22. Ibid., pp. 26, 23.
23. Ibid., p. 5.

24. Ibid., p. 41.
25. At one point Dubnick talks of the surfaces of cubist paintings as 'translucent', with a 'barely perceptible presence' behind them (ibid., p. 4), while elsewhere she describes them as 'opaque or translucent' (p. 27). How can a surface be *both* opaque *and* translucent? There is nothing *behind* the surface of a cubist painting: the whole point is that everything is there *on* the surface.
26. Ibid., p. 35.
27. Walker, *The Making of a Modernist*, p. 131.
28. Ibid., p. 132.
29. Ibid.
30. *Georges Braque: les papiers collés* (Paris: Musée nationale d'art moderne, 1982), catalogue no. 4.
31. I assume it is a table: the wood-grain *could* stand for a wall on which the guitar is hanging, but then where would the newspaper be?
32. Walker, *The Making of a Modernist*, pp. 132–3.
33. Daniel-Henry Kahnweiler, *Juan Gris: His Life and Work*, tr. Douglas Cooper (New York: Abrams, 1969) p. 141.
34. Ibid.
35. Ibid., p. 140.
36. Even when Gris 'rhymes' a book, a guitar and a mountain, the mountain can be seen through a window immediately behind a table on which the book and guitar are lying.
37. In Neuman and Wilson, *Labyrinths of Voice*, p. 93.
38. Walker, *The Making of a Modernist*, pp. 70, 71.
39. Ibid., pp. 65–6.
40. Lodge, *The Modes of Modern Writing*, p. 153.
41. Walker, *The Making of a Modernist*, p. 132.
42. Ibid., p. 141.
43. Lodge, *The Modes of Modern Writing*, p. 152.
44. Walker, *The Making of a Modernist*, pp. 162, 133.
45. Ibid., p. 127.
46. Ibid.
47. Neil Schmitz, *Of Huck and Alice: Humorous Writing in American Literature* (Minneapolis: University of Minnesota Press, 1983) p. 196.
48. Elizabeth Fifer, 'Is Flesh Advisable? The Interior Theater of Gertrude Stein', *Signs*, 4, 3 (Spring, 1979) 480–1.
49. What you have to 'hear', of course, are the 'hair pleas[e]' to be here.
50. Ulmer, *Applied Grammatology*, pp. 19, 26.
51. Jacques Derrida, 'Fors', tr. Barbara Johnson, *Georgia Review*, xxxi, 1 (Spring 1977) 108.
52. Jacques Lacan, *Ecrits: A Selection*, tr. Alan Sheridan (London: Tavistock, 1977) p. 158.
53. Terry Eagleton, *Literary Theory: An Introduction* (Oxford: Basil Blackwell, 1983) p. 167.
54. Ibid.
55. Lacan, *Ecrits*, p. 175.
56. Ibid., pp. 166–7.

8

Sneak Previews: Gertrude Stein's Syntax in *Tender Buttons*

SUSAN E. HAWKINS

Gertrude Stein is, like other great modernist figures, an innovator. She creates very early in the century a non-linear narrative technique, one that enables her to represent consciousness as process-ionally continuous. However, what Joyce and Woolf (at considerably later dates) accomplish in their most radical experimentations with 'stream of consciousness' is a psychologically complete representation of the human psyche, its machinations, meanderings, its subconscious depths. For Stein, consciousness does not have depth. This notion results, in part, from her conception of character as set, as psychologically typed or determined – a concept she acquired, and found very congenial, in William James's psychology classes at Radcliffe. If we are 'typecast', so to speak, from the beginning, then we do not change to any great degree through our contact with experiential reality; we pretty much *are*. Thus Stein's prose technique in *Tender Buttons* is not primarily concerned with the growth of human consciousness so much as it is to repeat, so insistently, a kind of phenomenological moment in which consciousness meets (but does not process) perceptual reality. Reality is repetition; the perceiving subject constantly re-enacts this moment. But, while in her earlier works she stressed, through syntax, the 'flatness' of character as perceiver of reality, in *Tender Buttons* she conveys the perceptual surface of reality itself. And, since reality and the moment in which it is perceived are the same thing, syntax must break its connection with linear logic. After all, syntax demands obedience to its own logic through grammar, a logic that is clearly at odds with perception. Stein's great project, then, is to free syntax from these traditional constraints through what I would call syntactic defamiliarisation, or the making new by casting in a strangely different way.

What Stein attempts in *Tender Buttons* is a revision of syntax, its power to order and hierarchise, and a dismantling of the place of the subject. To do this she creates, in part, a multiple point of view; at times it is almost as if the objects and rooms were speaking or thinking rather than a human being. By de-emphasising chronology (the dominant verb tense is the present), by employing verbs of being (the dominant verb choice is 'to be'), and by stressing process through repetitions and participials, Stein lessens the traditional subject's role and suggests instead a multivalent perspective. For instance, the third prose poem from the 'Objects' section is entitled 'A Substance in a Cushion', and the following is a sample paragraph:

> A cushion has that cover. Supposing you do not like to change, supposing it is very clean that there is no change in appearance, supposing that there is regularity and a costume is that any the worse than an oyster and an exchange. Come to season that is there any extreme use in feather and cotton. Is there not much joy in a table and more chairs and very likely roundness and a place to put them.　(*TB*, p. 10)

This paragraph exhibits a number of techniques found throughout *Tender Buttons*. The first and most obvious is what I might call 'down the rabbit hole'. We know things are normal only by comparison *after* we arrive in Wonderland. Here the opening sentence provides an unassuming beginning; we have an entirely reasonable thought. 'A cushion has that cover' seems an appropriate comment to include among a list of objects which might be found in the rooms of a home. But with the very next series of suppositions the reader knows, as Alice does, that something dizzyingly different is happening. The 'you' addressed in 'Supposing you do not like to change' is quite unknown; 'you' may be the speaker, an unidentified listener, the cushion (!), or the reader. Identity is impossible. I might add that the presence of this personal pronoun is very unusual. In *Tender Buttons* such pronouns are rare; I don't believe Stein ever employs the first person. Thus while we cannot identify who is being addressed, we none the less read this phrase as a complete thought; it has all the elements of a sentence and as such presents an aura of rationality, the *appearance* of sense. However, the next participial phrase presses our interpretative abilities. 'Supposing it is very clean' makes us wonder just what is the 'it is' here? While again we have the suggestion of syntactic completeness, it is going fast and is certainly gone by the time we reach the third phrase in this string – 'supposing that there is regularity and a costume' – run into an interrogative which has no grammatical sign to indicate a question. At this point, the subject – human or otherwise – has been left far behind. And the lack of appropriate punctuation marks only adds to our sense of unease and our desire for clarity.

This desire on the reader's part brings me to another technique which Stein employs here as well as throughout *Tender Buttons*. We might call this one 'dashed hopes'; it involves her use of interrogatives and negatives. Syntactic habits create particular expectations in readers. Generally when we hear a question, we anticipate an answer. Stein definitely works with such expectations in order to derive certain results. One of these, as I mentioned above, is reader unease – she would like to keep us guessing a bit. We stumble into that embedded question, no matter how odd it may seem, and we expect an answer. What we get for an answer, however, is *not* clarifying: 'Come to season that is there any extreme use in feather and cotton.' All we get here is another strange question, followed by yet *another* question, the final sentence of the paragraph.

Now the final sentence also contains a negative, and I think even more so than interrogatives, negative structures demand very precise responses and grammatical desires from readers. For one thing, negatives suggest the exclusion of certain choices or the dismissal of particular kinds of information. Such constructions strongly imply a narrowing of, or focusing on, an idea. For example, 'This did not determine rejoining a letter. This did not make letters smaller' ('Rooms', *TB*, p. 67). When a negative appears at the end of a sequence, its location again works on reader expectation. Its position suggests that it may clarify what has preceded it and has not made any sense. For instance, a short prose poem in the 'Objects' section is entitled 'A Time to Eat' and it consists of two sentences: 'A pleasant simple habitual and tyrannical and authorised and educated and resumed and articulate separation. This is not tardy' (p. 23). Finally, negatives tend to sound authoritative; we use them when we 'mean business'. And as syntactic structures they reinforce and emphasise the point we happen to be making: 'Startling a starving husband is not disagreeable. The reason that nothing is hidden is that there is no suggestion of silence. No song is sad' ('Rooms', *TB*, p. 66). The voice here is very definite, very controlled, very knowing (and weirdly funny) despite the actual content.

The notion of readerly expectation and writerly dashing of hopes is a major one in dealing with Stein's sort of experimentalism. We expect prose to be forthcoming, clarifying, informative, in short helpful, because it has always been so. We anticipate clear explanations, or at least concluding evidence of some kind which will make all that has come before fit into some sort of pattern. We expect the parts to fit the whole. What we receive from Stein is something other. To a great extent she uses the logic of syntax against itself, not so much because she wishes to *hide* all sense and pleasure from her readers, but because she wishes us to see how arbitrary, how odd and silly our syntax – and hence propensity for logical constructions – frequently is.

Gertrude Stein does not, as you have, no doubt, already noticed, build arguments of any sort, not even the poetic variety. Her sentences all sound familiar, and for good reason; she structures them paratactically: 'A sentence of a vagueness that is violence is authority and a mission and stumbling and also certainly also a prison' ('Roastbeef', *TB*, pp. 38–9). The sound and rhythm here are very like the sound and rhythm in the sentences of my first example. They all structurally repeat themselves, or contain repeated parts. No idea is really subordinate to another; no idea is really supported in the usual senses by pertinent detail. Stein's syntax depends on this equalising flatness. Ostensibly nothing has more value than anything else. But there is a cumulative effect after reading hundreds of paratactic constructions, and this effect consists of an odd slippage between the parts. The reader can never gain a completely sure understanding, a totalised interpretation. The destruction of the relationships of part to whole, surface and depth, blurs syntactically constructed categories of meaning and value. We can no longer fall back into old habits of thought. We are forced into new, albeit uncomfortable, territory.

Now there are those commentators who see her experimentalism here as much more semantically based than syntactic, but I would argue, again going back to my initial example, that Stein's technique of semantic *laissez-faire* tends to result in syntactic confusion due to illogical semantic fillers. 'Come to season that is there any extreme use in feather and cotton' functions to highlight the nouns 'feather' and 'cotton', and to make the reader aware of these two not totally incompatible substances, to make the reader aware, in short, of the differences between the two. The effect of reading such sentences, after even a short period of time, is to make the reader aware of many choices within existence, not just a limited few.

And the idea of choices, of differences, of variety brings me to a rather old-fashioned question: is there anything *else* going on in *Tender Buttons* besides innovative technique and radical syntactic experimentation? And the answer is, yes; at a very comprehensible level Stein reveals to us, in an extraordinary way, the house we live in every day.

Historically and culturally defined as *the* female domain, the house and its objects are often evoked negatively, particularly when a speaker complains about the retrograde activity of housekeeping: mopping, cooking, dusting, refrigerator-defrosting, ironing, toilet-scrubbing, all often done to the accompaniment of screaming children. This is the 'woman's work is never done' view. But the house, the home, its people and objects, may evoke a quite different response, one of caring love. A woman's domain is, after all, the arena in which she exercises her power (limited as it has been) and wields control of a given reality.

For Gertrude Stein, a consideration of this household space – its palpability, its food, rooms, objects – brings pleasure. It is within these rooms that we engage in some of life's most tactile and important activities: making love, cooking, eating, talking, listening, perceiving. We are nourished by dazzlingly different kinds of foods, which have multiple beauties; and we move, in so many significant ways, among objects which have a material life, but, more significantly, a conscious 'life' within our perceptions of them. This life is uninterruptable; we cannot *will* perception to stop. Given this flow of the experiential surface of existence, all our thoughts, our perceptions, are tender buttons. And mental buttons are as suggestive as any other kind. We *know* what buttons are for.

9

The Difference of her Likeness: Gertrude Stein's *Stanzas in Meditation*

NEIL SCHMITZ

Here are the first two lines of Gertrude Stein's *Stanzas in Meditation*:

I caught a bird which made a ball
And they thought better of it.

Before I put on my Gertrude Stein spectacles to read this poem, refocus my knowledge of her life, my knowledge of her theoretical practice, spectacles that enable me to see into these lines, I want simply to confront the bareness of this beginning, to remember other occasions, other problems, in my interpretation of her text. What is this bird, and how does the catching of it make a ball? Who thinks better of what? In *Tender Buttons*, where Gertrude Stein caught the singing bird of lyrical poetry for the first time, the initial entry poses a spectacular carafe, 'A CARAFE, THAT IS A BLIND GLASS', a carafe as outstanding and concentring as Wallace Stevens' jar, and, if we wonder what kind of carafe this is, the caution is prompt: 'All this and not ordinary, not unordered in not resembling' (*TB*, p. 9). Gertrude Stein wrote novels, plays, opera, poetry, portraits, wrote autobiography, lectures, geography, treatises, fairy tales, valentines, and each text, even the earliest, even the valentine, stops the reader at its entrance, makes a demand, insists on its difference, a difference that is radical, a difference that is severe. If the demand cannot be met, the 'not resembling' not accepted, what follows – the novel, the poem, the opera, the meditation – instantly becomes inscrutable, obstinate in its unmeaning, perverse in its equanimity. We may have thought to read it, but then we thought better of it. What follows this particular bird and ball in *Stanzas in Meditation*, sessions of brooding, of mulling, a semi-pastoral

124

excursion of 164 stanzas, is rarely traversed. It looks to be a long walk, a long listen, this poem, and the strange beginning gives one pause.

What does the text demand? What does this difference declare? Here it is in the first two lines of *Stanzas in Meditation*, in the poser of Stein's first sentence. If we figure it out, agree to Gertrude Stein's terms, assume what she assumes, will the text then open to our gaze, take us into its confidence, show us truth and beauty, the tree uprooting the garden wall, a poem torn in two? Will we come to understand the situation of her discourse, the wherefore of its cryptic utterance? In these stanzas, which speak on and on, nothing is obvious, everything is apparent. This much is certain: if we persist, are patient, if we traverse these 164 mental spaces, Gertrude Stein will greet us, with some irony, in the penultimate stanza. 'Thank you for hurrying through', she says in part v, stanza lxxxii (*SIM*, p. 151). The ending, semi-divine in its utterance, an elation, will give us back the beginning, which is, for all its mythy inference, cryptic, anxious, built around the phrase 'there is no repose' (p. 3). We shall have reached this point, this verge. The door is open, there she is – immediate, present in her composing, transfigured.

> I call carelessly that the door is open
> Which if they can refuse to open
> No one can rush to close.
>
> (p. 151)

Those who have come through the stanzas at an unhurried pace, who have stopped to consider the pansy, who have tolerated her difference, understood the travail in these lines, will see in this final offering a breathtaking finish, the clarity, the certainty, of Gertrude Stein's repose.

> I will be well welcome when I come.
> Because I am coming.
> Certainly I come having come.
>
> (Ibid.)

But that comes later, and we do not get there easily. Repose is not what we see or feel in stanza i. There is first Gertrude Stein's difference to accept, a seeming perplexity of absences and lacks, and we must decide our relation to it. It is a complicated piece of business, this acceptance, this deciding. The decision involves practically the whole of Gertrude Stein's discourse, which is all of a piece, a single insistent discourse, the same voice, her decision, her choice. The text is not for me. I have to be for it. To read the text, I must surrender certain aesthetic presuppositions, I must put myself outside the strictures of patriarchal poetry, I must cease to be its prejudiced reader. I must indeed see those presuppositions, those strictures (what is important, what is beautiful), as deep prejudices that blind me to the value of a contraposed poetry, a poetry deliberately written elsewhere. In 1927 Gertrude Stein writes a long poem entitled 'Patriarchal Poetry' that exactly measures her distance from the canon. A busy subject, patriarchal poetry is this, is that, is just about everything. It writes patriotic poetry: marches left right, left right. It writes sonnets: 'To the wife of my bosom' (*BTV*, p. 272). It is the name and the character of the text, a comic mask. The poem ends with singsong, with Mother Goose, with a 'Dinky pinky dinky pinky dinky pinky lullaby'. It is a wicked thing to do to Patriarchal Poetry, to show its dinky pinky, not take it seriously.

> Patriarchal Poetry not to try. Patriarchal Poetry and lullaby. Patriarchal Poetry not to try Patriarchal poetry at once and why patriarchal poetry at once and by by and by Patriarchal poetry has to be which is best for them at three which is best and will be be and why why patriarchal poetry is not to try try twice.
>
> (*BTV*, p. 294)

There is that, Gertrude Stein's refusal to come to terms with patriarchal poetry, and then there is the issue of the secret, the mystery of the referent in Gertrude Stein's discourse. Her harshest critic touches upon this point when he comes finally to deliver his summary opinion of her work. The story is beautifully told in *Everybody's Autobiography*. Leo Stein, who thought himself to be the genius in the family, had from the start coldly refused to discuss his sister's work, and then one day he gave his opinion. 'He said it was not it it was I. If I was not there to be there with what I did then what I did would not be what it was. In other words if no one knew me actually then the things I did would not be what they were' (*EA*, pp. 76–7). There is a double charge in Leo Stein's dismissal. The writing is solipsistic, too subjective, he argues, and the subject, the solipsist, is not in itself, in herself, sufficient. Leo Stein's low opinion of his sister's writing (all your things are just about you) is an annihilation of her existence, and she responded in kind. 'The only thing about it was that it was I who was the genius', she writes, 'there was no reason for it but I was, and he was not there was a reason for it but he was not and that was the beginning of the ending and we always had been together and now we were never at all together. Little by little we never met again' (p. 77). That is one version of Gertrude Stein's secret. To have the text, you must have her, and since she refuses to explain who she is, who she was, you will never have the text. Her densest critic, B. F. Skinner, finds the secret in her method. His article 'Has Gertrude Stein a Secret?', which appeared in the *Atlantic Monthly* in 1933, asserts that Gertrude Stein brought into her experimental composition a technique of automatic writing she had learned as a graduate student in psychology at Harvard. Skinner had studied her Harvard research papers and then re-examined certain puzzling sections in *Tender Buttons*. Everything that is inexplicable in her literary discourse, he decided, is the work of the automatic writer, a rambling, stuttering, 'split off' part of Gertrude Stein's 'conscious self'. He tells us

> This part of her work is, as she has characterized her experimental result, little more than 'what her arm wrote'. And it is an arm that has very little to say. This is, I believe, the main importance of the present theory for literary criticism. It enables one to assign an origin to the unintelligible part of Gertrude Stein that puts one at ease about its meanings.[1]

A happy solution, this one. When Skinner sent his article to the *Atlantic*, Ellery Sedgwick, the same Ellery Sedgwick who had genially solicited and gladly published selections from *The Autobiography of Alice B. Toklas*, hypocritically pounced on it. The article was a 'small classic of the dissecting-table', he promptly wrote to Skinner, just the thing he wanted, and he required only that Skinner change the title, 'Gertrude Stein and Automatic Writing'. 'The hook should be barbed with the right title', Sedgwick argued. 'Yours gives the case away, and also suggests a certain dullness wholly absent in what follows. I want to call the paper "Has Gertrude Stein a Secret?" and let it go at that.'[2] Here it is, then, cut out of her text, exhibited, Gertrude Stein's arm.

Neither secret, the secret life, the secret method, is the one Gertrude Stein poses in her text. In the almost placeless siting of her discourse, in her refusal to name names, to identify and describe, she is at play with the secret, with the unknowable, with what we expect to know, what we want to know. The door is open, she writes in *Stanzas in Meditation*, and there she is, introspective, thinking for herself about herself. We are privy to that mental drama; we observe Gertrude Stein bring the ordinary, her immediate, the particular, into the concentration of her thought; and what is the problem, since all this is written in the plainest English? Yet there is a problem, a semblance of code in the simplicity of the discourse. A part of speech, hitherto proletarian in its usage, is in revolt, telegraphing messages. If we mark the secret as the sign of her difference, compose ourselves before each confounding absence, each blanked reference, see in that unknowable not mystification, but the wise result of a deep analysis, partly philosophical, partly political, we are then inside the structure of her style, somewhere between decoding and discerning, between the *it* and the *I*. We hear her calling. We believe she is coming. She is, after all, great with secret, groaning with it, and in 1932, as she writes *Stanzas in Meditation*, about to deliver it. That secret, Gertrude Stein keeps telling us, showing us, is her genius. *The Autobiography of Alice B. Toklas* begins with this declaration: 'The three geniuses of whom I wish to speak are Gertrude Stein, Pablo Picasso and Alfred Whitehead' (*ABT*, pp. 5–6), a declaration that is nervously echoed in *Stanzas in Meditation*:

> She knew that she could know
> That a genius was a genius
> Because just so she could know
> She did know three or so
> So she says and what she says
> No one can deny or try
> What if she says.
>
> (p. 77)

What if? The hubristic self-declaration of genius in *The Autobiography* necessarily brought other secrets into view, the relation of Alice B. Toklas to Gertrude Stein, the issue of sexual identity, the question of names, an order of secrets that at once complicated and obscured Gertrude Stein's sense of the declaration, which, as she saw it, had very little to do with her nature and everything to do with her mind. We have only to recall the meanness of Ernest Hemingway's memoir 'Miss Stein Instructs' in *A Moveable Feast* to understand the posting of anxieties in *Stanzas in Meditation*. In Paris, some time in

the 1920s, Gertrude Stein received a salutary lesson in how the
unspoken, even among friendly colleagues, could suddenly be
voiced. 'Miss Stein thought I was too uneducated about sex',
Hemingway recalls. One evening, as she began to explain certain
niceties, the young Hemingway, unable to contain himself any
longer, promptly admitted to 'certain prejudices against
homosexuality'. He told her homophobic stories of homosexual
rape in the hobo camps and lake boats of the Midwest, told her
about the 'old man with beautiful manners and a great name' who
visited him in the hospital in Italy, who forced Hemingway 'to tell
the nurse never to let that man into the room again', gave her
instance after instance, compelling Gertrude Stein to concede at last
the sordidness of such activity, and then to state her difference: 'In
women it is the opposite. They do nothing that they are disgusted
by and nothing that is repulsive and afterwards they are happy and
they can lead happy lives together.'[3] After this 'dangerous
conversation', Hemingway tells us in *A Moveable Feast*, he went
home to his wife and that was the end of his affair with Miss Stein.

What did it mean, Gertrude Stein's proclamation of genius in
1932–3? Exposure, visibility, the hazards of manifestation, a testing
of her courage, the triggering of a mythical logic. 'No one knowing
me knows me', Gertrude Stein would stoutly insist in 1935, in *The
Geographical History of America*. 'I am I I' (*GHA*, p. 77). It is where the
Autobiography begins, where *Stanzas in Meditation* begins, already
past a certain repression, after the overthrow of an authority. *I am I I*.
She stands in that enabling discursive space, the ground of which is
Emersonian in American literature, speaking from that establishing
discursive act of self-love, the one that took Walt Whitman outside
Patriarchal Poetry. There is that grounding, that situation of the
text, and still another, which emerges when we consider the theme
of dismemberment that appears in her critical reception. Skinner's
article, Sedgwick tells us, is a dissection, and there is Gertrude
Stein's arm. B. L. Reid boldly asserts that his *Art by Subtraction: A
Dissenting Opinion of Gertrude Stein* (1958) is 'an essay in
decapitation'. The standard work on Gertrude Stein's canon is
unfortunately entitled *Gertrude Stein in Pieces* (1970).[4] Such is the fate
of Orpheus, who would not respond to the desire of the maidens,
who was torn to pieces and set adrift on the Hebrus. I have put on
my spectacles, and the trick now is to resist the temptation of story,
the temptation of deciphering. We are back at the entrance to *Stanzas
in Meditation*, considering the proper difference, the real secret.

> I caught a bird which made a ball
> And they thought better of it.

In his Preface to *Stanzas in Meditation and Other Poems [1929–1933]*, Donald Sutherland suggests that the first line means 'I captured a "lyricity" that constituted a complete and self-contained entity' (*SIM*, p. xiii). It is, he reminds us, one of the few instances in her work where Gertrude Stein consciously employs literary symbols. Here, then, is a declaration that restates the one given to Alice B. Toklas in the *Autobiography*. It thrusts her forward, evokes a *mythos*, places her in a lineage, but what kind of lyricity is it that Gertrude Stein declares in this scrupulously prosaic line? The very flatness of the statement, the reduction of the symbol to barest outline, at once ironises and transcends the conventional notion of lyricity, plays a certain wry plainness against the expected eloquence of such declaration. It tells us, finally, that her poetic achievement does not take place in the sacred grove where the mythical being of the lyric reveals itself clothed in sumptuous language, singing exquisite melody. Her place in that *mythos* is exceptional. The sweetness of Orpheus's song drives the maidens mad. The plainness of Gertrude Stein's song drives men mad. It is a constant concern in *Stanzas in Meditation*.

> I caught a bird which made a ball
> And they thought better of it.

Gertrude Stein strikes, as it were, two notes from the familiar song, and then returns to her averted discourse. This is a different kind of poetry, a poetry of the commonplace, a poetry in which the high-flown meanings of bird and ball are immediately relocated. Gertrude Stein speaks of her poetic strategy in the *Autobiography*. Alice reports,

> She began at this time to describe landscape as if anything she saw was a natural phenomenon, a thing existent in itself, and she found it, this exercise, very interesting and it finally led her to the later series of Operas and Plays. I am trying to be as commonplace as I can be, she used to say to me. And then sometimes a little worried, it is not too commonplace. The last thing that she has finished, Stanzas of Meditation, and which I am now typewriting, she considers her real achievement of the commonplace.
>
> (*ABT*, p. 276)

We are, then, to find bird and ball as things existent in themselves, as specifics, in a commonplace that is not too commonplace. Many different birds indeed appear in the text, among them the nightingale, and, as for the ball, there is an ordinary ball in *Stanzas in Meditation*, a bouncing ball, a purchased ball, a lost ball, a ball that comes finally to rest, stopped, in the mouth of a sleeping dog. This ball, in fact, comes bouncing into *Stanzas in Meditation* from another text, from 'For-Get-Me-Not. To Janet' (1929), where A BIRD and A BALL have separate sections in a sequence dedicated to Basket, Gertrude Stein's poodle. It is a familiar ball, the one in 'For-Get-Me-Not', the ball Basket loves to chase and chew. It is also, arguably, the metaphysical ball, Sutherland's ball, the ball that is an object for the contemplative, the ball as Entity, as Being, but this is a meaning that simply glistens as possible. At the time she writes of it, in 1929, Gertrude Stein's poetic line is staggered, abruptly punctuated, and the device gives her phrasing a portentous compaction. 'Let it alone. Any. Ball that is. Of course. Lost. Is not. It is. Not found. Because. At any cost. It is not. Lost Because. It is always there. Where' (*SIM*, p. 233). What seems to be a conversational exchange could also be, easily enough, the morning lesson in a Buddhist temple. The ball is always there.

Bird and ball belong to an ongoing consideration in Gertrude Stein's contemporaneous work, are motifs in a theme, and frequently sounded. As we have seen, she left to the patriarchal poets, to T. S. Eliot and Ezra Pound, the burden of the past, the esoteric and the mythical. Her concerns are the present, the commonplace and superstition. Superstition of course exists in the realm of the commonplace: red sky at night, sailor's delight; red sky in the morning, sailor's warning. She thought a great deal about the status of such superstitions, particularly this one, cited in *The Geographical History of America*: 'The cuckoo when he says cuckoo and you have money in your pocket and it is the first cuckoo you have heard that year you will have money all of that year' (*GHA*, p. 109). What is inside superstition, in this part of the commonplace, speaking, promising, warning? Obsession, phobic behaviour, insistence on priority (the *first* cuckoo is the only cuckoo that counts), belief in grace, dread of disaster (a shoe on the table, clothes put on wrongly in the morning), the profusion and conflict of signs, our first understanding of Nature. In *Ida A Novel* (1940), Gertrude Stein writes a magnificent coda to this long meditation on signs, at once politicising superstition (a number of militant superstitions hotly arguing their priority are at war) and subsuming it, gathering all the signs and portents up into a lyrical re-creation of the Creation Myth. But that is another matter. Superstition, adage, maxim, motto – these commonplaces are like prisms in her discourse, taken up, turned this way and that.

The cuckoo calls in *Stanzas in Meditation*, just once, in part v, stanza xvi, and the superstition is here the seeming sign of Gertrude Stein's breakthrough, of her public acceptance.

> It means wealth
> Moreover if the cuckoo to make sure
> Comes near then there can be no doubt if doubt there be
> But not by this to see but worry left for me
> Makes no doubt more.
> Does it can be it does but I doubt it.
>
> (*SIM*, pp. 106–7)

Yet the cuckoo comes near. It wants to hear the deserving jingle of coins in Gertrude Stein's purse 'to make sure'. The logic of her qualified repetition mimics the cuckoo's song: no doubt, no doubt, if doubt, I doubt. We are to see through the narrow focus of this superstition a complicated and ingenious attitude toward the literary uses of myth, and, so seeing, recognise that this depth of vision justifies her possession of the commonplace. In her lexicon, the commonplace means that which is classical. So her immortal bird sings. It is her destiny calling: cuckoo, cuckoo. It has come to tell her, 'thou wast not born for death'. The cuckoo is the emblematic bird of her 'lyricity', her nightingale, this bird whose monotonous note, repeating, repeating, typically signifies lunacy. In *Ida* this is the situation: there is a writer who 'had written a lovely book but nobody took the lovely book', and then one day in a spring the cuckoo sang to her. It sees the writer sitting on the grass and it chooses her. '[A]nd she said, Oh, a cuckoo bird is singing on a cuckoo tree singing to me oh singing to me. And the cuckoo sang cuckoo cuckoo and she sang cuckoo cuckoo to it, and there they were singing cuckoo she to it and it to her' (*Ida*, pp. 124–5). Cuckoos and nightingales; there are also barnyard fowl in *Stanzas in Meditation*, and robins and owls and kites.

> I caught a bird which made a ball
> And they thought better of it.

Sutherland gives us a usable reading of the first line, but goes no further with his explication. Something bars his way. It is time to turn to the second line of *Stanzas in Meditation*. The second line makes all the difference, poses the difficulty, for here is Gertrude Stein's undefining pronoun 'they'. What is it a pronoun is supposed to do? It is to stand in the place of, refer to, persons and things. 'They' will do many things in the succeeding lines:

> But it is all of which they taught
> That they were in a hurry yet
> In a kind of a way they meant it best
> That they should change in and on account
> But they must not stare when they manage
> Whatever they are occasionally liable to do
> It is often easy to pursue them once in a while
> And in a way there is no repose
> They like it as well as they ever did
> But it is very often just by the time
> That they are able to separate
> In which case in effect they could
> Not only be very often present perfectly
> In each way which ever they chose.
>
> (*SIM*, p. 3)

Who are 'they'? Richard Bridgman explains,

The 'Stanzas' have three main characters – 'they', 'she', and 'I'. Their identities are ambiguous, save that 'I' is most certainly the author. 'She' is probably Alice Toklas, although 'she' may also be that portion of Gertrude Stein's personality that consented to engage in this commercial undertaking [*The Autobiography of Alice B. Toklas*]. Similarly 'they' might be Gertrude Stein as a multiple personality, or Gertrude Stein and Alice Toklas.

He suggests 'they' might also be Sir Robert and Lady Diana Abdy, friends who had encouraged Gertrude Stein to write the *Autobiography*, or simply the 'verbal conservatives' who constitute the 'normal reading public'. There is ample evidence for this latter designation. 'Let me listen to me and not to them' (*SIM*, p. 30), Gertrude Stein writes, an admonition often repeated in *Stanzas in*

Meditation. As Bridgman sees the second line, 'they' are the 'verbal conservatives' who have rejected her work.[5]

So it is possible, with Sutherland and Bridgman, to see the first sentence as Gertrude Stein's declaration of the problem. It poses the subject of her contemplation. I have created a poetry, she says, it has supple form and solid content, lyricity and entity, I have done this in my own style, in my own voice, and I am still largely rejected, still generally ignored. If we see this much – her sense of her achievement, her sense of her rejection – if we see how it is stated – the august brevity, the compressed irony – then we shall also see that a great anxious space lies between the two lines, the two parts of the sentence, between the achievement and the rejection. We shall see that, for most of the discourse, Gertrude Stein is in that space. The cuckoo has sung to her, the time is opportune, she is writing something in an altered style that 'they' might like, think better of. She is, after all, middle-aged, 'in a hurry', and this is the reason for the change, for the 'decision in its entirety' (p. 3).

Yet if we take 'they' to mean Gertrude and Alice, remembering that Gertrude Stein's emblematic bird is the cuckoo, that she is adept at mimicry, is in fact at present writing in Alice B. Toklas's voice, then this singular plural, 'they', this joined mind, significantly alters our paraphrase. It is not a suspicious audience that scorns the bird and demeans the ball, but rather a congenial 'we' that has always regarded Gertrude Stein's poetry as the work of genius. She seems to be telling us this in the final line of the first stanza: 'Kindly have it joined as they mind' (p. 3). Bridgman's register of identities offers us a maze of possibilities, and what, other than a swiftly moving context, is our guide? Switches in designation would seem to occur from phrase to phrase. In part v, stanza xxxv, Gertrude Stein says in passing,

> What is a landscape
> A landscape is what they that is I
> See and look.
>
> (p. 124)

Is it then possible to substitute 'I' for 'they' and have the entire discourse leap into a sudden clarity of known reference? Such an effort at decoding must soon falter.

In the lecture 'Poetry and Grammar', Gertrude Stein talks at length about her displacement of the noun. She ingeniously personifies the parts of speech, politicises their function, so that we truly see in grammar a recognisable structure of power – hierarchies, classes, divisions of labour. Nouns (adjectives attend them, verbs impart their action) are magisterial, full of substance, what discourse is all about. 'Pronouns', she declares, 'are not as bad as nouns because in the first place practically they cannot have adjectives go with them. That already makes them better than nouns' (*LIA*, p. 213). Nouns take up all the meaning and then just sit there. Pronouns are, in some sense, free, never lodged in a thing, stuck to it. They are an activity of pointing, of referring, constantly on the move. 'They represent some one', Gertrude Stein observes, 'but they are not its or his name. In not being his or its or her name they already have a greater possibility of being something than if they were as a noun is the name of anything' (pp. 213–14). The parts of speech come alive in this lecture, take on character and personality. Here are rigid nouns always intoning the same thing, slavish adjectives, servile commas, redundant question marks, ugly quotation marks that 'spoil the line' (p. 215). Here is the semi-colon, a split personality. Gertrude Stein prefers the march and bustle of the working words. She respects the smart punch of a period, properly used. 'Verbs and adverbs and articles and conjunctions and prepositions are lively', she asserts, 'because they all do something and as long as anything does something it keeps alive' (p. 214). Why are nouns so bad? What's in a name? Death.

It is the anonymous personality of the pronoun that suits Gertrude Stein. She slips into it and becomes disembodied, invisible. It enables her to break 'the rigid form of the noun the simple noun poetry' (p. 237), to create without naming, and this, she assures her audience, has been her struggle as a writer from *Tender Buttons* to the present. 'I struggled I struggled desperately with the recreation and the avoidance of nouns as nouns and yet poetry being poetry nouns are nouns' (*LIA*, p. 238). She names her precursor in this struggle, Walt Whitman. 'He wanted really wanted to express the thing and not call it by its name' (p. 241). In the pronoun, with the pronoun, Gertrude Stein imaginatively escapes that nominal order where she perforce exists, bracketed, as Woman, Jew, Lesbian, but what is it finally, this bright pronominal subversion, this displacement of the noun? It is a literary enterprise, a mythic adventure, she is here to justify and explain herself, to teach her poetry, and all this is happening in a fierce world where nouns are nouns. Gertrude Stein, after all, delivers this lecture in

1934, while on her American tour, the same year as that in which
Adolf Hitler assumes the Name of the Father in Berlin. He is about to
impose his naming, his signs, on the world: yellow stars, pink
triangles, the twisted cross. What's in a name? Persecution and
death. 'Poetry and Grammar' points us back to the 'they' who pose
Stanzas in Meditation, who plant its abundance of pansies. Of the
editorial presence in the text, the sceptical reader who is scanning
the *Autobiography* in manuscript, who is 'he' and sometimes 'they',
Gertrude Stein reports, 'He likes it that there is no chance to
misunderstand pansies' (*SIM*, p. 8). There are indeed no tell-tale
pansies in the *Autobiography*, but here, in this text, they gaily border
the path, they are the way itself. There is, too, this happy sequence
in part II, stanza xii, now hard to read without thinking of Gertrude
Stein's and Alice B. Toklas's fortunate survival in wartime France:

> One fortunate with roses is fortunate with two
> And she will be so nearly right
> That they think it is right
> That she is now well aware
> That they would have been named
> Had not their labels been taken away.
>   (*SIM*, p. 36)

Who are 'they' in *Stanzas in Meditation*? 'They' variously signify
the several characters Bridgman describes in *Gertrude Stein in Pieces*,
and, more often than not, 'they' can be fairly discerned: the editorial
presence, the beloved 'she', the 'I' who is struggling between elation
and anxiety for repose. Such deciphering, however, only takes us
into the space where Gertrude Stein's life gives meaning to the line.
Stanzas in Meditation is a 'parallel autobiography' that speaks with
the 'immediacy of a diary', Bridgman tells us, and what it is about,
what it thinks on, is *The Autobiography of Alice B. Toklas*, the stuff of
Gertrude Stein's life. Bridgman's reading is helpful, a start, but it
ends up obscurely repeating Leo Stein's assessment of his sister's
writing. 'The irony is', Bridgman concludes, 'that were it not for the
attractiveness of the compromised *Autobiography*, about which she
worried for such a long period, "Stanzas in Meditation" would
never have been read.'[6] This approach, which effectively ignores
the poetry of the text, does not discover the mockery of Gertrude
Stein's ironic bird or lead us to the lost ball, the one that is there even
though we do not see it. Something else is going on in the text, a

constant practice of differing, a continual disclosure of likeness, and it comes to us pure and simple in single straightforward lines: 'It is a difference in which I send alike' (*SIM*, p. 126). That complication, perfectly balanced in this line, aptly poses the very issue of her poetry. If we undertake to recognise her difference, to understand its terms, shall we then see her likeness, and like it? The question of her difference indeed becomes the issue of her likeness.

Am I beautiful? *Stanzas in Meditation* repeatedly asks this question: 'Can they like me oh can they like me' (p. 30). Bridgman's halting reply to this question, the question at large in Gertrude Stein's work, comes to this: yes, in parts, in pieces. He admires the autobiographical narratives, but understands that she is essentially to be found in the other compositions, in her averted discourse. These compositions, Bridgman writes, 'memorialize that daily half-hour when she gathered what came to mind and randomly, incidentally, shaped it into a prose that was part free association, part mechanical variation, part revelation only partially revealed'. He respects the 'telling phrase' that emerges from the 'tumbling, shifting cargo of her consciousness' but the rest of it – the prose that is poetry, the long analyses of 'not only' and 'yet', of 'notwithstanding' and 'of course' – is apparently jettisoned. In the conclusion to *Gertrude Stein in Pieces* we see just a trace of Skinner's theory of the two Gertrude Steins, the rational one who speaks to us, the irrational one who is given over to, and this is Bridgman's expression, a 'cacophony of feelings, associations, and memories'.[7] I see these two quizzical fellows, Leo Stein and B. F. Skinner, everywhere in the criticism of Gertrude Stein. They stand, with signs around their necks, BEWARE OF LEO STEIN, BEWARE OF B. F. SKINNER, in my interpretation. Each in his exemplary fashion divides the issue of Gertrude Stein's writing, separates its difference from its likeness. 'I do not believe in the importance of the part of Miss Stein's writing that does not make sense', Skinner wrote in 1932.[8] What holds the text together, its lyricity, its entity, its form, its content? What organises the landscape of Gertrude Stein's work? 'They' do, Gertrude Stein tells us, 'they that is I' (*SIM*, p. 124). And the prospect, how fair is it, how appealing?

This much is certain: the discourse in *Stanzas in Meditation* is intricately patterned, a texture of interspersed and echoing repetitions. There is not a screw loose anywhere in the text. Because the ensemble is so intensely realised, so fluent, the extraction of lines and passages for separate scrutiny is extremely difficult, and this particular line, 'It is a difference in which I send alike' (p. 126), shows the hazard. The sequence in which it occurs begins with a meditation on the finality of death:

> What I wish to say is this
> There is no beginning to an end
> But there is a beginning and an end
> To beginning.
> Why yes of course.
>
> (p. 125)

Gertrude Stein then moves across stanzas (v.xxxviii–xxxix) considering 'of course' in two references – her impending death, her forthcoming recognition as a writer. The prepositional phrase swings like a hinge. A north wind is blowing, this is remarked, and there is the fact of winning:

> When they begin I did begin and win
> Win which of course.
> It is easy to say easily.
> That this is the same in which I do not do not like
>   the name
> Which wind of course.
>
> (p. 126)

In the midst of this reverie there is a sudden intrusion of an ominous butterfly. 'A broad black butterfly is white with this' (ibid.). It is, amid all the prepositions and pronouns, an immense butterfly. The density of this diverse meaning presses the relation of death and art into the 'difference' and 'alike' before us, and yet, as we shall see, the line itself is delivered in a passage that has the integrity of a completed thought. It is a teaching.

> This which I say is this
> Which it is.
> It is a difference in which I send alike
> In which instance which.
> I wish to say this.
> That here now it is like
> Exactly like this.
> I know how exactly like this is.
>
> (Ibid.)

There are still eight lines in the stanza, each one a drop from this certainty, a falling into 'if' and 'interference'. The stanza ends,

> They do not count alike.
> One two three.
>   (Ibid.)

Before I turn to this likeness, to count the three likes, I want briefly to mark the looping path that has brought us to it. In the first part of this essay, I focused on the difference and demand that confront us at the entrance to *Stanzas in Meditation*. Privileged readers of Gertrude Stein's discourse, those who have some learning in the specifics of her self-created legend, the meaning of her life as she saw it in her work, who know as well the history of her influences, her understanding and application of the venture and the discoveries of modernist composition in the first quarter of this century, have, as it were, some access to the seeming mystery of her style, and the ability to place it in the history of modernism. They will see in this principled figuration, these likes, the transfigured writing Gertrude Stein first discovered in *Tender Buttons* when she looked at the carafe and saw this:

> A kind in glass and a cousin, a spectacle and nothing strange a single hurt color and an arrangement in a system to pointing. All this and not ordinary, not unordered in not resembling. The difference is spreading.   (*TB*, p. 9)

Yet the apprehension of this difference, the understanding of its order, can only give us pause, bring us to this verge. It is a difference that wilfully challenges the received orders of literary value, a difference the alienation of which is deeply motivated, and it displaces the centrality of names and nouns in poetry. Here we are with it, and where are we? What is it? What is it like? We have been chasing birds, looking for balls, not unlike Gertrude Stein's poodle, Basket, and her chihuahua, Byron, eager to snatch and possess the object. But the line takes us elsewhere. We are led inescapably to estimate the virtue of her pronominal figure, led past the relatively cheap secrets of her life and her method to the beautiful secret of this disclosure. We are, in this instance, near, next to, the beatitude of union, the coincidence of opposites. Here, then, is this liking line, a posting in my reading of the text. We shall move next to this one, which occurs earlier in *Stanzas in Meditation*: 'A poem is torn in two' (*SIM*, p. 63), and then to closure, the opening of her finish: 'I call carelessly that the door is open' (p. 151).

> This which I say is this
> Which it is.
> It is a difference in which I send alike
> In which instance which.
> I wish to say this.
> That here now it is like
> Exactly like this.
> I know how exactly like this is.
>   (p. 126)

A message wrapped in difference, and, when we unwrap it, look into the difference, there it is, an 'alike'. It is, of course, possible to see Alice in that alike. She is probably there, inscribed in the activity of doubling, involved in the sensation of liking. An Alice-alike is being sent into the world with a winsome portrait of Gertrude Stein's genius. In the second stanza following, Gertrude Stein will serialise 'my dear – remiss – kiss – bliss – this' (pp. 126–7). There is always that in Gertrude Stein's text, the continual inscription of the beloved, tribute and testimony. Yet in this passage we are swiftly into a scene: the master speaks, the pupil questions, the master speaks again. She will only say this, that it is a difference in which she sends alike. The pupil's question is urgent: give me an example, show me a case. Where in all this difference will I see a likeness? The master, disdaining to say *what* this alike is like, repeats her message, *that* there is an alike. The exchange itself, it might be said, is the first likeness, and, were the pupil an adept, he or she would quickly recognise the situation. The *what* of 'this' is never given, but is rather to be realised.

What is it like, this 'alike'? Let us restate the question, and move from the shade of the Bo tree. It is like 'this', that which is present in the 'here now' of the discursive instant, intensive, self-referential. The line invokes the literature of logical and linguistic paradoxes, the literature of *sententia*, evokes Parmenides, evokes Saussure, the Saussure who reminds us that difference is the functional condition of the sign. 'This' also points to a blankness, and we know exactly what blankness is in American literature – it is full of meaning. It is the 'mystic sign' that gives forth hints. 'A broad black butterfly', let us remember, 'is white with this' (p. 126). In that sense, this 'alike' is the very likeness of a sustained immanence. The text poses a discourse relatively independent and complete, containing within itself its own terms and processes. It poses the averted discourse of the other. It is for itself, about itself, reluctant to be apportioned, named, illustrated, brought into cases and examples, into rhetoric. In the hold of this discourse, Gertrude Stein will not, for the sake of being liked, for the sake of a public, derange what she chooses to see, to think, and yet there is a shiver of mortal dread in the purpose. There is always interference. An egotistical *I* edges into and upon the magisterial *I*:

> Now there is an interference in this.
> I interfere in I interfere in which this.
> (Ibid.)

It is a struggle constantly admitted, brought into the compass of thought. As we contemplate what cannot be represented, that august secret, the unknowable, the ungraspable 'this', we observe, easily enough, the radiant object that appears in all contemplative writing, and the problem of the ego, the *I* caught in the meshes of the perishable world that is always dying, the *I* distracted by the desire for approval.

A religious intonation is strong in the statement of this passage, but the writing is not scripture. The text is generally too full of itself, of its concerns, what it admits, what it engages, too full of its anxieties, resentment, suspicion, to set itself up as pronouncement, and yet there are epiphanies, there are magisterial instances. The first two lines of *Stanzas in Meditation*, as we have seen, pose the fundamental tension in the text: I did, they thought. It is repose, not rapture, that Gertrude Stein seeks in her line, and to find it she must confront Death, Ambition, Integrity, the principal dreads in the text. She is fifty-eight, the *Autobiography* is the big chance, an advertisement, a text in which she points to this one, her proper likeness. The sequence we have been examining begins, after all, with a consideration of death, marks the north wind, a black butterfly, her impending triumph, all of which comes to 'this'. So much depends on 'this', the beauty of her line, the virtue of her pronominal figure. Here, then, is an austere, relatively nounless verse that clearly shows us something. To get to the commonplace, Gertrude Stein's 'real achievement' in *Stanzas in Meditation*, the literal place of likeness, we must embrace tautology, puzzle through her equivocation, equably regard the immanent, indwelling, intrinsic meaning of this discourse, that which is on the other side of the pronoun, the density of its private, particular reference. All this, she insists in *Tender Buttons*, is 'not unordered in not resembling' (*TB*, p. 9). It exists in the commonplace of language, appears in the seam, in the trace, that marks the coincidence of opposites. The text's implicit appeal is to the integrity of its intelligence, to what is manifest in the articulation of the line. Gertrude Stein's poetry, in brief, is not to be torn in two.

Who are 'they' in *Stanzas in Meditation*? What is 'this'? These questions, open to the play of interpretation, are virtually solvable. What are 'they' doing with 'this'? That is the productive question. Gertrude Stein's pronoun, 'they that is I', breaks into the sovereign place of the noun and seizes its signifying power. 'They' represent representing. 'They' represent an enjoining and projective mind. What is a landscape? Gertrude Stein asks. It is what I see. 'I can look at a landscape without describing it' (*SIM*, p. 50), she asserts. What are we looking at in *Stanzas in Meditation*? Not the sights, but the seeing. The names, the sights, that we may see in the *Autobiography* which 'they', Gertrude and Alice, are collaboratively composing. In this text, 'they' will give us no repose until we enter into the play of its presentation, into the rationale of its defamiliarising effect. And, yet, here are the ligatures, the relays, the qualifiers, the connectives: not only, yet, however, not only not, notwithstanding, but, in which. What is poetry doing? Poetry, she tells us in 'Poetry and Grammar', 'is doing nothing but using losing refusing and pleasing and betraying and caressing nouns. That is what poetry does, that is what poetry has to do no matter what kind of poetry it is' (*LIA*, p. 231).

So instructed, we should not forget the ball in 'For-Get-Me-Not', the one that is there even though we do not see it. That ball is here in *Stanzas in Meditation*, in six mentions. Here, too, is a veritable aviary: chickens and ducks, kites and owls, the robin, the nightingale. Here are trees too close to walls, flowers, fruit, garden vegetables, the plod of homecoming cows, distant mountains, 'a cloud', the autumnal activity of gathering, of mowing, the detail of a rural landscape, the things of the pastoral. We are in the countryside where the quiet of the ode inheres, where the daily walk that is full of *notitia* takes place, where the actual landscape is always framed by the concept and history of landscape. Part I begins with a bustle of

comings and goings, with minding and blinding 'in and on account'
(*SIM*, p. 3), and then, near the end of stanza iv, this:

> We learned we met we saw we conquered most
> After all who makes any other small or tall
> They will wish that they must be seen to come.
> After at most she needs be kind to some
> Just to like that.
> Once every day there is a coming where cows are.
>
> (p. 7)

What follows in stanza v is the pansied path. It takes us into a
garden, into the countryside. The greenery of Gertrude Stein's
thought is spatially distributed, a matter of instances, of
recollection, and everywhere interrupted by other concerns, but it
constitutes all the same the age-old greenery of garden verse,
establishes a pastoral context. At times the garden in *Stanzas in
Meditation* looks like a Chinese garden, full of precepts. Then again it
looks like a Persian garden, with its allegorical cuckoo. Often it
resembles Emerson's Concord, that small comfortable space, the
convenient site of his transcendental botanising. In that space
Emerson took his stand: 'I ask not for the great, the remote, the
romantic; what is doing in Italy or Arabia; what is Greek art, or
Provençal minstrelsy; I embrace the common, I explore and sit at the
feet of the familiar, the low.'[9] In the ordinaries posed in *Stanzas in
Meditation*, we shall get Gertrude Stein's version of the meal in the
firkin, the milk in the pan, just so, and then meaningfully turned.
Some figures are briefly touched, planted as it were, to reappear
later in the text. Brought back to mind during her nocturnal
composition, moonlit, Gertrude Stein's garden is simply the
pregnant commonplace. It is good to know that

> Fifty percent of the roses should be cut
> The rest should bloom upon their branch.
>
> (p. 149)

To those who seek repose, gardens give such reassurance. The
garden talk in *Stanzas in Meditation* gives us crevice and cranny, a
gathering of flowers, the certainties of the almanac, respite, in a
discourse otherwise rigorously self-centred and cerebral:

It might be very well that lilies of the valley have a fragrance
And that they ripen soon
And that they are gathered in great abundance
And that they will not be refreshing but only
Very lovely with green leaves.

(p. 15)

So the lilies of the valley are cut and placed, the little question of
their fragrance answered by their look, and Gertrude Stein comes
back to the 'question of their arrangement', not the floral
arrangement but the human arrangement, in her text. With these
interposed, repeated commonplaces – what she sees, this and this
only, the natural fact in its setting, the cut flowers – she summons a
repose, she marks the therapeutic function of garden verse. Now
and then, here and there, the garden appears, Gertrude Stein looks
up from her manuscript, she sees her garden, there as it is, and the
great garden, the one that gave birth to patriarchal poetry, that
structures our experience of the countryside, our concept of
landscape. It is the garden of names and knowledge.

Known makes it plain I shall
Think birds and ways and frogs and grass and now
That they call meadows more
I have seen what they knew.

(p. 17)

With these green instances, then, Gertrude Stein establishes a
system of nounal themes in *Stanzas in Meditation*. A floral theme is
stitched into the text, and the pansy is one of its motifs. As we shall
see, the tree and the wall are in the weave of a certain theme. So, too,
is the sound of birds singing, and the interconnections, when
perceived, are invariably rich with the sweetness of autumnal
melancholy. For with the tree and the wall, and the sound of birds
singing, there is the wind and wind, the wind as in north wind and
wind as in winding sheet, emblems of bliss, *memento mori*, and there
are others, the mower, the faun, the fireside, just as closely
articulated. Across the field of pastoral reference, we see the zigzag
of a butterfly. Such is the space of the noun in *Stanzas in Meditation*.
Here are things from the garden, notations from a country walk, and
old mossy tropes. Gertrude Stein's fleeting pronominal verse is
constantly in touch with the old noun poetry, its ruins, its remnants,

using it, abusing it, caressing it. Garden observance clearly holds a
depth of meaning.

> Hours of a tree growing. He said it injured walls.
> We said the owner and the one then here preferred it.
> Imagine what to say he changed his mind.
> He said it would not matter until ten years or five.
>
> (p. 12)

What is the significance of this seemingly prosaic anecdote? It
occurs in part ɪ, stanza viii, a stanza that is mostly a love lyric. 'Out
from the whole wide world I chose thee' (ibid.), she sings. The
politics of the situation is immediately rendered. This 'he' is the
visiting editorial person, the agent of authority, the reader of their
dissimulated 'account', the person before whom 'they', Gertrude
and Alice, feel great anxiety. 'He' causes the 'what if' that twists and
turns throughout *Stanzas in Meditation*. In this exchange, 'he'
authoritatively asserts, renders an opinion, 'they' disagree, and he
abruptly changes his mind, complies, seems eager to please. This is
what is at the surface in the exchange, the surprise of his collapse,
but the distinction of hours and years, the relation of tree to wall,
these elements, these aspects, are rooted in larger – one might say,
ancient – considerations. There are at least two conceptions of the
garden implicit in the brevity of the anecdote, the tended and the
left-alone, each of which differently poses the value of the tree, the
value of the wall. A prior dispute, a familiar opposition, is instant in
the first line. We know what Robert Frost thought of this problem,
and how far back in time this wall extends. It marks properties,
imposes distinctions, stands between the Me and the Not Me. Here,
too, amid this gnarly issue, it is possible to see a figuring of Gertrude
Stein's literary reputation, slowly reaching up, thrusting aside,
displacing the inert of indifference, though this identification is not
immediately stressed. As she stops here to reflect, to consider the
event, she plants a figure.

In part v, hundreds of lines later, hours of reading later, Gertrude
Stein wonders how 'they changed apart alike', wonders, in stanza ii,
if

> They could should they under any circumstance
> Understand differ or differs.
>
> (p. 92)

It is a reflection that surely has to do with the game of identity in the *Autobiography*. 'I have often thought', Gertrude Stein writes, thinking of Alice, 'that she meant what I said' (*SIM*, p. 92). The stanza reiterates the play of difference and alike, and it ends abruptly with this striking repetition:

> When they thought how often about a wall.
> When they thought how often about a wall.
>
>   (p. 93)

How is it possible to find repose before this wall, which here looms large? We are in part v, near the end of the discourse, approaching the opened door, and there is a forthcoming resolution, one that humorously displaces the character of the wall by putting it next to love and butter:

> They will gather love is mine.
> Butter is mine.
> Walls are not only mine
> Will they or if they had rather
> Been when they were to find mine.
> They will not either leave it all to chance
> Or yet no one knows movements which having fallen.
>
>   (p. 148)

A constant practice of differing, a continual disclosure of likeness. What emerges in *Stanzas in Meditation* is a network of inter-dependences: the new pronominal verse, the old noun poetry, a collocation of themes, forms, languages, held together by an activity of seeing, of thinking, that breaks down walls, conformities. Should we count the lines in each stanza, we should see their arbitrary measure, a long lingering here, a rapid overstepping there. 'It is a difference in which I send alike', so Gertrude Stein writes. Beside the major nounal themes that stretch like intermittent paths through *Stanzas in Meditation*, there are other, shadowy nounal tracks. Gertrude Stein invokes the shades of a number of great men, principally the great conqueror – 'I came, I saw, I conquered' – and the great emancipator:

> They find it one in union.
> In union there is strength.
>
>   (p. 30)

Here, then, the riddle, and beyond it the actual door, the literal cry: *it is open*, Gertrude Stein's transpierced present particular.

> Now I ask any one to hear me.
> This is what I say.
> A poem is torn in two
> And a broom grows as well
> And which came first
> Grows as well or a broom
> Of course any one can know which of two
> This makes it no accident to be taught
> And either taught and either fight or fought
> Or either not either which either
> Can they be either one not one only alone.
> (p. 63)

What this says, I suppose, is this: *I am not in pieces*. It is, of course, the oldest riddle in the world, and Gertrude Stein reconstructs it with a branch from garden verse. Broom is a bush, a thorny bush, a blackberry bush. Which came first, the chicken or the egg, the noun or the verb, the man or the woman? She addresses 'any one', and everyone knows which came first, who has priority and therefore privilege. So it is taught, 'which came first', and here the fight begins, history begins. The riddle is unanswerable, circular. It leads the question around and back to the coiled serpent whose tail is in its mouth, the original circle, the great unbreakable ball of being. Does duality resolve itself into unity? Can masculine and feminine be enjoined? What does she tell Picabia later in the text?

> Oh yes I said forget men and women.
> Oh yes I said I said to forget men and women.
> And I was not melancholy when I thought of everything.
> (p. 45)

Repose. We are at the ending Gertrude Stein writes as a beginning.

> Why am I if I am uncertain reasons may inclose.
> Remain remain propose repose chose.
> I call carelessly that the door is open
> Which if they can refuse to open
> No one can rush to close.

Let them be mine therefor.
Everybody knows that I chose.
Therefor if therefor before I close.
I will therefor offer therefor I offer this.
Which if I refuse to miss can be miss is mine.
I will be well welcome when I come.
Because I am coming.
Certainly I come having come.

These stanzas are done.

(p. 151)

She is coming, I am going. Goodbye, Gertrude Stein. I shall conclude with a modest epiphany. When I was a student, no one taught Gertrude Stein. She was encountered in Hemingway, cited as an influence. She had no standing as a poet. We all led comfortable lives inside patriarchal poetry. The chairs were good, the rugs plush, the bookcases lined with Uniform Editions. The study of literature was the study of sure things. We were told to read and reread *The Great Chain of Being*, and didn't at first recognise the feel of its manacle. Yvor Winters, who had the face and the voice of a hanging judge, taught me poetry at Stanford, taught me 'which came first', who was in the Great Chain of Poets and who was without. Those who know Winters' criticism know that he hanged many excellent poets, and left them hanging there, exposed to the elements, to the derision of the claque that was always in his courses. We were shown their disgraceful forms – Wordsworth, Whitman, the early, middle and somewhat late Victorians. Some poets, I must say, deserved Winters' judgement – Edgar Allan Poe, Algernon Swinburne – and I didn't mind seeing them swing in the breeze. I do not believe that Winters ever mentioned Gertrude Stein, at least not in my hearing. She was, I suppose, too absent in her presence. One afternoon, at a friend's house in Berkeley, I happened to catch the final act of a play on television. The play was set in post-war France, the dialogue was exquisitely patterned, the speech at once easily fluent and deftly stylised. It was the work of a master. I had never heard anything quite like it. Who wrote this, I wondered. It sounded like a serene Harold Pinter, without any sacrifice of toughness. Then the credits came on: *Yes Is For A Very Young Man, by Gertrude Stein*. Having heard the call, I went to see, and that was that. At first I saw difference, then I saw likeness, and this was the lesson. Goodbye, Gertrude Stein.

Notes

1. B. F. Skinner, 'Has Gertrude Stein a Secret?', *Atlantic Monthly*, Jan 1934, p. 56.
2. Quoted in B. F. Skinner, *The Shaping of a Behaviorist* (New York: Alfred A. Knopf, 1979) pp. 135–6.
3. Ernest Hemingway, *A Moveable Feast* (New York: Charles Scribner's Sons, 1965) p. 20.
4. B. L. Reid, *Art by Subtraction: A Dissenting Opinion of Gertrude Stein* (Norman: University of Oklahoma Press, 1958) p. vii; Richard Bridgman, *Gertrude Stein in Pieces* (New York: Oxford University Press, 1970).
5. Bridgman, *Gertrude Stein in Pieces*, p. 214.
6. Ibid., p. 217.
7. Ibid., p. 347.
8. Skinner, 'Has Gertrude Stein a Secret?', *Atlantic Monthly*, Jan 1934, p. 57.
9. Ralph Waldo Emerson, 'The American Scholar', *Complete Writings of Ralph Waldo Emerson* (New York: William H. Wise, 1929) i, 35.

10

Masterpieces, Manifestoes and the Business of Living: Gertrude Stein Lecturing

ALAN R. KNIGHT

Gertrude Stein, for whatever psychologically, socially or culturally induced reasons, needed to be famous, to make a conquest of power and tradition, to experience what she referred to as *la gloire*. However, when large-scale 'best-seller' fame finally came to her with the 1933 publication of *The Autobiography of Alice B. Toklas*, she quickly realised that it was not the sort of *gloire* she was looking for. She was all too conscious of the fact that she was the most widely known unread author in America. For a writer who felt that she had written one of the three great works of the twentieth century (*The Making of Americans* joined *Ulysses* and *A la recherche du temps perdu* – *LIA*, p. 184) this was unacceptable. She wanted to be read and to be lionised for her creative genius; she did not want to be lionised only for the force and appeal of her personality. After all, she had been well known for years as the 'Sybil of Montparnasse' – as the friend, patron, and promoter of many of the early twentieth century's most famous artists and writers, and, while this role occupied her, she did not consider it either fulfilling ('governing is occupying but not interesting' – law 65) or her life's work. She was a writer. And it was as a writer that she would have herself lionised.

Henry McBride, a New York journalist and friend of Gertrude Stein's, had warned her against striving for too large a measure

---

Law 1 [S]omething . . . printed . . . [is] no longer the property of the one who wrote it . . . .[1]
Law 2 [T]alking essentially has nothing to do with creation.
Law 3 [T]he essence of being a genius is to be able to talk and listen to listen while talking and talk while listening . . . .
Law 4 [O]ne has no identity . . . when one is in the act of doing anything.
Law 5 Identity is recognition.

150

of fame instead of developing a small audience capable of understanding and appreciating her. He argued that in the process of achieving a wider fame she would experience growing pressures to conform to traditional conventions. He warned that this would stifle her creative impulse. In 1933 Stein discovered that he had in large part been right. After having written almost every day for thirty years she was unable to write anything. As she later wrote, 'Nothing needed any word and there was no word inside me that could not be spoken and so there was no word inside me' (*EA*, p. 64).

This block, along with her lack of satisfaction in the fame she had achieved, started her thinking about the relationship between the writer and her audience, and among the writer, her audience and the 'business of living' (*WAM*, p. 88). She came to realise, as she later wrote in 'What are Master-pieces and Why Are There So Few of Them', that 'After the audience begins, naturally they create something that is they create you' (law 67). Stein did not want to be shaped by her audience; she did not want her writing to be reduced to a 'business'; she wanted to do the shaping herself. Her meditations on these relationships resulted not only in theoretical discourse but also in pragmatic action. She had two problems of a practical nature to resolve. She had to break through her block and begin writing again and she had to convince her large new audience that they should actually read her and not just 'about' her.

Stein's realisation that the major reason for her block was this pressure to conform to her audience's desires was important. She now had a concrete obstacle to overcome. At first this audience pressure seemed to exclude from her writing process any external stimuli. Naturally, she found this a very barren point of view. Only when she began to reformulate for herself a difference between external stimulus as demanding subject (or audience) and external stimulus as undemanding object (or raw material) was she once again able to place herself in a position where she did not feel that she was undermining her integrity during the act of writing. This

---

Law 6 I do not care who it is that has or does influence me as long as it is not myself.
Law 7 [T]here is always the same subject . . . each one in his or her way knows all of them . . . it is not this knowledge that makes master-pieces.
Law 8 At any moment when you are you you are you without the memory of yourself.
Law 9 [I]n lecturing . . . one ceased to hear what one said one heard what the audience hears one say.

distinction eventually evolved into the theory of human mind and human nature which she wrote about at length in 1935 in *The Geographical History of America*. It was also at the heart of her 1936 lecture 'What are Master-Pieces and Why Are There so Few of Them'. In this theory, a masterpiece is a text which deals with the world but bears no necessary relationship to it; it aims for a textual 'purity' in which text is an 'entity' or unnecessary product (in terms of its relation to the business of living) of the human mind; all other writing is concerned first and foremost with its relation to the world, is the product of human nature and is 'identity'.

Stein spent the summer of 1933, the summer immediately following the success of *The Autobiography of Alice B. Toklas*, at her summer home in Bilignin as usual. Two unexplained deaths in the neighbourhood provided the undemanding-external stimulus which was extraordinary enough to be easily separated from the demands of her audience and which was jarring enough to start her writing again. First, Madame Pernollet of the well-known Hotel Pernollet in the nearby town of Belley died after she had apparently fallen out of a second-storey window of the hotel. Second, the English friend of Madame Caesar, who lived on a chicken farm close to Gertrude and Alice, was found dead in a ravine with two bullets through her head. Neither of these deaths was ever confirmed to be murder, though both of them raised suspicions. In any event, in puzzling out these two events Gertrude Stein had begun to write again. The result was *Blood on the Dining Room Floor*, Stein's version of the detective story.[2] Her first pragmatic action then was her decision to use an external stimulus as a starting point for writing 'entity'. As she later wrote, 'a picture [or a text] exists for and in itself and the painter [or writer] has to use objects landscapes and people as a way the only way that he is able to get the picture [or text] to exist' (law 15).

Her second pragmatic action was the decision to enter the 'business of living' – that is, to write texts aimed at making readers out of her new audience, texts which did not pretend to be masterpieces. She decided to give a series of lectures that would, she

---

Law 10 [O]ratory is practically never a master-piece . . . .
Law 11 [H]istory deals with . . . orators who hear . . . what their audience hears them say.
Law 12 [T]he letter writes what the other person is to hear and so entity does not exist there are two present instead of one and so once again creation breaks down.

hoped, not only convince people that she was readable but also that she was worth reading. In these lectures she set out to define the ground rules for reading that her public complained they lacked. It is these lectures that I call her manifestoes.

Recent work done by semioticians on the generic configuration of the avant-garde literary manifesto provides a useful context within which to consider Stein's lecture/manifestoes.[3] The manifesto is a text uniquely suited to a period of Foucauldian rupture: that is, to a period of shift from one cultural, historical or social strata to another – a rupture and shift which require both a new formulation and a new understanding of rules, codes and conventions.[4] The peculiar nature of the avant-garde modernist rupture was that it did not separate itself from traditional systems in order to establish the authority of a better system; rather, it separated itself from traditional systems in order to demonstrate the inadequacy of any system. The avant-garde literary manifesto does not attempt to constitute or reconstitute coherence and meaning; instead it is a text which, to use Foucault's term, 'compensates' for this loss of coherence and meaning.[5] This compensation takes the form of self-consciously providing a collection of rules, codes and conventions in a way that makes evident their provisional status.

In Stein's terms, the manifesto is a text of identity because it provides a business-like connection between the necessities of 'human nature' and the free-play of 'human mind'. It is useful then to consider here the conventions of that text which concerns itself with 'convention'. For the purposes of clarity I shall divide my discussion of the generic conventions of the manifesto into three *ad hoc* categories. I shall place the manifesto in relation to time and place, power and tradition, and discourse.

Law 13 [A]ction is necessary and anything that is necessary has to do with human nature and not with the human mind.
Law 14 [A] master-piece has essentially not to be necessary.
Law 15 [A] picture exists for and in itself and the painter has to use objects landscapes and people . . . to get the picture to exist.
Law 16 [T]he minute one is conscious deeply conscious of these things as a subject the interest in them does not exist.

TIME AND PLACE

The first thing to assert is that the manifesto is an *act*. This act is dependent upon the contingencies of time and place, which is to say that time and place, during this textual act, are translated into a unique synchronic space of consciousness. Stein produced her lecture/manifestoes expressly for the audiences to whom they were delivered. Without the perceived need for these lectures and without the many requests by friends and the various interested parties (such as publishers and agents) that they be given, it is unlikely that they would ever have been written. And without some prior success and notoriety it is unlikely that the requests would have been made. (The requests here stand for the forces demanding such an act: the social, cultural or political mix of forces which the manifesto writer sees as demanding the announcement of a break with the past and the declaration of new laws. These forces may be perceived in many ways and not just as requests.)

Another important convention of the manifesto is that it does not precede a new form but rather follows it. Stein wrote these lectures not in the process of creating her aesthetic but rather in the hope of convincing others that her aesthetic was worthy of note and of emulation. These lecture/manifestoes are not the sort of textual meditations in which she clarified for herself what she was attempting to do. They were written for her audience, to be performed before them. Others of her theoretical writings, such as *How To Write* and *Four in America*, are more exploratory and meditative – written more for herself and not expressly for her audience – and are therefore not to be considered manifestoes. (A manifesto is not simply any text which deals with theoretical issues. It is a genre of text which deals with theoretical issues in a certain way and for certain reasons.)

Brought together at one time and in one place the manifesto is necessarily a performance. It is not an immutable 'ideal' or 'essence' which exists independently of its 'living' in the world. The audience

---

Law 17 [W]hat is happening [in the world] is not really interesting . . . it excites them
    a little but it does not really thrill them.
Law 18 [T]alking is really human nature . . . .
Law 19 [H]uman nature has nothing to do with master-pieces.
Law 20 In real life people are interested in the crime more than they are in
    detection . . . .
Law 21 [I]n the story it is the detection that holds the interest.

is as necessary as the performer and the text. The participants in the performance of a manifesto can be on either the performing side of the text or the audience side of the text. If they are on the performing side they desire to shock and create scandal by committing an act of rupture which undermines the traditional conventions of meaning and/or power. If they are on the audience side then they are necessarily unaware of what the manifesto will declare to them; they are allied with the extant powers and traditions (or at least unallied with the 'movement' performing the manifesto); and they will be shocked and scandalised by these declarations which will attempt to undermine the codes and conventions they live by. However, since the manifesto is a function of time and place, this shock value quickly disappears. Time and place are no longer 'now' but 'then'. The new 'now' contains the 'now' of 'then' and therefore cannot be scandalised by it. The manifesto quickly becomes a museum piece to be dissected and analysed – just as I am doing here. It is no longer a placed and primary textual act but a displaced one made secondary in a meta-literary act. Stein herself contributed to this quick 'fossilisation' by publishing all of her lectures. (This does not mean that a manifesto cannot be reactivated – although this would require a certain naïveté in the audience: to reactivate a manifesto a person would have to have had no exposure to whole areas of culture.)

POWER AND TRADITION

The avant-garde manifesto is not written from a position of power. One way in which it attempts to make its position appear more than spurious is to appear under the banner of a movement. A movement can claim more power than an individual simply because of numbers. If one man is a nut he can easily be dismissed as a nut because he has no support and is isolated; but once his particular brand of 'nuttiness' is shared by others it becomes a norm or convention which must be taken seriously (that is, recognised as a

---

Law 22 [T]he master-piece . . . has to do with the human mind and . . . entity . . . .
Law 23 [T]he master-piece . . . has to do with . . . a thing in itself and not in relation.
Law 24 The moment it is in relation it is common knowledge and anybody can feel and know it . . . .
Law 25 [E]very one . . . sooner or later does feel the reality of a master-piece.
Law 26 [T]here is in the thing that we call the human mind something that makes it hold itself just the same.

power to be reckoned with). But how then can Stein, a single person, be called a movement? It seems to me that, if we look at the situation surrounding the composition of these lecture/ manifestoes, it is not too ingenious to suggest that all of the people surrounding Stein, all of the people whom she had collected over the years who were actively promoting her, writing letters to publishers on her behalf, sending out her manuscripts for her, in essence working as *de facto* (albeit unpaid) agents, constitute a movement of like-minded persons working toward the same ends.

The characteristics of the avant-garde modernist movements corroborate this. Those involved in a movement consider themselves set apart (if not among the elect) because of the special knowledge they possess. Stein's promoters certainly felt that they had acquired a special knowledge which allowed them to understand Stein. In addition, a movement may claim power and legitimacy but is never institutionalised. A movement is a collective and not an institution. It is not an institution because it must remain marginal and precarious in its relation to power and tradition. Which is not to say that a movement may not become an institution. However, if it does it can no longer create manifestoes (it will create constitutions or charters of rights instead) and the manifestoes it created before its institutionalisation become historical, venerated museum pieces. Stein's relation to power and tradition at the time of her lectures was definitely precarious. Her texts were the 'other' attempting to scandalise 'sameness'.

The writers of manifestoes, then, must always remain on the outside. Their power and authority is self-professed and not granted them by the general populace, by those who demand and support institutions. To imbue themselves with even a limited measure of authority (a measure large enough to make scandal felt) manifesto writers must pass themselves off as prophets who claim that the future has arrived – in the sense that they are inspired teachers and law-givers. They feel no need to explain the truth of what they say, which they take as self-evident; they demand only that what they say be accepted. For vatic pronouncements – that is,

---

Law 27 [Master-pieces] exist because they came to be as something that is an end in itself and in that respect it is opposed to the business of living which is relation and necessity.

Law 28 [But a master-piece may talk about the business of living.]

Law 29 [A master-piece] does not begin and end if it did it would be of necessity and in relation . . . .

the pronouncements of a prophet – are by definition infallible, since received through divine inspiration.

In the modernist sense this infallibility is a human dimension, limited by our conceptual or textual horizons, and therefore provisional. This paradox is necessary and unavoidable and gives to divine inspiration a new context and a special meaning. For, although some avant-garde writers and artists, such as the dadaist Hugo Ball and the Russian futurist Alexei Kruchenykh, did become conventional religious mystics, in general the 'divine' should not be given an overly religious connotation. It does not refer to a known source or named God but simply the 'unknown' inherent in any 'limited' conceptual horizon. It invokes the 'mystery' behind religion and not the doctrinal explanation of that 'mystery'. Thus inspiration is that which results from contact with this alogical, chaotic 'mystery'. This is, of course, religious in the larger sense of the word but not religious in the sense that it pertains to any specific religion – that is, unless we accept Matthew Arnold's prophecy and see literature as the religion of our age, in which case any inspiration from an undefined source which contributes to literature (that is, which expands the textual horizon) is religious since literature is our religion. The manifesto does not provide a new sense of coherence. It merely provides (through 'divinely inspired' contact with 'mystery') a compensatory textual identity (prophetic laws which can be formed into many patterns of relations and not just one logical episteme[6]) for the 'coherence' it has scuttled.

Stein's lecture/manifestoes are studded with vatic pronouncements, with unsupported declarations which are to be taken as law. A typical pattern of relation begins in the second paragraph of 'What are Master-pieces and Why Are There So Few of Them': 'I was going to talk to you but actually it is impossible to talk about master-pieces and what they are because talking essentially has nothing to do with creation' (law 2). We are never given any logical argument in support of this conclusion. It is presented as a self-evident law. If we read further on in this lecture/manifesto we learn that 'talking is really human nature' (law 18) and that 'human

---

Law 30 [Y]et . . . like the subject of human nature master-pieces have to use beginning and ending to become existing.

Law 31 [A]nybody who is trying to do anything today is desperately not having a beginning and an ending but nevertheless in some way one does have to stop.

Law 32 [S]econdary writing . . . is remembering . . . .

nature has nothing to do with master-pieces' (law 19). This does not
'explain' why talking is not creation. It is simply another law in a
chain of interconnected laws.[7] Further on we learn that human
nature is identity (law 40), that identity is recognition or
remembering (laws 5, 35), that recognition is placing things in
relation (laws 8, 32) and that 'the moment it is in relation . . . it is not
a master-piece' (law 24). This new 'explanation' is once again just
another series of laws. Not only that but it completes a tautology.
We are told that talking is not a masterpiece because talking is in
relation and that a masterpiece cannot be talked because a
masterpiece is not in relation. The tautology is typical of the
manifesto, where what 'is' is so because it 'is' and not because it
follows logically from the central premise of a coherent system. Each
law in a pattern is related contiguously and not hierarchically.[8] All
that can be said is that a is a and b is b.

Thus a manifesto is not a mystical document full of arcane
knowledge which attempts to solve the mysteries of the unknown –
although this might often seem to be the case; and it is not a
document in the dialogue between those who would discover first
principles. It is a document directed to the common man; it is a
document which states that 'what is, is'; it is a pragmatic attempt to
challenge power and tradition which employs the conventions of
prophecy as its strategy. The manifesto, in its struggle for power,
allows 'desire' to dominate 'knowledge'. The exposition of the
logical foundations of the knowledge which it professes is sacrificed
to rhetorical strategies which respond more immediately to the
desires (to accommodate 'mystery' 'chaos' and 'silence') of the
avant-garde modernist manifesto writer.

However, this does not necessarily mean that all of the ideas
contained in a manifesto are entirely new. This is far from the case.
The ideas themselves may simply be a reshuffling of old ideas. What
counts is that the impetus to change constitutes an act of rupture
given the specific circumstances of a specific time and place. It is an
act of prophetic self-legitimisation and is therefore a privileging

---

Law 33 If you do not remember while you are writing, it may seem confused to
others but actually it is clear . . . .

Law 34 [A] master-piece . . . may be unwelcome but it is never dull.

Law 35 [M]ostly people live in identity and memory . . . when they think.

Law 36 [M]emory is necessary to make them exist and so they cannot create
master-pieces.

machine which wishes to establish not so much order as a post-rupture identity.

DISCOURSE

J. L. Austin's distinction between a constative utterance and a performative utterance provides a useful starting point for a discussion of the manifesto's discourse.[9] A constative utterance claims to be a statement of fact which can be either true or false. Thus, 'The sky is blue' is understood to be a true statement of the colour of the sky. A performative utterance is neither true nor false but rather an actual performance. Thus an utterance such as 'I promise to pay' is an *act* of promising. Austin goes on to show, however, that the constative utterance is not a separate and equal classification of utterance but actually an utterance subordinate to the performative utterance. For, although the sentence 'The sky is blue' appears to be a true or false statement of fact, what is actually understood is the utterance, 'I *promise you* that the sky is blue'. The utterance is no longer clearly true or false but a performed promise. (This sense of discourse as performance is different from, although parallel in implication to, the sense of physical performance which I introduced into the discussion of the manifesto in relation to power and tradition. Whenever performance is valorised, the ideal is invalidated.)

Therefore to say, as semioticians say, that the customary mode of the manifesto is declarative, is to say that the manifesto stresses the performative (since a declaration is a promise of factuality) rather than the supposedly constative nature of utterance. A manifesto is a promise. It is a promise to fulfil certain desires. And as a promise it is a mode of discourse which courts scandal, since any language-constituted promise is a promise to fulfil the desire for meaning. This is a promise that can never be fully kept, and an unkept promise is scandalous. Each new promise reveals both the scandal

---

Law 37 [T]he boy and the man have nothing to do with each other, except in respect to memory and identity.

Law 38 It is not extremely difficult not to have identity but it is extremely difficult the knowing not having identity.

Law 39 [Master-pieces] are knowing that there is no identity and producing while identity is not.

of the old promises – the old laws and conventions – and, self-reflexively, the scandalous nature of its own promising.[10]

Not only do manifestoes use many overtly performative verbs, such as 'promise', 'assure' and 'declare', but they also make insistent use of the copula, as is the case with Stein, whose laws use them almost exclusively. As Derrida has shown us, the copula, in which the subject of an utterance is declared 'equal' to its object, is a promise of meaning that is both at the centre of the metaphysics of presence and the weakest link in that metaphysics. It is the weakest link because the most easily undermined. To say that *a* is *b* can easily be turned into *a* is not *b* by qualifying *a* in a way that disqualifies its equality with *b*. The copula then is the most spartan of the linguistically performed promises.

Thus the manifesto's relation to discourse reflects its relation to power and tradition. It is a discourse of challenge and rupture, of 'otherness' (new promises) attacking 'sameness' (old promises). The manifesto not only challenges and ruptures the scandalous ideational or ideological framework of power and tradition but also the capacity of discourse to be factual (the self-reflexive recognition of the scandalous nature of its own discourse). By being so forthrightly performative the manifesto is rupturing – that is, decentring or deconstructing – the claim that what linguistic signs signify is or ever can be fully understood. It is not enough simply to disrupt conventional grammar, although this is useful; the manifesto also performs in a way that brings the understandability of discourse into question.

This performance is essentially naïve, as are the pronouncements of any prophet. It is not the sophisticated argument of a metaphysician or theologian, where sophisticated implies the attempt to forestall all logical objection. It is not a completed discourse, but a discourse placed in an open field which may thus stand as preface to a fuller text and a larger textual field.

Law 40 Everything that makes life go on makes identity and everything that makes identity is of necessity a necessity.

Law 41 The pleasures that are soothing . . . [and] exciting all have to do with identity . . . .

Law 42 [T]here is more identity that one knows about than anything else one knows about . . . .

Law 43 [T]hinking is something that does so nearly need to be memory and if it is then of course it has nothing to do with a master-piece.

Gertrude Stein was not the only avant-garde writer pragmatically to use the manifesto for the 'business of living' with language, literature, society and culture. The phenomenon was widely spread. Numerous manifestoes were written by the Italian futurists, the Russian futurists, the various dada groups, the surrealists, the vorticists, the imagists – the list goes on and on. It might even be said that one of the things which separates the avant-garde modernist from the more conservative modernist – which is to say, those modernists who recognised the problems inherent in metaphysics but who tried to compensate for this loss of externally reinforced meaning by creating internally coherent and autonomous universes – was the need to write prophetic manifestoes. For the avant-garde modernist the need to recognise rupture is more important (is more desired) than the need to recognise continuity – the point being that continuity can be readily formulated but that the act of formulating continuity is a self-deception, whereas a declaration of rupture is a self-conscious act of self-creation. The act of formulating continuity is an act within metaphysics; the act of declaring rupture is a *script*ural act de*pict*ing the absence at the heart of metaphysical presence. The more conservative modernists did, of course, write much in the attempt to justify their various aesthetic postures. But their writings cannot be considered manifestoes since in the end they seek to establish continuity. They follow very much in the textual tradition of the artist/critic which has been with us at least since Horace's *Ars Poetica*. They are writings which attempt to enter an ongoing aesthetic–metaphysical debate. They are not 'otherness' attacking 'sameness'; they are doubters refining 'sameness'.

The manifesto then, as a textual act which identifies the avant-garde modernist, is a text in which the issues of 'post-rupture' literature are made apparent. Stein's lecture/manifestoes can be read as declarations concerning various of these issues.[11] 'What are Master-Pieces and Why Are There so Few of Them' concerns itself with a key issue (and the one at issue here): the status of textual and self-creation. In other words, this lecture/manifesto deals not only

---

Law 44 [M]ostly . . . [a master-piece] is about identity . . . and in being so it must not have any.

Law 45 Moments are not important because of course master-pieces have no more time than they have identity although time like identity is what they concern themselves about . . . .

Law 46 Once when one has said what one says it is not true or too true.

Law 47 [W]hat . . . women say [is] truer than what men say.

with the status of the masterpiece but, by implication, with the status of all other texts as well, including the manifesto.

Stein begins this lecture by telling us how she set out to put it together and in what way she considers it a text. She begins, in effect, by describing the status of her lecture/manifesto, which she then proceeds to set off against what she considers to be the status of the masterpiece. As it turns out, in her view there are very few masterpieces or texts of 'entity', but the manifesto as a text of 'identity' is a member of an enormous group of texts.

This declaration of Stein's on textual creation does not concern itself with generically delimiting the lecture/manifesto. I have borrowed this pattern of conventions from semiotics and imposed it upon Stein because of the manner in which it allows us access to Stein's texts – and indeed the texts of other avant-garde writers, who can now usefully be viewed in the same textual field. She does not concern herself with anything so easily (and self-deceivingly) defined as a genre. Her lecture concerns itself with the ontological (or, in Derrida's terminology, ontotheological) status of *script*(ur)ing. The only true scrip*tur*ing is the masterpiece; all other writing is worldly scripting and part of the business of living.

In her lecture/manifesto on masterpieces Stein prophetically declares the postures which allow her to create masterpieces – that is, what I have abstracted as her laws. Such postures inevitably entail evasions. Without these motivating evasions (an evasion being a posture which allows one to sidestep silence) we would be lost forever in the inactivity of the silence of aporia. An identifying characteristic of post-rupture literature is that these self-evasions are self-consciously performed; they are presented not as truths arrived at by logic but as an option chosen. For this reason they are very easily discovered and deconstructed.

The nature of Stein's evasion tells us much about her views on the ontotheological status of the creative as well as the business-like text. She divides texts into two categories: 'writing identity' and

Law 48 [A] thing goes dead once it has been said . . . because of there being this trouble about time.
Law 49 [T]ime does make identity . . . .
Law 50 [I]dentity does stop the creation of master-pieces.
Law 51 If you do not keep remembering yourself you have no identity . . . .
Law 52 [I]f you have no time you do not keep remembering yourself.
Law 53 [Y]ou create yes if you exist but time and identity do not exist.
Law 54 We live in time and identity but as we are we do not know time and identity . . . .

'writing entity'. Writing identity requires that a self-deception (myth or episteme) be placed firmly within the text, just as firmly as the text is placed within society and culture. The masterpiece as 'writing entity' is that text which requires no assistance from existing networks of codes and conventions in order to exist. It is a text which 'is' but which is not necessary; it is not motivated by existing social and cultural exigencies. The masterpiece is a 'pure' text. It is that pure text which Renato Poggioli saw as inevitably posited by avant-garde modernists.[12] It is Barthes's zero-degree writing. Ostensibly zero-degree writing or pure writing or entity writing avoids the need for an underlying episteme because it is what it is and nothing else; it is not what it is because it is in relation to something else. These pure texts have the same ontotheological status as do the two poles of Yeats's system in *A Vision*, the only two positions in his system to which no historical personage or text was assigned. They are necessary but ideal positions which anchor the orbits of the other positions but which can never, in themselves, be achieved. They are the absent centres recognised by Derrida. Inevitably, they are positions or postures of silence.

There is therefore some confusion in Stein's lecture/manifesto on masterpieces as to whether or not this posture of pure text is simply an element in the process of writing or an achievable type of text. On the one hand there is her well-known connection with writing as process: her connection with Jamesian 'stream of consciousness'; her use of the continuous tenses to portray the 'ing'-ness of being; her belief that composition is a spontaneous meditative 'act' and not something to be thought out beforehand. In her lecture/manifesto on masterpieces she tells us that, 'one has no identity . . . when one is in the act of doing anything' (law 4); that 'it is the detection that holds the interest' and not the solution (law 21); and that a masterpiece 'does not begin and end' (law 29). All of these things suggest that the posited pure text is simply a tactical evasion which

---

Law 55 [T]o know what one knows is frightening to live what one lives is soothing . . . .

Law 56 [T]here are very few master-pieces because to be able to know that is not to have identity and time but not to mind talking as if there was because it does not interfere with anything and to go on being not as if there were no time and identity but as if there were and at the same time existing without time and identity is so very simple that it is difficult to have many who are that.

Law 57 [A] master-piece does not continue it is as it is but it does not continue.

Law 58 [T]he fact that they all die has something to do with time but it has nothing to do with a master-piece.

aids the process of writing. On the other hand, in this same lecture/manifesto we are told that the masterpiece 'has to do with the human mind and the entity that is with a thing in itself' (law 23); that 'master-pieces have no more time than they have identity' (law 45); and that 'a master-piece does not continue it is as it is but it does not continue' (law 57). All of these laws suggest that the pure text is an achievable product.

A critic can do one of two things with this confusion. He can emphasise it in order to demonstrate Stein's inadequacies as writer and theorist and use it as ammunition to warn us away from wasting our time. Or he can look for some way of demonstrating that the apparent confusion is really no confusion at all and thus reclaim Stein for a reading public that demands coherence and identity: in other words, he can collaborate with Stein's manifesto in the business of living. The first response is the response of a critic who still feels the scandal of the manifesto; the second response is the response of a critic who acquiesces to the power of play.

To respond in the second way it is necessary to demonstrate that process dominates product in Stein's manifesto; it is necessary, once again, to read something into the text. First, it is necessary to add that, in order for a posited ideal effectively to influence a process, it is necessary that that ideal be believed in. If it is not believed in then it has no power to motivate the creative process, because it can be made to disappear too easily and so to dissipate any energy that it had induced. Stein was primarily a writer who believed in process. But in order to believe in process she had to have a motivating concept of product. The critic who provides such a formulation inevitably creates a hierarchy out of Stein's laws. In this case the idea of 'entity text' is subordinated to the idea of composition as process. As a creative writer and a manifesto writer Stein is not obliged to acknowledge such a hierarchy. She is able to present her laws contiguously.

In this necessary evasion (this sidestepping of aporia by allowing to exist contiguously two beliefs that on the surface appear

---

Law 59 The word timely as used in our speech is very interesting but you can anyone can see that it has nothing to do with master-pieces.

Law 60 [I]dentity consists in recognition . . . .

Law 61 [I]n recognizing you lose identity because after all nobody looks as they look like.

Law 62 [N]o master-piece can see what it can see if it does then it is timely . . . .

Law 63 If there was no identity no one could be governed . . . .

contradictory without attempting to resolve them in a formula that is too easily deconstructed) there is a silent admission that it is in this problematic play that whatever bliss (Barthes's *jouissance*) can be derived from the text is to be found. ('The pleasures that are soothing . . . all have to do with identity' – law 41: Barthes's *plaisir*). To accept this is to accept the pathos inherent in language. That is, language is our prime means of communication and yet the most outstanding characteristic of this communication is that it always falls short of what it aims for. Post-rupture texts look for *jouissance* by playing in the gaps of this falling short. For Stein, the gap is between identity and entity. To say that there is sadness here is not to contradict the presence of *jouissance*; rather, it reminds us that the original lofty aim of any language is to communicate without any possibility of misinterpretation and that our pleasure is located in the gap between this ideal and the inevitable falling short.

In her more obscure and oblique texts, Gertrude Stein is moving ever closer to her sense of entity and of thingness where the text is unnecessary and is the product of 'one' not in relation. It is, for whatever psychological, social and cultural mix of reasons, moving deeper into the universe of a private language that can have a reading or interpretation imposed upon it but can never communicate any sense of its own self-deception (its own self-conscious choice of episteme). In her more accessible writings, such as her lecture/manifestoes, she is moving closer to identity, giving us language that is still in relation, still recognisably part of the business of living, but still with enough private language to force us to question the foundations of language as a transparent vehicle for communication. What we do when we try to find theoretical coherence in Stein is try to find the stages that connect the public use of language to the private use of language and thereby develop a lexicon that will enable us to decode what were once seen as unreadable texts. Many such interpretative lexicons exist, most of them ingenious. They constitute the self-deceptions (creative and useful) of our shared critical activity. At their best they contribute to

---

Law 64 [G]overning has nothing to do with master-pieces it has completely to do with identity . . . .

Law 65 [G]overning is occupying but not interesting . . . .

Law 66 When you are writing before there is an audience anything written is as important as any other thing . . . .

Law 67 After the audience begins, naturally they create something that is they create you, and so not everything is so important . . . .

our pleasure (*jouissance*) in the text. And yet, if it were not for Gertrude Stein's need to be famous, and the manifestoes that tried to make of that fame something more than a personality cult, it is possible that we might not even make the effort to impose ourselves on her more private texts.

Notes

1. These laws have been abstracted from *WAM*.
2. Interestingly, her lecture/manifesto on masterpieces claims that the detective story comes very close to fulfilling the criteria she has set. 'In real life people are interested in the crime rather than the detection' (law 20), while 'in the story it is the detection that holds the interest' (law 21). Since the only necessary action is the death and since this comes at the beginning of the detective story, what follows – that is, the detection – is unnecessary and therefore potentially a masterpiece, since necessary actions are human nature and unnecessary actions are human mind and only human mind can produce a masterpiece (laws 27, 28, 29 and many more).
3. Three journals have devoted special issues to the manifesto: *Littérature*, 39 (Oct 1980); *Etudes françaises* 16, 3–4 (Oct 1980); and *L'Ésprit créateur*, XXIII, 4 (Winter 1983).
4. See Michel Foucault's *The Order of Things: An Archaeology of the Human Sciences* (London: Tavistock, 1970).
5. Ibid., p. 44.
6. To say that there are many patterns means that they will contradict one another (otherwise they would inevitably be part of the same pattern). But then we must admit that contradictions are always defined in the context of a controlling pattern (or episteme). If the controlling episteme is removed, then so also are the contradictions. These different patterns now stand as signs of textual plurality.
7. Many similar patterns can be found, almost at will, throughout the laws.
8. This reflects, perhaps a little too neatly, the idea that the structural trope for modernism is metonymy, where signs are related contiguously, rather than the metaphor, where signs are related hierarchically.
9. See J. L. Austin, *How to Do Things with Words*, ed. J. O. Urmson (New York: Oxford University Press, 1962).
10. For an excellent study of the relationship between the textual body, promising and scandal, see Shoshana Felman, *The Literary Speech Act*, tr. Catherine Porter (Ithaca, NY: Cornell University Press, 1983).
11. 'Composition as Explanation' concerns itself with representation, borders, framing, context and trust; 'Plays' concerns itself with discontinuity, fragmentation, signification/force, desire and need; 'The Gradual Making of the Making of Americans' self-consciousness,

self-reflexivity, narcissism and the fall into the present; 'What is English Literature' concerns itself with textual fields, intertextuality, conceptual horizons and dialogics; 'Pictures' concerns itself with figuration; 'Poetry and Grammar' concerns itself with valorisation, privileging, and private and shared languages; 'Poetry and Repetition' concerns itself with repetition compulsion, and the fall into time/history.

12. See Renato Poggioli, *The Theory of the Avant-Garde*, tr. Gerald Fitzgerald (Cambridge, Mass.: Harvard University Press, 1968).

11

'Would a viper have stung her if she had only had one name?': *Doctor Faustus Lights the Lights*

SHIRLEY NEUMAN

IDA A NOVEL BECOMES AN OPERA

'[I]n a kind of a way novels are still a puzzle to me',[1] Gertrude Stein explained as she began *Ida A Novel*. The puzzle proved difficult. Between mid-May and December 1937 she wrote at least three brief and unsatisfactory drafts of an opening for *Ida*.[2] By early December she thought that a conversation with Thornton Wilder had given her 'a scheme for Ida which [would] pull it together'.[3] But when, after Christmas festivities and a move to a new apartment, she resumed work in the beginning of February 1938, it was not *Ida* but *Doctor Faustus Lights the Lights* that occupied her (*GS–CVV*, II, p. 590): 'Ida has become an opera, and it is a beauty, really is, an opera about Faust', she would report.[4]

Stein read some of the libretto to Gerald Berners, who was to score the opera, when he visited Paris in April[5] and by 11 May she had completed the first act,[6] with the exception of the overture and the beginning of scene ii. She would complete the last two acts and send the manuscript off by 20 June (*GS–CVV*, II, p. 598). Although she would later add, at Berners' request, an 'overture' and additional material for the monologue opening Act I, scene ii,[7] by the end of June 1938 Stein thought of *Doctor Faustus Lights the Lights* as finished. Once more, she turned her attention to her novel, writing a second, much more developed version she called 'Arthur and Jenny' (YCAL).

What made Stein turn from a novel she could not yet write to an operatic re-presentation of the questions of knowledge and evil symbolised by the figure of Faustus? And what was there in the realisation of that opera that enabled her to return to her novel, to write its lengthy 'Arthur and Jenny' version? The three drafts of the first, unsuccessful 'Ida' version provide a clue. This passage, with slight variations, recurs in all of them:

Ida had a little dog his name was Iris. Iris is the name of a flower it might be the name of a girl it was the name of a little white dog he jumped up and down. Bayshore was not near the water that is unless you call a little stream water or quite [a] way off a little lake water, and rocks beyond it water. If you do not call all these things water then Bayshore was not at all near any water but its name was Bayshore and it was in a country where there are vipers only most of the time nobody sees them. Ida almost did not nor the little white dog Iris but on the path there must have been a yellow viper and as Ida watched the little dog Iris jump up and down bouncing like a ball she must have trod on the tail of the viper because she felt a sharp thing that was not like a sting on the side of her foot and as she stooped to look she saw something disappearing, she did not think it could be a viper but she looked down and took down her stocking she was wearing stockings while she was walking and there were two sharp little marks and she remembered that she had read that that was what a serpents bite looked like.
    Therefor she went on meditating and then as she went on she met some woman who belonged there, Ida of course did not, and Ida said to her could I have been bitten by a viper, yes said the woman not often but it does happen, well said Ida what shall I do, better go and see a doctor, so Ida went back to where she had come from and pretty soon she found a doctor and he said oh yes and injected a serum into her, it did not hurt her but it made a big red patch where the sting had been, it will make another one where the poison has been stopped higher up said the doctor and it did. Some one said sometimes the big red patch comes back every spring said some one they knew some one to whom this did happen but this did not do this to Ida. Then there was the dog Iris he had not been stung by the viper.
       (Quoted from 'Ida' notebook IV, YCAL; other versions are in
                                     notebooks III and VI)

The passage begins in a manner characteristic of Stein by calling into question the reference of proper nouns. But the rhythms soon become flat, and both the anecdote and the language which describes it are uncharacteristic: Stein seldom uses so un-American a word as *viper*; she rarely uses similes and never uses one so banal and intrusive as 'bouncing like a ball'; and she does not lean upon archetypal narratives of the sort called up by the serpent's bite. The passage is badly written *because*, I suggest, the intrusiveness of mythic associations distracts Stein from her usual concentration on the *words* she is writing. When Stein herself had been bitten by *une vipère*, she had felt it as 'quite biblical',[8] an analogy she is still explicitly making in the second 'Arthur and Jenny' version of her novel. In short, the mythic associations of her anecdote were a crux and a challenge to Stein, intruding as they did on the total concentration on *present* knowing and experiencing that governed her in the act of writing. What were the implications of a character's feeling 'biblical'? Unresolved, these implications were one of the things preventing Stein from 'pull[ing] together' *Ida*; faced, they were the genesis of *Doctor Faustus Lights the Lights*.

The serpent's tooth had very specific literary as well as personal and mythic associations for Stein: suffering snakebite, she wrote, had made her 'want to reread Elsie Venner'.[9] As Oliver Wendell Holmes himself pompously explained, in *Elsie Venner* he had wanted 'to test the doctrine of "original sin" and human responsibility for the disordered volition coming under that technical denomination'.[10] He did this by writing a reversal of biblical allegory. Mrs Venner, while carrying Elsie, has been bitten by a rattlesnake and her daughter shows it: her unblinking eyes glitter coldly, she bears on her neck the stigmata of the serpent's sting, she moves with a graceful but threatening sinuosity, and she exercises an unchecked and knowing malevolence throughout her childhood and adolescence. Holmes's point is not that we inherit Original Sin; instead it is that Elsie is not responsible for the tragedy of her life. Moreover, when she loves for the first time, the stigmata disappear and her reptilian beauty softens to resemble the saintly features of her dead mother. Holmes rewrites the biblical story to show Elsie's progress, through acts of love, from a guiltless evil to a self-elected innocence. Stein too needs to discover such a transposition – that is, needs to show that things are not always what their names or myths suggest (just as *Bayshore* is not near the water and Iris is not a girl, a flower or an eye). That she needed and had not found a comparable theology and narrative structure is evident in her decision to channel this first version of *Ida* into *Doctor Faustus Lights the Lights*. That she found Holmes's solution suggestive is intimated by the numerous reversals of convention she effects in the plot of her opera.

Stein was a writer completely committed to using language in such a way that her reader could not substitute habitual associations and ready-made cultural meanings for concentration on the words themselves. Ordinarily, she is the last writer to draw attention in her work to the intertextuality of writing – or what she, with her gift for clear statement, simply called the last 400 years of English literature. Why, then, did she choose the figure of Faustus with which to confront the crux presented by Ida's snakebite?

Three factors make the choice, if not quite inevitable, at least unsurprising. First, Stein several times noted that she had conceived *Ida* as a study of the effects of publicity on a personality. The media's obsession in 1937 with the Duke and Duchess of Windsor[11] contributed to this focus but critics have also been quick to connect it with her own 'stardom' during her 1934–5 American tour. Stardom and hubris are first cousins and Stein was self-scrutinising enough to see the kinship. Faustus, as he re-enacts the fall into Original Sin, weds the Christian plot of the quest for unlawful knowledge to the hubris of the Greek tragic hero. Stein has her Mephisto, in fact, openly compliment Doctor Faustus in terms of pride of knowing: 'and now are you not proud Doctor Faustus yes you are you know you are you are the only one who knows what you know' (*DF*, p. 90). Secondly, although Stein was far more interested in knowledge than in sin and not the least given to identifying the two, the question of the *nature* of knowing which is so large a part of the Faust tradition was attractive to her: her Doctor Faustus stands against Mephisto with his assertion that 'What I know I know, I know how I do what I do when I see the way through and always any day I will see another day and you old devil you know very well you never see any other way than just the way to hell, you only know one way' (p. 91). Finally, Faustus has almost as much mythic presence as the serpent himself and it is precisely the serpent's presence that Stein is trying to dislodge in order to clear a space in which she can realise her own perceptions about Ida's snakebite.

Stein's libretto descends from two operatic and literary Faustus traditions: one derived from Goethe and used by Gounod and Berlioz, the other derived from the German puppet plays and Marlowe and modified by Ferruccio Busoni. Those traditions both characterise Faustus as desiring the powers of a demiurge and settling for the antics of the devil. In a direct allusion to Genesis, Stein's Doctor Faustus asserts that, even unaided, he could, god-like, have created original light: 'What am I. I am Doctor Faustus who knows everything can do everything and you say it was through you but not at all, if I had not been in a hurry and if I had taken my time I would have known how to make white electric light and day-light and night light' (*DF*, p. 89). But Stein's Faustus, pleading lack of time, is already a less tragic figure than that of tradition. While Stein does permit him light, with its allusions to both Genesis and knowledge, she is slyly humourous in allowing him to invent *electric* lights: creating the theatrical illusion of the stage on which 'he' stands, electric lights suggest illusoriness itself and their very mysteriousness, as they 'glow', 'go . . . out' and 'begin to get very gay' in response to the action, introduces commentary that is comic as well as mysterious.

Indeed the 'overture' to the opera soon becomes carnivalesque. The opening tableau reveals Faustus, arms raised to the door lintel, his silhouette strongly backlit by the light he invented. The visual allusion is to a 1938 production of Berlioz's *The Damnation of Faust* at the Académie Nationale de Musique et de Danse in Paris: Stein drafted the opening of a portion of her libretto beginning with 'Doctor Faustus' song' (*DF*, p. 92), in the Académie's 23 February 1938 programme for Mozart's *Don Giovanni*. In that draft, she presents Faustus 'sitting alone' (YCAL). The programme, however, included a photograph of the set of *The Damnation of Faust*, a set dominated by a tall cross, strongly backlit, at the top of a rise: the image clearly remained in Stein's mind when she wrote her own 'overture' many months later. However, she immediately undercuts the iconography of crucifixion by the wordplay and colloquialism, as well as by the petulance, of Faustus's first speech: 'The devil what the devil do I care if the devil is there' (*DF*, p. 89). Nor is Stein's Mephisto a worthy antagonist: he calls Faustus 'dear' and pats his arm as a placating woman might; his only defence against Faustus's accusations is the dubious distinction that the devil 'deceives' but 'never lies' (p. 90); and he is finally kicked 'to hell' (p. 91) by Faustus. The language throughout the scene mocks conventional theology by its rhymes, puns, colloquialisms and allusions to children's hymns. Not the Bible but 'the devil tells you so' (p. 89), and Faustus claims of electric light that 'I wanted to make it and the devil take it' (p. 90). Even the devil's legendary redness has less significance than the superstitious rhyme about sailors and sunsets: 'oh devil . . . now you are red at night which is not a delight and you are red in the morning which is not a warning' (ibid.). All this comic play points to the more serious theological inversions figured in Stein's Doctor Faustus and to the knowledge constitutive of his despair. He lives in a world without symbols, knowing that 'light however bright will never be other than light' (p. 91), and concludes that there is 'no snake to grind under one's heel' and no afterlife: 'there is no hope there is no death there is no life there is no breath, there is just every day all day and when there is no day there is no day' (p. 90).

That it should be *electric* light that Doctor Faustus invents and that leads him to this despair opens into a network of operatic and personal references that suggest what *is* at stake as Stein so quickly up-ends so much in the Judaeo-Christian tradition. Recalling her youthful attendance at the opera, she remembered seeing, or being told about, 'the fight in Faustus' (*LIA*, p. 113). The reference seems to be to the 'Scène des épées' in Gounod's *Faust*, a scene Méphistophélès provokes by his knowing song – 'Le Veau d'or' – about humankind's adoration of Mammon. The struggle in Stein's libretto involves no weapons so pointed as rapiers; however, she does assimilate the scene to her own concerns with identity, publicity and worship of the golden calf of Mammon when she makes the decision to have Doctor Faustus invent electric light. For he surely owes his inventiveness to Sir Henry Irving's Mephistopheles in W. G. Wills's 1886 adaptation of Goethe, which toured widely in America after its first London run. Sir Henry hooked the duellers in the fight scene up to a primitive battery; whenever, in his role as Mephistopheles, he intervened on Faustus's behalf by using his rapier to disengage those of the fencers, sparks flew. The first use of electric 'flashes' on the stage, the duel was admired as one of Irving's most sensational scenic effects.[12]

The link between 'Le Veau d'or' and electricity would have been richly resonant for Stein. As Richard Bridgman notes,[13] she was discomfited when New York paid tribute to her celebrity by announcing her arrival in Broadway's electric lights (*EA*, pp. 112, 175). The connection with the Gounod–Irving scene is obvious: *The*

Autobiography of Alice B. Toklas – the book written, as none of her previous books had been, to earn money, the book which lit up her name in electricity – lays her open to the self-accusation of 'serving Mammon'. That service, described by Stein in her *Lectures*, involves the writer's relationship to the language she uses. '[S]erving god', she was at pains to point out, the writer writes 'directly, . . . the relation between the thing done and the doer must be direct'; serving the golden calf of Mammon, he writes 'indirectly he says what he intends to have heard by somebody who is to hear' (*LIA*, pp. 22–4). Or, as Faustus puts it, 'oh no thought is not bought', and to have sold one's soul for knowledge, to have bought thought, is to have served Mammon (*DF*, p. 100), to have become the creature of those who light one's name in electricity.

To turn night into day is one of the antics Faust performs for the Duke and Duchess of Parma in both Marlowe's play and in Ferruccio Busoni's 1925 opera *Doktor Faust*, which had been revived in concert performance in London in March 1937. Although Stein was not present at the performance, Busoni's opera, as well as those by Gounod and Berlioz, clearly figured in the discussion between herself and Gerald Berners.[14] Moreover, Stein did go to London on 23 April for the 27 April première of the Stein–Berners ballet *A Wedding Bouquet*. There she moved in musical circles in which she would certainly have heard discussion about the Busoni revival. The performance was reviewed in several places; in the April issue of the *London Mercury*, for example, Desmond Shawe Taylor stressed the 'intense and rarefied spirituality' of Busoni's Faust. He also described in detail the final scene, in which Faust wills his own life into his dead child, who is then resurrected as a naked young man bearing a flowering branch and striding 'with uplifted arms over the snow into the town and into the night'.[15]

While the visual presentation of Busoni's resurrected child is not in Stein's style, she would certainly have been alert to the political allegory of *Doktor Faust*. Busoni had begun his libretto in 1914; his use of Faustus as emblematic of man's self-destructiveness and his pointed recasting of Faustus's death to prophesy the possibility that a new order might rise out of the ashes of the Great War would have been particularly poignant in 1937, when Stein was in England and Europe seemed daily more menaced, and even more so a year later as she was writing *Doctor Faustus* and Hitler was annexing Austria. That Faustus and war were linked in her mind is clear from the allusion of her title to a 1915 piece, 'He Didn't Light the Light', in which 'he', 'they', a soldier, an electric light, a match and Palma de Mallorca figure in a conversation, the context of which seems to be First World War blackouts, about when, where and whether a light is lit. Busoni's suggestion that Faustus, however damned, could by an act of will be life-giving, particularly when combined with her association of snakebite with Holmes's earlier revision of the doctrine of Original Sin in *Elsie Venner*, is crucial to Stein's libretto.

Stein's retelling of the Faust story rests on the reasoning that, if hell is the torment of the soul, then a man without a soul (having, perhaps, sold it) cannot go to hell: 'I have made it [electric light] but have I a soul to pay for it', her Faustus worries (*DF*, p. 90). That question is the basis of the connection and the struggle between Faustus and the Ida character.

Connection and struggle are intimated in the parallelism, contrasts and comic timing of the first two scenes of the play. In 'The Ballet' of Act i, Stein's Doctor Faustus, in keeping with tradition, seems to anticipate a visitation, perhaps an epiphany, presented initially as an indeterminate but epistemological question: 'If I do it / If you do it / What is it'. Then as entity: 'Will it be it / Just it.' And finally as confrontation and 'shocked' recognition: 'It is it' (p. 92). 'It' turns out to be Marguerite Ida and Helena Annabel, who has questions of her own.

Stein added the opening action of the scene which introduces her heroine[16] in late September or early October 1938 while she was writing her children's story *The World Is Round*. The scene repeats the double register of comedy and terror[17] of that story and reaches its climax in a frantic inability to repudiate id/entity:

> Would it do as well if my name was not Marguerite Ida and Helena Annabel . . . I would give up even that . . . to be not here but there, but (and she lets out a shriek,) I am here I am not there and I am Marguerite Ida and Helena Annabel and it is not well that I could tell what there is to tell.   (*DF*, p. 96)

When the troublesome viper intrudes on this terror, her response echoes Faustus's: 'what is it', she asks (ibid.). Just as the first scene ends in farcical quarrelling between Faustus and his companions, the boy and the dog, so here also, at the moment of the serpent's sting when we expect crisis and revelation, events become farcical.

A passing country woman echoes Marguerite Ida and Helena Annabel's every question: 'have I been bitten, . . . have I says Marguerite Ida and Helena Annabel have I have I been bitten. Have you been bitten answers the country woman, why yes it can happen, then I have been bitten says Marguerite Ida and Helena Annabel why not if you have been is the answer' (p. 97)

Stein undoes a good deal of the traditional import of both the Faustus and the serpent figures by this sort of comedy and she keeps it up even while implying a mystic connection and a struggle between Doctor Faustus and Marguerite Ida and Helena Annabel. For the event productive of dramatic tension in this act is not the serpent's sting but the approach and confrontation of Doctor Faustus and Marguerite Ida and Helena Annabel. The merry ballet of Faustus's electric lights, which glow, flicker and fade in response to her 'presence' and vitality, suggests a mystic connection between the two characters. And her question as she approaches Doctor Faustus implies the ensuing struggle: 'Am I Marguerite Ida or am I Helena Annabel' (ibid.), she asks, suggesting that she chooses a 'self' to suit the occasion. But Faustus's query is the more shattering, for, where she queries identity ('Who am I'), he queries entity ('What am I'). The comedy continues: as she approaches him, she responds with comic patness to each of his queries. 'Oh what am I', Doctor Faustus repeats and, as if on cue, she calls from off-stage 'Doctor Faustus' (p. 98). Boy and dog and Faustus dream a dream that calls into question the signifying function of signs – 'somebody says there is where is it where is it where is it where, here is here here is there somebody somebody says where is where' – only to be answered by the off-stage query, 'are you there Doctor Faustus say where Doctor Faustus' (p. 99). [18]

The playfulness of this dialogue displaces the traditional values of the story so as to make room for the serious debate about knowing that Stein's characters are about to enact in their struggle with one another. In the ensuing, less comic, struggle *each* represents knowledge to the other. Faustus's is the acquired medical and technological knowledge that can cure the sting, a knowledge that carries with it the larger power to let there be electric light. Hers is the knowledge Stein defined as 'knowing', the knowledge to 'see' and name him:

> And then she says in a quiet voice.
> Doctor Faustus have you ever been to hell.

Of course not she says of course you have not how could you sell
your soul if you had ever been to hell . . . .   (p. 99)

That she can go to hell is her present fear and the basis of Doctor
Faustus's future envy, and this difference between them points to
the mutual exclusiveness of their two kinds of knowledge. Their
struggle is dramatised as 'seeing'. Doctor Faustus, who has 'bought
thought' and sold his soul 'here there and everywhere' cannot see
Marguerite Ida and Helena Annabel (pp. 100–1). She, needing his
knowledge, fears it: 'and you you have the light cure me Doctor
Faustus cure me do but do not see me, I see you but do not see me
cure me do but do not see me I implore you' (p. 101). The chorus
sums up this struggle: 'And he says / He can but he will not / And
she says he must and he will' (p. 102). And, just as the lights 'flicker
and flicker' (ibid.), he does cure her, *because* her entity, the fact that
she is what she is, is stronger than his will:

> The boy has said will you
> The woman has said
> Can you
> And you, you have said you are you
> Enough said.
> You are not dead.
>
> (p. 103)

As the subsequent action makes clear, Stein is making a distinction between innocent and guilty knowledge that involves not
only source but also motive and use. For, while Faustus's 'cure' of
Marguerite Ida and Helena Annabel effects a transfer to her of his
knowledge of how to make light, it does so without her having to
make a pact with Mephisto. And, not unlike Busoni's Doktor Faust
or even Holmes's Elsie Venner (who, when the man she loves is
about to be struck by a rattlesnake, uses her own snake-like gaze to
quell it), Stein's Faustus has used his fatally acquired knowledge to
life-giving ends. No doubt remembering the medical training she
had in common with Oliver Wendell Holmes, Stein invokes *two*
traditions of the serpent: that of the symbol of guilty knowledge and
death and that of the healing symbol on the cadeucus.[19]

'WOULD A VIPER HAVE STUNG HER IF SHE HAD ONLY HAD ONE NAME?': AN ENTR'ACTE

The question is asked by one of the chorus near the beginning of Act II. In fact, in the beginning, she was only 'Ida'. In the first draft of the first version of *Ida A Novel* Ida is her whole name. By the second draft of this version, she 'knew another Ida who was thirty' (YCAL) and, with that doubling, Stein has the first inkling of the strategy by which she will describe the effects of publicity and of her own experience that a public demands and creates a public and a divided person. 'I did not know myself, I lost my personality', she wrote in a 1934 piece ('And Now') about the public attention her first autobiography garnered for her, 'So many people knowing me I was I no longer' (*HWW*, p. 63).

Manuscript fragments that belong to the transition from the first version of *Ida A Novel* to *Doctor Faustus Lights the Lights* indicate that Stein only slowly realised that her character should have a double name. One fragment outlines an obviously tentative notion: 'Supposing she goes away part time the other half. – she is at home. she could have lots of adventures, —— I do not see how she could be different but she is, which is best of all' (YCAL). On the back of this sheet is the title 'Is she a twin'. Of four other sheets in the same bundle, two recount the things 'Ida Isabel' (a name that would have appealed for its obvious pun, 'Ida is a belle') and her dog Love see. The other two sheets in this bundle are a draft of a passage in which a 'young girl' decides 'to have a sister a sister who looks as like me as two peas (not that peas do) and no one will know which is she and which is me' (cf. *Ida*, pp. 17ff.).

While these fragments come to nothing in themselves, they are indications of the growing importance of the twin in Stein's conception of her novel and of her linking of the twin's creation to a moment of public recognition. Two pieces originating in late April and May 1938 were crucial to her realisation of the possibilities of the twin and, therefore, crucial to the completion of *Doctor Faustus* and to her taking up the 'Arthur and Jenny' version of her novel. In the unpublished 'A Portrait of Daisy To Daisy On Her Birthday',

> Daisy was a twin. That is she made herself one . . . .
> Daisy began to sit and write.
> She made Daisy.
> If you made her can you kill her.

Not if she is Daisy.
And Daisy made Daisy.
One one one.
            (YCAL)

The Daisy of the piece was Daisy Fellowes, whose birthday, Stein noted in a letter to W. G. Rogers,[20] was very near to Alice Toklas's (30 April). 'A Portrait of Daisy' was written at the end of April or beginning of May 1938 and was very quickly canalised into 'Lucretia Borgia' (published October 1938), a play which, even in Stein's *oeuvre*, is remarkably self-reflexive: in it 'Jenny began to sit and write. / Lucretia Borgia – an opera' (*RAB*, p. 119). The play consists of three first acts each offering a different explanation of Lucretia's creation of her twin and a different combination of names that will reappear in the 'Arthur and Jenny' version of *Ida A Novel*. A fourth Act I raises the crucial question which finds its way into the published version of *Ida*:

They called her a suicide blond because she dyed her own hair.
They called her a murderess because she killed her twin whom she first made come.
If you made her can you kill her.
One one one.   (*RAB*, p. 119; cf. *Ida*, p. 11)

To dye one's hair is to create another identity and is a way of killing oneself. That the 'twin' represents the public self and that that self is productive of anxiety is signalled in the text by the use of the collective 'they' for the public and by the desire to kill/fear of killing that twinned self. This becomes even more evident when we realise that this piece was written in close conjunction with the short sketch 'Ida' published in November the same year in *The Boudoir Companion: Frivolous, Sometimes Venomous Thoughts on Men, Morals and Other Women*.[21]

In *The Boudoir Companion* sketch 'dear Ida', who has always lived a quiet life, suddenly becomes famous as a result of a narrative she writes or tells. But the rising chant of public acclaim – 'Dear Ida, sweet Ida, Ida, Ida' (*HWW*, p. 44) – changes her identity. She *had* been two people, one a public and iconic identity (admired recipient of a beauty prize), one a private entity ('not remembering any one or anything' – p. 45). Being 'one of two, . . . sometimes she went out as one and sometimes she went out as the other' (ibid.); that is, she chose whether to act in terms of her public identity or of her own personality. But fame makes it temporarily impossible for her to act except in the image of the publicly created identity:

> Ida was no longer two she was one and she had every one.
> Everybody knew about her.
> Oh yes they did.
> And why
> Ida was her name
> That was her fame.
>
>   (Ibid.)

Appropriating and appropriated by her audience, she is only Identity, her public self, 'no longer two' but only 'one'. The *folie* of Ida's popularity, simultaneously gratifying and disquieting, is given parodic expression in a syncopated allusion to 'A Portrait of Daisy', the piece in which Stein had finally realised the significance of a doubled self to the Ida of her novel and the Ida of *Doctor Faustus Lights the Lights*. For the 'tune' which we hear syncopated behind the description of Ida as 'Stored and adored. / Bored and reward / All for love of Ida' (*HWW*, p. 46) is 'A Bicycle Built for Two', that popular version of American readiness to place its Daisies on ped(est)als. While the words and rhythm of the song alluded to evoke a gay *folie* of excessive adoration, the syncopation of Stein's tune introduces an unease into her description that is consistent with the unexpected inclusion of 'stored' and 'bored' among Ida's attributes. The first suggests that public adoration makes her into a commodity; the second that it is less than interesting. While the gratifications and anxieties of public adoration hum, like the tune, beneath the surface of the *Boudoir Companion* 'Ida', at the explicit narrative level Ida quickly recovers the circumstances in which she can choose whether to act in terms of public identity or of her own personality. 'Not that they loved Ida' (*HWW*, p. 46), the narrator hastens to correct the heady illusions worked by acclaim. As quickly as her fame flared up, it dies down: 'now again they say dear Ida', 'Once more dear Ida' (pp. 46, 47). The last sentence of the text sees her with both her selves restored and acting once again as protective coloration: 'remember me to Ida. Dear Ida' (p. 47), the narrator instructs, but that 'Dear Ida' functions ambiguously, both descriptively and vocatively. Is this 'dear Ida' the person to whom the narrator is to be remembered? Or the person addressed, who is to remember the narrator to that other character 'Ida'? Ida/dear Ida triumphs, for we no longer know which Ida has gone out.

Would a viper have stung Marguerite Ida and Helena Annabel if she had had only one name? The texts written at the same time as *Doctor Faustus Lights the Lights* suggest not. In them, two names are a character's way of not losing her personality in the face of the public's attempts to appropriate her and to assimilate her into the single, public name. For Marguerite Ida and Helena Annabel did have two names from the opera's inception: in the manuscript she is 'Ida and Annabel' throughout the first act and the beginning of the second. This is consistent with Stein's realisation of her Ida character when she began the libretto with the questioning title 'Is she a twin'. But the fact that Marguerite Ida and Helena Annabel becomes a very publicly worshipped saint in Act II *after* being bitten suggests that publicity is one of the opera's associations with venom, that having one name might be the fatal consequence of being bitten, and that, while Faustus's cure has saved Ida's life, it has also, by catapulting her into fame, made it necessary for Ida and Annabel to double her already doubled name in order to ensure the distinction of the private from the public self. By 11 May 1938 Stein had finished Act I and begun Act II. At precisely this point she wrote 'A Portrait of Daisy', 'Lucretia Borgia' and the *Boudoir Companion* 'Ida'. In those pieces she discovered the significance of the doubled name and released the possibility of the 'Arthur and Jenny' version of the novel with its specific focus on publicity through the character of Arthur, who is deciding whether or not to be a king in an obvious allusion to the public Edward VIII and the private Duke of Windsor. And at this point too, immediately after 'One sun / And she is one' in Act II (*DF*, p. 107), 'Ida and Annabel' begins to be written in the manuscript as 'Marguerite Ida and Helena Annabel' and Stein goes back over her manuscript and inserts 'Marguerite' and 'Helena' into previous occurrences of the name. The double name has been playfully doubled as a result of the liberating surge of creativity in early May which led Stein to a means of characterising a resistance to becoming a public 'one'. For Stein had made explicit her conviction that that doubling is a fundamental human strategy when the narrator of the *Boudoir Companion* 'Ida' stops to explain what Ida's story means:

Now let us make it all careful and clear.
Everybody is an Ida.
Dear Ida.

(*HWW*, p. 46)

'SHE HAS EVERYTHING / AND HER SOUL': WORSHIPPING MARGUERITE IDA AND HELENA ANNABEL

In Act II of *Doctor Faustus Lights the Lights*, the chorus in its adoration of Marguerite Ida and Helena Annabel joins the theological drama of Act I to the drama of publicity Stein had been working through in the shorter pieces she was writing as she finished Act I and began Act II. Her chorus is the most active since Euripides'. It gossips and gapes, speculates and surmises, spreads rumours and creates enormous public pressure. The opening song sung by 'Some one' suggests a method in which choric frivolity carries serious undertones:

> Well is well and silver sell
> Sell a salted almond to Nell
> Which she will accept
> And then
> What does a fatty do
> She does not pay for it.
> (*DF*, p. 103)

A silver salt cellar, displaced onto 'silver sell / Sell a salted almond to Nell . . . / [who] does not pay for it', is the most glancing of allusions to the sale of knowledge for thirty pieces of silver and to Faustus, who, having sold his soul, cannot pay, so to speak, his electric bill. But the chorus quickly turns to its primary dramatic function: to seek out Ida most volubly and, when they have found her, to gaze at her:

> There she is
> There there
> Where
> Why there
> Look and see there
> There she is.
> (p. 105)

Their collective *folie* echoes to the tune of 'Three Blind Mice': 'See how they come/See how they come/To see her' (p. 106). This chorus, like the Greek chorus relaying what 'they say', embodies the public voice and, by extension, the voice of publicity. To be a subject of the chorus's conversation and an object of its gaze is necessarily to be a creation of publicity, and Marguerite Ida and Helena Annabel, enthroned as an icon and adored as she is in this act, not only parodies religious worship but also characterises 'a person . . . so publicized that there isn't any personality left'. 'I want to write', Stein had written to W. G. Rogers in summer 1937 when she began her work on the first version of *Ida*, 'about the effect on people of the Hollywood cinema kind of publicity that takes away all identity.'[22]

Stein's concern with the way publicity overturns the balance between public identity and private personality, the concern she has been working out in shorter pieces as she began Act II of *Doctor Faustus Lights the Lights*, is one of two thematic strands entering into the presentation of the hallowed and worshipped Marguerite Ida and Helena Annabel. The second is a reconsideration, in terms of the female character, of the theological argument connected with Doctor Faustus in Act I. Stein's scenario for Act II begins, 'Ida and Annabel has become a legend, she sits as a legend' (YCAL) – that is, she has become a quasi-sanctified figure. In the libretto, 'The curtain at the corner raises and there she is Marguerite Ida and Helena Annabel and she has an artificial viper there beside her and a halo is around her not of electric light but of candle light, and she sits there and waits' (*DF*, p. 104). Two things have happened here. If Faustus was given the powers of a technological god in Act I, Marguerite Ida and Helena Annabel clearly embodies the natural correlative of those same powers in Act II, where she is not only worshipped but can, like him, make light (though she shows no interest in doing so).

This is to suggest that part of the theological argument of *Doctor Faustus Lights the Lights* involves an extended allusion to matriarchal religion.[23] That the Greek (sun) gods had displaced a prior matriarchal (moon-identified) pantheon, and that vestiges of the goddesses remained in the Virgin Mary, was current theory in the anthropology and classicism of Stein's generation, beginning with Sir James Frazer, and continuing with writers such as Jane Harrison in her influential *Prolegomena to Greek Religion* (1903) and *Themis* (1912) and Richard Briffault in his three-volume *The Mothers* (1927). The visual iconography of Stein's libretto invokes these matriarchal goddesses: they were often represented as associated with snakes, sometimes as holding them, just as Marguerite Ida and Helena Annabel is seen to do when the curtain to her sanctuary is raised. The snake itself had plural and simultaneous significations, both creative and destructive: so too the viper in *Doctor Faustus Lights the Lights* becomes the agent of both the heroine's knowledge and power and of the boy's and dog's deaths. Sometimes the symbol of the goddess herself, at others of the male fecundating principle, the serpent was figure for the goddess's immortality. The iconography would be appealing to a writer wishing to invert the premises of the Christian doctrine of Original Sin: the serpent, associated with the matriarchal goddess, is the symbol of her immortal wisdom, not of her mortal guilt.

The point in the libretto at which Stein presents her heroine as holding the viper – that is, in terms of the ancient imagery of the matriarchal goddesses – is the point at which she doubles her names. That doubling, I have already argued, was Stein's way of signalling a necessary division between public icon and private personality and belongs to the libretto's publicity theme. But her *choice* of names for her character belongs both to this theme and to the theological argument: the doubly compound name has associations with Greek matriarchal religion, with its traces in Christianity, with the Faustus story, and with Stein's discovery in 'A Portrait of Daisy' of the possibilities of twinning her character. And each pair of names pairs worldly temptation and matriarchal religion.

'Marguerite' obviously derives from the Faustus story, where her fall re-enacts Eve's. One of many fallen flowers in literature and opera, her name evokes the courtesan Marguerite in Dumas's *La Dame aux camélias* and the woman Faust seduces in Gounod's libretto; the generic name for *daisy* in French, it also has an active life in argot, where *cueillir une marguerite* is to deflower a virgin. That her new knowledge brings Stein's Marguerite power and 'immortality', and not sin and death, is one of the theological inversions of this libretto. (It is also an inversion of Stein's own earlier plotting in 'Melanctha', in which the heroine, in the grand tradition of nineteenth-century opera, pays for her 'wandering' and her 'knowing' by dying a consumptive's death.)

'Ida' most obviously suggests, as Allegra Stewart first noted,[24] *Mount Ida*, the Olympus of Greek matriarchal religion, and home of the Great Mother. Ida's dog, in the first version of *Ida A Novel*, and one of two dogs in the published version (the other is 'Love'), is named 'Iris' and is frightened by thunder and lightning. That the dog Iris should be afraid of Zeus's bolts ceases to be mysterious when we recall that the Greek goddess to whom she owes her name (a goddess thought to be the mother of love) was one of many matriarchal goddesses displaced by worship of Zeus.

'Helena Annabel' is similarly suggestive and has connections with the twin who becomes a public icon by winning a beauty prize in 'Lucretia Borgia. A Play' and in *Ida A Novel*. The association with Helen of Troy is obvious, while 'Annabel' is merely another version of the earlier pun on *Isabel / is a belle*. But both also have sacred connotations. In that Greek religion which antedated the celebrations of Apollo the sun god, Anna evidently personified both the Old Year, as a crone, and the New Year, as a bride; she survives in her crone aspect as mother of the Virgin Mary.[25] In *Doctor Faustus Lights the Lights* her name stands as that aspect of Marguerite Ida and Helena Annabel's character that prefers moonlight and candlelight to Doctor Faustus's electric light and that resolutely sits with her back to the sun represented by the man from over the seas who comes to court her. Helen has similarly sacred connections: indeed, some readings of representations of her 'rape' argue that it was in fact her sanctuary rather than her chastity or her husband's rights that was violated. Stein presents her character in a similar manner: while Marguerite Ida and Helena Annabel is directly related to the Idas who win beauty contests in Stein's writing of the period, she is also about to be displaced from her sanctuary by a male wooer.

In Act II of *Doctor Faustus Lights the Lights*, Marguerite Ida and Helena Annabel is perceived by the chorus/public as a female rival to Doctor Faustus,[26] as one who, having been cured by him, has put on his knowledge with his power. A woman complains,

> Here we know because Doctor Faustus tells us so, that he only he can turn night into day but now they say, they say, (her voice rises to a screech) they say a woman can turn night into day, they say a woman and a viper bit her and did not hurt her and he showed her how and now she can turn night into day. (*DF*, p. 112)

Complaint becomes the plea of 'Doctor Faustus oh Doctor Faustus say you are the only one who can turn night into day' (ibid.), but Stein is rewriting the Bible that tells us so.

When we read the action of the libretto in terms of a 'temptation' by and subsequent 'knowledge' of publicity, in terms of Christian theology, or in terms of the displacement of early matriarchal cults – and all these possibilities co-exist in the text with no one privileged over the others – then we understand Marguerite Ida and Helena Annabel as both strengthened by her knowledge and undermined by her position as public idol. The precariousness of her position is foregrounded by the man from over the seas who trivialises it by courting her with a Valentine's Day rhyme:

> She is all my love and always here
> And I am hers and she is mine
> And I love her all the time
> Pretty pretty pretty dear.
>   (p. 107)

Where she sits with her back to the sun and is associated with the moon, he is associated with the sun and with the displacement of the female goddesses by the patriarchal religion of the sun/son god Apollo. When he approaches Marguerite Ida and Helena Annabel, he is confident that 'I am your sun oh very very well begun, you turn your back on your sun, I am your sun, I have won I have won I am your sun' (p. 108). She has, at first, the strength to resist; she responds by holding the symbol of her power, the viper, and charging that he is Doctor Faustus. Stein makes this a moment of dramatic struggle in the libretto, for when the man from over the seas ignores her charge to insist that he is the one and only true man/god – 'I am not any one I am the only one, you have to have me because I am that one' (ibid.) – Marguerite Ida and Helena Annabel temporarily weakens and drops the viper. Troubled, she hastily recovers it. An early manuscript fragment of a scenario for this scene casts it plainly in terms of female abnegation of power in the sexual relationship; Stein summarises: 'The love scene gets more xciting and just at that moment when they make love with the viper and the lights and she says she would *but not quite* sacrifice all for him Mephistopheles enters' (YCAL, emphasis added). In the final version, this conventional sexual temptation is intimately linked to temptation by the snares of publicity. For, in this final version, it is Marguerite Ida and Helena Annabel's retrieval of the viper, the symbol of her public power, that allows her to 'see' that the man from over the seas is shadowed by Mephistopheles, whom she defies by asserting that 'Lights are all right but the viper is my might' (*DF*, p. 109).

None the less, the man from over the seas has 'won'/one(d) her and the viper is no longer *her* might. For, once she has become an icon, she is no longer two, a public identity and a private personality, 'she is one' (p. 107); and, when the man from over the seas appears, shadowed by Mephistopheles, he is the new and sinister embodiment of strength, of two in one. He brings with him a new, adoring chorus/public, a boy and a girl, whose song of marked libidinal longing makes plain that they are 'two' as he would have himself and Marguerite Ida and Helena Annabel be. But they sing not *to* Marguerite Ida and Helena Annabel but to her symbol, which they address as 'Mr Viper', suggesting that it is already in transition from her to the man courting her. They sing,

> Mr Viper dear Mr Viper, he is a boy I am a girl she is a girl I am a boy we do not want to annoy but we do oh we do oh Mr Viper yes we do we want you to know that she is a girl that I am a boy, oh yes Mr Viper, please Mr Viper here we are Mr Viper listen to us Mr Viper, oh please Mr Viper it is not true Mr Viper what the devil says Mr Viper that there is no Mr Viper, please Mr Viper please Mr Viper, she is a girl he is a boy please Mr Viper you are Mr Viper please Mr Viper please tell us so.   (p. 109; cf. p. 118)

This song catches extraordinarily the complex impulses of adulatory crowds, whether their worship is religious or of the 'Hollywood cinema' variety: the joy, the sexuality, the sense of mystery and demand for explanations, the elegiac quality, the longing to be one of the elect. Serving to articulate the change in the object of public worship from Marguerite Ida and Helena Annabel to the man from over the seas, its singers belong to the plot which finds an analogy for publicity in worship, which sets out to overturn theological doctrine, which records a struggle for power and its loss and which looks in bleak silence to the still unknown consequences of the transfer of that power.

'ALL DARK'

By Act III the transition is well under way and its consequences are beginning to unfold. When we next see Marguerite Ida and Helena

Annabel she is 'sitting with the man from over the seas their backs to the sun' (*DF*, p. 114). He proposes to alter this arrangement by 'forget[ting]' that she is 'one', but she hangs on to her public image, stiffening and reasserting her presence: 'here I am, yes here I am' (ibid.). But her public is no longer so interested as it was and the power of the moon goddess is rapidly waning: the music in this scene is to express a '*noon-day* hush' (ibid.; emphasis added) and chorus associates the viper entirely with the man from over the seas and talks almost entirely of him:

> come any one come, see any one, some, come viper sun, we know no other any one, any one can forget a light, even an electric one but no one no no one can forget a viper even a stuffed one no no one and no one can forget the sun and no one can forget Doctor Faustus no no one and and no one can forget Thank you and the dog and no one can forget a little boy and no one can forget any one no no one.   (Ibid.)

What everyone can and does forget in this chorus is Marguerite Ida and Helena Annabel. Like the Ida of the *Boudoir Companion* sketch, her moment of being 'stored and adored' by her public is over; her worshippers are displacing her in favour of a new idol. As the scene continues, electric light once again covers the stage and the viper is once again natural and lethal: 'The dog says / Thank you, the light is so bright there is no moon tonight I cannot bay at the moon the viper will kill me. Thank you' (*DF*, p. 116).

With Ida forgotten, the action turns once again to Doctor Faustus and to the theological questions about the nature of knowing focused by his characterisation. His new quest is 'to be again alright and go to hell' (ibid.), for, to be able to go to hell would be, as Marguerite Ida and Helena Annabel seemed to be, to have everything and his soul too. Urged by the chorus, who, true to its character as the public, has now turned against Marguerite Ida and Helena Annabel, and by Mephisto, who advises him that he can get to hell without the devil's help if he commits a sin, he inquires further, 'how can I without a soul commit a sin'. Mephisto's answer is brutally direct and undiscriminating: 'Kill anything' (ibid.).

When Doctor Faustus makes his choice, the viper as symbol and agent undergoes another transformation and deals literal death – 'you are forever ever ever dead' (p. 117) – on a night when electric light eclipses the moon. The comic possibilities of *Doctor Faustus*

Lights the Lights have been changed into a despair as dark as the electric lights are bright. For Doctor Faustus kills to go to hell because his invention no longer interests him or anyone else and he kills, however deceived he may be about it, to become human once more, to have a soul. His decision to kill his only companions, the boy and the dog, the fact that even Mephisto counts himself as 'deceived' by the act, the indifference of the public, the continuing insistent song of innocence and longing sung by the boy and girl: these mark the gratuitousness of the act and the darkness of its motivation.

And Doctor Faustus kills not only to be able to go to hell but also to revenge himself on Marguerite Ida and Helena Annabel by taking her to hell with him. With obvious reference to previous Fausts, the devil makes him youthful to enable him to persuade her, but finds himself deceived one last time when she refuses to go with Doctor Faustus. This refusal effects the final ironic inversion of the traditional Faust plot and the end of Marguerite Ida and Helena Annabel's power to 'see'. For refusing to be deceived – not believing that the young man before her is Doctor Faustus – she is in fact deceived. With the end of an order in which the viper was symbol of healing as well as of death, with the death of the boy and the dog, and with the failure of her own discernment, her eclipse is complete. She succumbs to the stranger/sun god: 'fainting into the arms of the man from over the seas' (p. 118), she clearly does not become again a private personality as her public worship evaporates; instead, she loses the last trace of either public identity or private entity. Meanwhile, the man from over the seas 'sings', tenderly, sexually, condescendingly, about standing in her place: 'pretty dear I am here yes I am here pretty pretty pretty dear' (ibid.). In Stein's rewriting of the Faust operatic tradition, no choir of angels sings as Marguerite ascends into the radiance that lies on the other side of the heavenly gates. Instead the curtain falls on darkness: Faustus 'sinks into the darkness and it is all dark and the little boy and the little girl sing' (ibid.) their strangely pleading, suspenseful, unknowing song.

Busoni's *Doktor Faust*, I earlier suggested, was a reflection of the political history of the period of its composition, begun in 1914 and completed in 1925. Stein wrote *Doctor Faustus Lights the Lights* as Hitler annexed Austria, completing it as the last Jews to escape that country fled to France and England, and in the daily expectation of the outbreak of war. Busoni's *Faust*, an allegory suitable to the peace following what was believed to be the war to end all wars, ends in resurrection. Stein's *Doctor Faustus Lights the Lights* begins there as Faustus, however reluctantly, 'cures' Marguerite Ida and Helena Annabel. It ends with his self-determined act of murder, an act that balances and negates the opening. Her opera links technological knowledge, sexual knowledge and the knowledge of the crowd to ask what happens when the viper, symbol of the 'temptation' of all three and of their simultaneously healing and destructive capacities, changes hands. The deaths and the pleading uncertainty of the children's voices singing in the dark bode ill for its use in the hands of the new sun god. 'There is too much fathering going on just now', Stein had written two years earlier of political authority,

> and there is no doubt about it fathers are depressing. Everybody nowadays is a father, there is father Mussolini and father Hitler and father Roosevelt and father Stalin . . . and father Blum and father Franco is just commencing now and there are ever so many more ready to be one. . . . The periods of the world's history that have always been most dismal ones are the ones where fathers were looming and filling up everything.   (*EA*, p. 133)

Such a period seems to begin at the conclusion of *Doctor Faustus Lights the Lights*, finished as Stein, with the rest of the Western world, waited for war. 'It is all dark' and her libretto does not let us see what will happen now that the viper is the possession of a new public idol; but it does work through the significance of the serpent's sting, it does tell us what it means, in terms of her contemporary experience and perception, to feel 'biblical'. Knowing that, Stein was able to return to the manuscript of *Ida A Novel*.

Notes

1. Letter, Gertrude Stein to Robert Haas, postmarked 17 May 1937 (YCAL).
2. *Ida A Novel*, MS notebooks III, IV, VI (YCAL). The eleven MS notebooks of *Ida* have been numbered at Yale in the order in which their passages appear in the published novel and not in the order of their composition. The interconnections and overlaps of the several MSS, including *Doctor Faustus Lights the Lights*, that Stein was working on during the period of the several drafts of *Ida* are both extensive and informative as to her

working methods. I outline them fully in Shirley Neuman, *Gertrude Stein* (London: Macmillan, forthcoming). For the purposes of this essay, I give an abbreviated chronology.

May 1937–December 1937: (1) three, possibly four, drafts of openings of the first version of *Ida A Novel* (described in this essay as the first version of the novel); (2) *Picasso*.

February 1938–4 May 1938: (1) Act I of *Doctor Faustus Lights the Lights*; (2) 'A Portrait of Daisy/To Daisy On Her Birthday', incorporated almost immediately into (3) 'Lucretia Borgia'.

4 May–20 June 1938: (1) a sketch 'Ida', published in *The Boudoir Companion: Frivolous, Sometimes Venomous Thoughts on Men, Morals and Other Women*, ed. Page Cooper (New York: Farrar and Rinehart, 1938); (2) Acts II and III of *Doctor Faustus Lights the Lights*.

Summer–December 1938: (1) 'Arthur and Jenny' (which proves to be the second version of *Ida A Novel*); (2) overture for *Doctor Faustus Lights the Lights* and additional monologue for Act I, scene ii (written either in early October 1938 or January/early February 1939); (3) *The World is Round*.

January–June 1939: (1) 'Arthur and Jenny', further work; (2) French nightclub owner Agnes Capri is interested in using 'Deux Soeurs qui ne sont pas soeurs' for a musical setting and Stein writes for her instead 'Superstitions', incorporated into the published version of *Ida* in 1940.

July (?)–November 1939: (1) *Paris France*; (2) 'Arthur and Jenny', or the third version of the novel, *Ida A Novel* (developed out of 'Arthur and Jenny').

December 1939–June 1940: (1) 'My Life with Dogs', incorporated into the published version of *Ida A Novel*; (2) *To Do: A Book of Alphabets and Birthdays*; (3) the third and published version of *Ida A Novel*.

3. Letter, Gertrude Stein to Thornton Wilder, postmarked 8 Dec 1937 (YCAL).
4. Letter, Gertrude Stein to Thornton Wilder, postmarked 11 May 1938 (YCAL).
5. Berners, who had written the music for the 1937 production of Stein's *The Wedding Bouquet*, had commissioned the libretto. When the Second World War began, he found it impossible to write music and the score for *Doctor Faustus* was never composed.
6. Letter, Stein to Wilder, postmarked 11 May 1938 (YCAL).
7. The 'overture' is the opening of the opera to 'The Ballet' (*DF*, pp. 89–91); the additional material for Act I, scene ii, is the lines from the beginning of the scene to the second recurrence of 'oh dear yes I am here' (pp. 95–6).
8. Letter, Gertrude Stein to Lindley Hubbell, 4 Nov 1933, quoted in Richard Bridgman, *Gertrude Stein in Pieces* (New York: Oxford University Press, 1970) p. 292. The association of snakebite with the Bible makes its final appearance in Stein's writing during the months following the completion of *Doctor Faustus*, in the opening chapters of 'Arthur and Jenny'. But there the incident is simply a statement that

Jenny was bitten, with the added remark that 'It felt like the Bible' (YCAL). The implications of this feeling having been worked out in *Doctor Faustus*, it no longer proves a stumbling block.

9. Bridgman, *Gertrude Stein in Pieces*, p. 292.
10. Oliver Wendell Holmes, 'A Second Preface' to *Elsie Venner: A Romance of Destiny* (1861; New York: Dolphin Books, Doubleday, n.d.) p. 9.
11. Hence the title of the second version of the novel: 'Arthur and Jenny'. Arthur is a king and Ida/Jenny first makes a career out of remarrying in this version. The media's mythologising of the royal romance is also signalled by the name *Jenny*, a diminutive of *Guinevere*.
12. Laurence Irving, *Henry Irving: The Actor and his World* (London: Faber and Faber, 1951) pp. 468–9.
13. Bridgman, *Gertrude Stein in Pieces*, p. 290.
14. All three, for example, are cited by Gerald Berners in a letter to Gertrude Stein, 15 Oct 1938 (YCAL).
15. *London Mercury*, xxxv, 210 (Apr 1937) 622–3.
16. See n. 9.
17. The simultaneous pathos and comedy of Stein's libretto found a response in Berners, who wanted to make the music for the opening of this scene very romantic so as to increase the comic effect of anti-climax when Marguerite Ida and Helena Annabel wishes for a chair (undated letter to Gertrude Stein, YCAL).
18. The printed text is in error here; I follow the MS and TS.
19. Allegra Stewart, *Gertrude Stein and the Present* (Cambridge, Mass.: Harvard University Press, 1967) p. 165, notes the dual creative and destructive aspects of the viper.
20. Gertrude Stein to W. G. Rogers, in W. G. Rogers, *When This You See Remember Me: Gertrude Stein in Person* (New York and Toronto: Rinehart, 1948) p. 23.
21. The only extant complete manuscript of the *Boudoir Companion* 'Ida' is a fair copy of thirty-one single sheets (YCAL) to which was clipped a letter (since catalogued) from Page Cooper, editor of the volume. That letter lets us date the piece very exactly. Itself dated 9 May 1938, it describes the projected *Companion* and asks Stein for a contribution. Stein wrote the sketch in response to the request; she drafted some of it on the letter itself. A further letter from Page Cooper, dated 29 May 1938, acknowledges its receipt. Allowing time for the letters to travel between New York and Paris, this means Stein wrote 'Ida' in the third week of May 1938.

    The *Boudoir Companion* 'Ida' has previously been confused with the first draft of *Ida A Novel* and erroneously dated 1937. Stein listed 'Ida' as a 1937 piece in the draft of a bibliographical update, a copy of which is in the YCAL uncatalogued papers. But the 'Ida' referred to in this bibliography and in the letters of 1937 was in fact the first draft of the novel, titled *Ida A Novel* (in its second version it became 'Arthur and Jenny', and in its third, published version reverted to the original title). The circumstances favouring this error were compounded by the fact that Page Cooper's initial letter of inquiry had been clipped to the manuscript of the *Boudoir Companion* 'Ida' which remained for many years among the uncatalogued Stein papers (YCAL).

22. Gertrude Stein to W. G. Rogers, in Rogers, *When This You See Remember Me*, p. 168. The icon of Ida, haloed and holding the artificial viper, may owe more than a little to the 1930s logo of Columbia Pictures with its sentimentalised allusion to the Statue of Liberty, whom it represents holding a torch which sinuously replicates the coils of a serpent and from which electric lights 'halo' out across the screen.

23. Such an allusion seems more consistent with the interests of contemporary feminists than with most of Stein's *oeuvre*. And, in fact, critics have been careful about feminist readings of Stein's works, concluding that she identified herself with male roles in both her professional and personal life. But, as her renown gave her a financial and personal power greater than any she had ever known, she did begin to write in her own female person. Throughout the 1930s, she associated war-mongering with patriarchal government and eventually she would wittily and subversively appropriate patriarchal religion to feminist ends (using, for example, Augustine's description of the Church as 'the mother of us all' to title her opera about Susan B. Anthony).

24. Stewart, *Gertrude Stein and the Present*, p. 162.

25. Ibid., p. 163.

26. Betsy Alayne Ryan, *Gertrude Stein's Theatre of the Absolute* (Ann Arbor: University of Michigan Research Press, 1984) p. 128, notes 'parallels' between the character of Faustus and Stein in her 'identity' crisis. Like Bridgman (*Gertrude Stein in Pieces*, pp. 289–96) and like Stewart in her Jungian interpretation (*Gertrude Stein and the Present*, pp. 141–87), Ryan reads Doctor Faustus as the central (or the only) character in the play, to whom all other characters are secondary or of whom they are even a part (Stewart). My own reading, grounded as it is in the development of the opera out of the temporarily abandoned novel, stresses the 'Ida' character as equal to Doctor Faustus in the dramatic action of the libretto.

12

When the Time Came

bpNICHOL

AN ENTRANCE MONOLOGUE

My original ambition was to take the first chapter of *Ida* & go thru it showing how the construction of Stein's sentences & paragraphs is twinned to what it is she is saying; how, in short, her saying says. I'd thot 'first chapter' because in an earlier essay ('Some Sentences, Paragraphs & Punctuation on Sentences, Paragraphs & Punctuation'[1]) I'd gone into the first page of *Ida* fairly thoroughly, albeit from a different point of view, & the sheer symmetry of moving from the first page to the first chapter definitely appealed to me. The reality of what I'm going to do has turned out differently from its intended reality largely because of the approach I elected to take, which is to say the approach I elected to *try* (& I'll put the emphasis there – I'm going to *try*) – to deal thoroughly with the first five pages of *Ida*. I want to deal with Stein's writing in its *real* context which is the flux & flow of her actual texts. I *don't* want to extract her meaning so much as slow your reading of the text down thru the use of that ancient & beneficent device, the extensive commentary, forcing you to linger over the deliberateness of her craft, & show you how, tho she was whimsical & had a highly developed sense of play, the whimsy & the play were part of an over-all & continuous strategy of engagement with some of the central issues of any writer's writing: the role of the I; the relationship of the role of the I to the function of narrative time; the whole issue of narrative time in general. I confined myself to five pages because I decided finally that what I was interested in developing was a general strategy for reading Stein, trying to convey to you the excitement I feel when I read her & why I feel it, & given that, that I was more interested in doing a few pages carefully, at a pace we *all* could absorb them, than doing a whole bunch of pages hastily. I'd also like to emphasise that I include my own I in there when I say 'all', because my guide was the feeling in me after five pages that that was a hell of a lot to absorb, & why didn't I leave the next few pages for another lecture, or another critic even, but leave off at a point where the I & the we could both see clearly what was happening.

When I was much younger than I am now, chronologically speaking, but about the same age mentally, tho without the experience I've accumulated since then, I started writing a book on Gertrude Stein's theories of personality as revealed in her early opus *The Making of Americans*. The general scheme was to go thru & extract the many & very clear things she'd said about personality types & demonstrate both the consistency & accuracy of her particular classification system. This is easy to do; it would just take a gross amount of time – say two years or so if you were working at it full tilt. I finished two chapters of the work, sketched out an additional four, even published the initial two, & then abandoned the project. It took me awhile to see why I'd abandoned it, but the why is very important to what I'm going to talk about today, so it's worth taking a moment or two to talk specifically about that point. Now you'll have noticed I said 'talk' when here I am rather obviously reading to you from some prepared notes, prepared sentences in this case, so right away you're grasping the principle of a real-time fiction. The writer is finally a writer. She/he is not a talker. Even tho this is only the third time I've presented these words to an audience, I am *presenting* them – virtually the same ones as in the other times – I am not talking/creating in any spontaneous sense. Tho it's clearly this I addressing you, this I is using the words the I managed to write down in its hotel room on English Bay one late November afternoon (tho of course right now, in the time of the writing, it's today on English Bay & I'm imagining a you which is tomorrow & other days in the future & me saying, or you reading, these words). Therefore I say, & I just said (whether in an oral or a print sense), this whole talk is a kind of fiction. And it's precisely this borderline between the real life of the I & the I's existence in narrative time, any narrative's time, that was one of Stein's central concerns. She was exploring the continuous present & she wanted writing to occupy a continuous present. She very specifically asked us all in her *Geographical History of America*, 'Oblige me by not beginning. Also by not ending' (*GHA*, p. 157). I.e. – continue. Continue continuously. Give the text the reality of its existence as an object & let that object be continuously present to you – timeless in that sense. So how could I continue extracting? I was violating Stein's text when I did that, the very spirit of her text, & I was, of course, proving the validity of Heisenberg's Principle of Uncertainty as it applied to literature. By extracting I was bringing the text to a dead halt & we were no longer observing it as it was & therefore our observations ceased to have any validity. We're in danger of that even in what we're going to do today but at least in this case I'm going to encourage you to, if you feel like it, read on ahead of me & just let what I'm saying drift in & out of your own relationship to the text. Don't let me stop the particularity of that relationship. Just let me help if the help's helpful. That was one of the things that struck me in Grade 8 when Miss Nethercut, our English teacher, would be reading from Charles Dickens' *Oliver Twist* & we weren't supposed to read on ahead, we were supposed to stay with her & she'd stop every few minutes & say 'Barrie' or 'June' she'd say 'where am I?' & you'd have to have your finger on the correct spot. Don't keep your finger on the spot. It doesn't matter if you miss what *I'm* saying because it's what Stein's saying that's important. I'm going to be insisting the same information in different ways because that's what Stein did & you'll get the real flux of the definite particles if you simply read away. Okay. Here we go. This is a reading of the first five pages of *Ida* entitled 'When the Time Came'.

THE DEFINITE PARTICLES

Resist the temptation to jump too far ahead in terms of knowledge.
i.e. Let the net of information arise mainly from the text at hand.
Read the book you're **reading.**

This is the announcement of what Stein proposes to deal with, that the self, the Id(e)a of I, & tIme, are inseparable, but that the I exists beyond notions of sIngularity.

THERE WAS a baby born named Ida. Its mother held it with her hands to keep Ida from being born but when the time came Ida came. And as Ida came, with her came her twin, so there she was Ida-Ida.

The mother was sweet and gentle and so was the father. The whole family was sweet and gentle except the great-aunt. She was the only exception.

But the exception becomes the rule. Stein allows us some foreshadowing here by implication.

This whole opening is very rich & dense. What is being dealt with is the notion of 'self-consciousness' & the idea that the 'self' also births the 'not-self', that those who never confront the I/I remain sweet & gentle, that only the great-aunt, who bore twins & buried them under the pair tree, the one who faced the **issue** of a doubleness, is different, & makes others feel funny.

This is the reannouncement of the 'two', picking up from the opening page's Ida–Ida twins theme & echoing the pun on pair as where the two's been buried. These types of punning, underlinings & recapitulations are underlined in the grandfather's statement about trees – 'tree' is always the same (repeats itself) but then 'in a little while' you come to see how each 'tree' is unique (insists itself) & 'a cherry tree does not look like a pear tree'. Stein is drawing on a natural model to once again insist her distinction between repetition and insistence.

This figure of the old woman becomes oracular precisely because she is old & has, therefore, knowledge of what *both* young & old mean.

The cherry tree can be taken as a pun on 'cheery' & hence 'sweet & gentle' & hence, too, 'innocence' in all its senses which loops back to 'cherry'.

An old woman who was no relation and who had known the great-aunt when she was young was always telling that the great-aunt had had something happen to her oh many years ago, it was a soldier, and then the great-aunt had had little twins born to her and then she had quietly, the twins were dead then, born so, she had buried them under a pear tree and nobody knew.

Nobody believed the old woman perhaps it was true but nobody believed it, but all the family always looked at every pear tree and had a funny feeling.

The grandfather was sweet and gentle too. He liked to say that in a little while a cherry tree does not look like a pear tree.

It was a nice family but they did easily lose each other.

So Ida was born and a very little while after her parents went off on a trip and never came back. That was the first funny thing that happened to Ida.

The days were long and there was nothing to do.

Here we expect the word 'trees' to occupy the fourth position but instead we find it buried in the word 'streets'. 'trees' become 'streets' even as a 'cherry tree' does not become a 'pear tree'. In each insistence of a thing some transformation must take place. Otherwise it is simply a repetition.

She saw the moon and she saw the sun and she saw the grass and she saw the streets.

The first time she saw anything it frightened her. She saw a little boy and when he waved to her she would not look his way.

She liked to talk and to sing songs and she <u>liked to</u> **change places. Wherever she was she always** <u>liked to</u> **change places. Otherwise there was nothing to do all day. Of course she went to bed early but even so she always could say, what shall I do** <u>now, now</u> **what shall I do.**

Here is part of Stein's theory of narrative & her theory of personality. The I(da) is always changing places. And indeed in this story each time an Ida is mentioned you are never sure which Ida. Each recurrence is *not* a repetition but a fresh insistence & hence a fresh revelation.

Once you realise & accept that Stein is dealing with **insistence,** not repetition, then it's clear that two different 'now's' are being pointed to – two different time periods. The comma between them is used to mark the time shift, to underline the time shifts any narrative contains.

And thus arises this entire paragraph, a commentary on time.

Thus also the following paragraph's insistence that *Ida* is not *idle* but is as a day is – 'always the same day'. Yet it is important to remember that Ida *is* Ida, & that the *now*, *now* structure parallels the *day*, *day* & *Ida*, *Ida* samenesses & differences. Each is a discrete unit of time & being, tho they have the same name. *Ida* is not *idle* but she is *Ida* & these are not exactly the same.

Some one told her to say no matter what the day is it always ends the same day, no matter what happens in the year the year always ends one day.

Ida was not idle but the days were always long even in winter and there was nothing to do.

Ida lived with her great-aunt not in the city but just outside.

Ida was not idle, &, in fact, as the earlier sentence made clear, 'always could say, what shall I do now, now what shall I do'. Which of course is a graphing of the I in motion, the I insisting Itself.

Here we see how the exception becomes the rule, becomes the ruler of Ida's life, as the great-aunt, who is linked to Ida–Ida thru the pair tree, becomes the one who raises Ida & Ida, the one by whom her days are ruled.

Everything is **transformed.** Things become like other things. Each thing/episode/experience has its separate existence & is transformed within it. This is the notion 'insistence in narrative', that as you move forward & encounter the same words/ideas in new constructions and configurations they are different & have a new existence. It is this very difference in each moment that must be conveyed if one is to have a complete description.

She was very young and as she had nothing to do she walked as if she was tall as tall as any one. Once she was lost that is to say a man followed her and that frightened her so that she was crying just as if she had been lost. In a little while that is some time after it was a comfort to her that this had happened to her.

She did not have anything to do and so she had time to think about each day as it came. She was very careful about Tuesday. She always just had to have Tuesday. Tuesday was Tuesday to her.
They always had plenty to eat. Ida always hesitated before eating. That was Ida.

She has time to contemplate the natural insistence – each day as it comes. And these days, as we have seen, are I days, the discrete units of the I's existence. They are also Ideas.

to do,
Tuesday, which is, of course,
Two's day or Ida, I day which is also the 'They' that opens the next pair-agraph (& each is the graphing of that pair Ida/Ida). 'Tuesday was Tuesday to her'; the same & different each time she encountered it.

Stein makes use of the doubleness of this little logic loop. Everything is *not* Two, yet *is* Two & yet, too, is one. Really, of course, it is 1 plus 1. But it is not Two.

Indeed here is a third 1 who restates the theme of I & I's desire to dIalogue with self. I talks to I. Thus for any of us there is an experience within self of 'I?' 'da?'. Q & A.

One day it was not Tuesday, two people came to see her great-aunt. They came in very carefully. They did not come in together. First one came and then the other one. One of them had some orange blossoms in her hand. That made Ida feel funny. Who were they? She did not know and she did not like to follow them in. A third one came along, this one was a man and he had orange blossoms in his hat brim. He took off his hat and he said to himself here I am, I wish to speak to myself. Here I am. Then he went on into the house.

Ida remembered that an old woman had once told her that she Ida would come to be so much older that not anybody could be older, although, said the old woman, there was one who was older.

Orange blossoms were & are associated with marriage (my mother's wedding ring had them clustered on it) & thus a third fruit/tree/sexual &/or romantic word is added (i refer here to its *associational* net & *not* to some private symbolism of Stein's). The 'or' of 'orange' (part of the 'either/or' *two* term formulation) is also important.

This reiterates a point Stein made in *The Making of Americans*, that we are never to ourselves as anything other than young men & women in our consciousness of self. That the idea of 'older' is something only the 'old' can convey to us. This is underlined later in the text by Ida's growing older leading to her being sixteen. It is those from whom time is almost over that the concept 'old' is fully revealed to.

Ida began to wonder if that was what was now happening to her. She wondered if she ought to go into the house to see whether there was really any one with her great-aunt, and then she thought she would act as if she was not living there but was somebody just coming to visit and so she went up to the door and she asked herself is any one at home and <u>when they that is she</u> <u>herself</u> said to herself no there is nobody at home she decided not to go in.

That was just as well because orange blossoms were funny things to her great-aunt just as pear trees were funny things to Ida.

Here the theyness of the she is drawn out as is indeed the whole question of whether anyONE is in the house with the great-aunt. The I's continual strategy of creating a not-I, another self which comes to visit the house in which the I lives, & then abiding by its judgements, is sketched.

And only a few paragraphs earlier we'd heard how the orange blossoms in the one person's hand 'made Ida feel funny'. Since they are funny things to both Ida & her great-aunt we are pointed back to that sense of how the *one* has the potential to become more than one. One pair-agraph about pair trees &/or ange blossoms, the potential for more than one in one. Particularly when we remember it is *one* of the *two* who come in *one-by-one* (one bi one (& hence *two*) that has the orange blossoms, & the man who wishes to speak to himself.

The other point here is that 'orange blossoms' are not 'orange blossoms' when they mean 'marriage'. i.e. 'When is a door not a door? When it's ajar'. This is a transformation that happens thru the *insistence* of multiple meanings (i.e. *NOT* symbolism).

The one-bi-one pun leads us into this whole statement about, specifically, sexual choice &, more generally, the notion of what constitutes choice (as in the earlier choosing to be Ida Ida, or I/not-I). Love is blind, and blind to the issue him or her. Determinist & absolutist psychologies do not allow for that. Love is born blind. Age has nothing to do with it. (It is also worth remembering Stein's aphorism: 'I am I because my little dog knows me.' There is the notion that in the twinning, the recognition of the other, the not-I, is what brings the I into its true existence. And what is Love but that recognition, that blind sighting.)

And so Ida went on growing older and then she was almost sixteen and a great many funny things happened to her. Her great-aunt went away so she lost her great-aunt who never really felt content since the orange blossoms had come to visit her. And now Ida lived with her grandfather. She had a dog, he was almost blind not from age but from having been born so and Ida called him Love, she liked to call him naturally she and he liked to come even without her calling him.

It was dark in the morning any morning but since her dog Love was blind it did not make any difference to him.

It is true he was born blind nice dogs often are. Though he was blind naturally she could always talk to him.

This is Stein's statement of pronominal choice (a continuation of the one-bi-one), that some she's quite naturally want to call *him* she, that Love, that dog, is blind to the categories people would place on it . . . 'it did not make any difference to him'.

(I'll pause briefly simply to point out that this line is also an injunction to the reader & as such reinforces the approach we are taking to the text here.)

One day she said. Listen Love, but listen to everything and listen while I tell you something.

Yes Love she said to him, you have always had me and now you are going to have two, I am going to have a twin yes I am Love, I am tired of being just one and when I am a twin one of us can go out and one of us can stay in, yes Love yes I am yes I am going to have a twin. You know Love I am like that when I have to have it I have to have it. And I have to have a twin, yes Love.

The house that Ida lived in was a little on top of a hill, it was not a very pretty house but it was quite a nice one and there was a big field next to it and trees at either end of the field and a path at one side of it and not very many flowers ever because the trees and the grass took up so very much room but there was a good deal of space to fill with Ida and her dog Love and anybody could understand that she really did have to have a twin.

She began to sing about her twin and this is the way she sang.

On a 'One' day she says to him 'now you are going to have two'.

Here there is the double notion that the self has selves (six Is in three IIves) & that in love we are twinned ('yes Love yes I am yes I am'), that the beloved is a twin I (en-*twin*-ed). Love is the twin ('I have to have a twin, yes Love').

There both is & there isn't space. It is a question of point-of-view. Point-of-view is itself a means of transformation, the 'given' in translation.

Stein is also playing here with the whole notion of description & its inaccuracy on the level of language. Even as she moves out to describe the house her description keeps contradicting itself . . . 'the trees and the grass took up so very much room but there was a good deal of space to fill . . .'.

This is the opening theme restated, that time enters with the I, & here the additional complexity or notion that it enters with the death of the not-I. The possibility of the not-I is born with the I & inside time is not-I whereas tIme is I.

Following on the heels of the earlier 'I have to have a twin' (the anticipation), we have the birth & the contemplated death of Ida Ida.

Oh dear oh dear Love, that was her dog, if I had a twin well nobody would know which one I was and which one she was and so if anything happened nobody could tell anything and lots of things are going to happen and oh Love I felt it yes I know it I have a twin.

And then she said Love later on they will call me a suicide blonde because my twin will have dyed her hair. And then they will call me a murderess because there will come the time when I will have killed my twin which I first made come. If you make her can you kill her. Tell me Love my dog tell me and tell her.

This is a rather complicated play on 'love me, love my dog' but the dog *is* love & in love the I is twinned & the instruction is to both I's & to the I that is other, that love must flow both ways, that tho she made her she didn't make her. The I must love the other I.

But there is also a warning not to take this as autobiography ('tell me and tell her') because in fiction (& *Ida is* a novel) you create all kinds of not-I's. A little later on in the novel she says, 'Little by little she knew how to read and write and really she said and she was right it was not necessary for her to know anything else.' Everything she or you or I could want to know is there in the writing. The writing is, in that sense, self-contained.

Thru all the punning & word play we are constantly reminded that there is nothing funny about Ida but that funny things do happen to her, & certain things give her, & other people, funny feelings. This constant emphasis on the meanings of the word 'funny' points to the doubleness of all the play. Stein knows the doubleness of her entendres but she is not trying to be funny ('There was [is] nothing funny about Ida [the novel, in this case] but funny things did happen to her.' Serious punning).

This is rhyme, a reassertion of the issue of sexual choice, & a play on the classic palindrome 'a man, a plan, a canal – panama'.

Like everybody Ida had lived not everywhere but she had lived in quite a number of houses and in a good many hotels. It was always natural to live anywhere she lived and she soon forgot the other addresses. Anybody does.

There was nothing funny about Ida but funny things did happen to her.

Ida had never really met a man but she did have a plan.

That was while she was still living with her great-aunt. It was not near the water that is unless you call a little stream water or quite a way off a little lake water, and hills beyond it water. If you do not call all these things water then there where Ida was living was not at all near water but it was near a church.

It was March and very cold. Not in the church that was warm.

By this point in the narrative Stein is playing with the **language** of description. Each assertion is followed by its flaw if considered as a logical statement & the useless generality & hence uselessness of most description (precisely because it is inaccurate on the level of language) is pointed to.

Similarly in her discussion of where Ida lived, Stein asserts that in the flow of life (& there is an equation here to the flow of reading) one quite simply forgets one's former address. You are moving on & 'it was always natural to live anywhere she lived'. So in the reading, as you move on you are forgetting things addressed to you as reader &, unless you are going to extract plot, this is natural.

AN EXIT MONOLOGUE

There is no conclusion to all this which is exactly as it should be since what we have been dealing with here is a beginning. Indeed I have found that each time I do this with a group of people additional meanings emerge. In a recent presentation Marlene Goldman pointed out how, when Stein says (or has Ida say), 'I am going to have a twin yes I am Love, I am tired of being just one and when I am a twin one of us can go out and one of us can stay in . . .', she is also addressing her own shift away from the autobiographical works & back towards fiction. She is precisely interested in the interface between the authorial I and the fiction's I (the I of Ida &, as a contracted statement, 'I'd'a done it if I had time' shows us how the I of the character is the I of 'I would have', the I of the conditional phrase, the phrase in which we express the fictional possibility). Kris Nakamura[2] also pointed out how the Ida in the first Random House edition is decoratively glyphed at the top of each page as follows:

$$I^D{}_A$$

In this way both the I & the A achieve their singularity & the D is brought into question. She proposed it as the first letter of a two letter configuration viz:

$$I^D{}_A{}^L$$

where D is Death (& one condition of the not-I) & L is Love (another condition of the not-I). These exist at this moment simply as thots stirred by that most recent talk. There are more. Obviously I do not agree with critics like Marianne Hauser who said in her review of *Ida* at the time of its first appearance, 'To look for an underlying idea . . . seems as futile as to look for apples in an orange tree.'[3] Once you accept that everything in Stein is deliberate gesture, forms part of a consistent & evolving whole, Stein makes sense, an almost perfect sense.[4]

Notes

1. *Open Letter*, 5th ser., 3 (Summer 1982) 17–23.
2. Marlene Goldman's and Kris Nakamura's observations were made after I delivered this lecture to David Young's 'Dream Class' (North York, spring 1983). Kris's suggestion of 'IDAL' is, perhaps, contradicted by Stein when she says that 'Ida was not idle'.
3. Marianne Hauser, 'Miss Stein's Ida', *New York Times*, 16 Feb 1941, section 6, p. 7.
4. As a final note I would add my thanks to the people at Simon Fraser I first delivered this lecture to, & particularly to Juliet McLaren & Barry Maxwell who helped me clarify the business of the orange blossoms.

   Passages from Gertrude Stein's *Ida* are reproduced from the first (1941) Random House edition. 'When the Time Came' has previously been published in *Line*, 1 (Spring 1983) 46–61.

13

The Mother of Us All and American History

ROBERT K. MARTIN

Critical appreciation of Gertrude Stein's last major work, the opera *The Mother of Us All*, has been hindered by a simplistic view of it as barely disguised autobiography. The work convinces any reader or listener of Stein's deep sympathy for her principal character, Susan B. Anthony, and its place at the end of her career encourages a reading of the text as Stein's 'valedictory'.[1] None the less, to read the opera as a work about Stein herself, in which Anthony is simply 'equivalent to Gertrude Stein',[2] is to rob the text of its rich historical allusiveness and to diminish Stein's attempt at a commentary on American history. A careful reading of the opera makes it clear that this work is a part of Stein's last creative stage, in which she moved beyond her modernism to an art that was both representational and firmly situated in historical space.

What little commentary there has been on the opera has regularly denied the work's reflection and refraction of history. Michael Hoffman's account is the most misleading, and it also indicates the way in which the autobiographical reading of the opera is part of a general accusation of self-serving: 'Stein's point in this opera has little to do with history, American or otherwise, except in the way history can be made to buttress her assessment of herself.'[3] Since Stein's presentation of time is not linear nor disjunct, since she in other words makes regular use of a 'continuous present' (*CE*, p. 31)[4] that ultimately derives from Henri Bergson's *simultanéité* by way of William James, she might be thought to have no place for an exploration of history. However, it is precisely her concept of time, in which past and present merge into one, that enables her to see a living relationship between characters drawn from 150 years of American history. Her central metaphor for this relationship is generative and maternal, a way of stressing the organic nature of the interplay between now and then, in which then remains alive through memory and consciousness.

Although the idea of an American identity had been important to Stein throughout much of her career, it gained particular importance for her during the Second World War, when she felt a strong identification with the American soldiers fighting in her adopted France. The origins of *The Mother of Us All* can be seen clearly in *Brewsie and Willie*, her book devoted to those American soldiers. It is in them, and through their awakening, that Stein places her hope for the future. In *Brewsie and Willie* Janet is reading a book about Susan B. Anthony, and she reports to the others that Anthony's liberation of women is to be seen as an act equivalent to the emancipation of black slaves: 'before she came along women were just like Negroes, before they were freed from slavery' (*B&W*, p. 88). The lesson to be learned from Anthony's life is the need 'to make a noise, a loud noise' (p. 89). Stein does not identify the principal accomplishment of Anthony as the narrower goal, achieved only after her death, of voting rights for women, but rather as the creation of a new sense of self, the ability to make oneself heard and to speak for oneself. This achievement by women is for Stein a fulfilment of the original democratic and emancipatory mission of the United States.

The Mother of Us All is in many ways Gertrude Stein's return to America, in spirit if not in flesh. It is an offering to her compatriots reaffirming her belief in a democratic America and defining the terms in which that American heritage can be reclaimed. The conclusion of *Brewsie and Willie*, Stein's address 'To Americans', suggests the continuity of American history and the nature of the post-war crisis facing America. Stein begins by remarking on the effect the G.I.s have had on her: 'they have made me come all over patriotic' (*B&W*, p. 113). But this response is not a new one, for 'I was always in my way a Civil War veteran' (ibid.). The claim is a fascinating one. Of course as a woman Stein, even had she been alive at the time, could not have been a veteran unless she had been disguised as a man. Men make wars and women survive them. But the events of the Civil War provided for the emergence of the Northern economic boom in which Stein's family prospered, as well as the westward expansion that brought them to California. Stein is thus in many ways the *product* of the Civil War, if not actually a veteran of it. At the same time, she is a veteran of that other, more enduring civil war, in which men regularly proclaim their dominance over women.

Stein's claims for the rights of women are thus based on her sense of herself as an American – that is, as a free individual with fundamental rights. 'Alice B. Toklas' in the *Autobiography* calls attention to 'how completely and entirely american' Stein was, and links this to her interest in the civil war, calling Stein 'a civil war general of either or both sides' (*ABT*, p. 19). The recognition of women's rights is thus the third stage in a tripartite revolution already marked by two principal events: the American Revolution, with its assertion of national rights to self-determination, and the American Civil War, with its accomplishment of the emancipation of black slaves. The final stage of American history's revolutionary programme will come with the freeing of women, an accomplishment that Stein identifies with the achievement of selfhood. The period following the Second World War is crucial for Stein because it offers the challenge of the decline of industrialism. European industrial societies such as England, she writes, 'have gone poor', while communism and socialism will not 'save you', since they are mass movements denying individual liberty. What she asks Americans of the post-war years to accomplish is 'to learn to produce without exhausting your country's wealth' and to turn from thinking of themselves as 'mass job workers' to 'learn[ing] to be individual' (*B&W*, p. 113).

Anthony is an appropriate heroine for Stein's 1946 works because she illustrates the failure of the Civil War to realise its potential for the union of black emancipation with women's freedom and because her own unconventional life represents the commitment to individual fulfilment joined with a sense of social justice that Stein believes may offer an alternative to the group identities of mid-twentieth-century America. Further, Anthony's own life showed the fallibility of a prosperity based on rapid industrial growth and cut off from the renewable resources of the earth. Stein's experiences as a war refugee in the French countryside reminded her of the fundamental necessity of the land, even as technology collapsed under military attack.

The maternal metaphor of the title of Stein's opera offers a particularly striking irony. It is indeed this single woman, whose most enduring relationship was with another woman, who is in the end 'the mother of us all'. Anthony's presentation of this idea of creativity is based upon the offering up of one life for others: one gives of oneself so that others may live ('I give my life, that is to say, I live my life every day' – *MOUA*, p. 65). Against this extraordinary spiritual fertility there is the sterility or impotence of traditional authority. As Lawrence puts it in *Brewsie and Willie*, 'we are being ruled by tired middle-aged people, tired business men, the kind who need pin-ups' (*B&W*, p. 89). The business men whose sexuality can be restored only by an artificial image of a woman are representative of an entire society lacking the ability of continued renewal. Against this false sexuality stands the figure of Susan B. Anthony, 'sexless' in conventional (male) terms, but ultimately restorative through a selfless power of love and sympathy.

The assertion of Anthony's fecundity is an important way of reaffirming a positive and self-sufficient sensuality for women. She is, however, not only the source of women's new identity, but also the 'mother of us all', as she offers the possibility of reclaiming what Stein has defined as an American heritage and has located in her simple G.I.s uncontaminated by the power drives of politics or property. Thus Richard Bridgman's claim[5] that the opera ends bleakly in the recognition of Anthony's sterility is outrageously misguided. What Anthony recognises at the end is not her failure, but the need to measure success or failure of the endeavour in the creation of new, free individuals rather than in particular material accomplishments. The new free self (free even to repudiate her memory) can be the only adequate tribute to her efforts. As Anthony's contemporary, Whitman, put it to his own *élève*, 'He most honors my style who learns under it to destroy the teacher. / The boy I love, the same becomes a man not through derived power but in his own right.'[6]

The Mother of Us All is a tribute to the memory of Susan B. Anthony, not merely as a disguised form of self-praise (although Stein certainly saw many similarities in their situations), but in recognition of her historic role. Anthony is important in the history of the American women's movement not only because of her long struggle for female suffrage, but also because she was the leader of those in the suffrage movement who wanted to enlarge their struggle to include 'the legal inequalities of marriage and the double standard of morals'.[7] Stein makes use of her figure in the opera not so much to depict a specific historic figure at a given point in her career as to capture the essence of a revolutionary spirit that figure incarnates.

The technique employed by Stein for this purpose is partly

linguistic. She makes use of the set phrases of American public life and political rhetoric in order to show, on the one hand, their possible realisation in the hands of a real democrat, and, on the other, their abuse when they become mere surface, cant phrases repeated without meaning. The words thus come alive again or are revealed as the mindless rote of the unthinking. This tactic is again foreshadowed in *Brewsie and Willie*, when Stein writes in her conclusion,

> Find out the reason why, look facts in the face, not just what they all say, the leaders, but every darn one of you so that a government by the people for the people shall not perish from the face of the earth, it wont, somebody else will do it if we lie down on the job . . . .   (*B&W*, p. 114)

Stein brilliantly mixes the clichés of popular advice ('look facts in the face'), folksy locutions ('every darn one of you'), and fragments from Lincoln's Gettysburg Address in a manner that both recalls the origins of her message in American political heritage and warns of its transformation into the blank phrases of Fourth of July rhetoric. It is a call for a radical democracy that is true to its past, and that can be awakened by an undermining of the surfaces of an abused language. At the same time the conclusion of the passage quoted suggests the dangers to that very tradition she is invoking.

In addition to this rhetorical strategy, the opera makes use of the American (and English) folk form of the pageant as a means of confronting history. This technique allows her to confront a single, largely static, timeless figure (Susan B. Anthony) with a series of minor, timebound characters. Thus Anthony confronts characters from John Adams, evoking the foundation of the American republic, through Daniel Webster and the pre-Civil War period, Andrew Johnson and Reconstruction, to Stein's own contemporaries and friends Virgil Thomson and Donald Gallup.

Although Anthony's final words are delivered from the grave, as it were, through her statue (or the public figure she has become), Stein does not allow her to become a mere historical presence. Instead, she humanises the character by her interest in the psychology of power, by her attribution to Anthony of a recognition of the limitations of the satisfaction of success. This in itself amounts to what we may think of as a feminising of historical inquiry, through a shift from the external to the internal, an insistence upon the importance of the personal along with the public. (The tactic is feminist, since it undercuts the usual assumptions of male discourse that success in the public sphere brings satisfaction, but it is of course by no means exclusively female: Whitman's 'When I heard at the close of the day', from 'Calamus', offers an interesting parallel.)

Stein also subverts traditional (male) historical narrative by her inclusion of a domestic interlude, in which Susan B. Anthony is portrayed at home with her companion Anne (based on the historical Anthony's friend Anna Shaw). The interlude divides the opera's two acts, and is a 'short story' rather than a dramatic text. The generic subversion is analogous to the thematic: Stein uses the interlude as a way of asserting the power of the personal and domestic. Creating her 'mother' to offset the historical 'fathers', she is not content to make her a male figure in skirts, for whom the private must be sacrificed to the public. Instead, her personal life is placed at the centre of her political life. (The effect of this strategy is somewhat diminished in the performing version of the opera, where the interlude is rewritten in dramatic form and placed as the prologue.) At the same time, that domesticity, in its imitation of heterosexual marriage, offers a reproach to Anthony and her belief in the necessity of individual action. As she puts it, despite her 'marriage' to Anne, 'I could never be one of two I could never be two in one as married couples do and can, I am but one all one, one and all one, and so I have never been married to any one' (*MOUA*, p. 75).

As Anthony herself, in the historic split in the women's movement in the post-Civil War years, placed the emphasis on marriage laws and the denial of women's property rights, so Stein's text centres not on the suffrage movement but on the nature of marriage as a social institution. She recognises that marriage is, as Engels pointed out, fundamentally a relationship of property. Early in the play, Jo the Loiterer's story of his marriage establishes, in a comic way, the connections. Drawing upon the traditional metaphors of nature, Stein creates this conversation:

Jo the Loiterer.	My wife, she had a garden.
Chris the Citizen.	Yes
Jo the Loiterer.	And I bought one.
Chris the Citizen.	A wife.
	No said Jo I was poor and I bought a garden.

(p. 54)

As long as women are seen as a means of production, they are a garden to be planted and reaped – cared for, yes, but only for their ability to produce. But Jo's wife is not content to be his property. As he explains, 'my wife said one tree in my garden was her tree in her garden' (ibid.). Jo assumes that purchasing the garden makes it his, while his wife argues for a community of property, in which the sharing of possessions becomes a model for the elimination of property altogether. Jo's wife was, as he says, 'funny', defining that quality in this way: 'you have to take all your money and all your jewels and put them near the door you have to go to bed then and leave the door ajar' (p. 55). Anthony's own experiences underlay this discussion: although her mother had inherited property, it was not placed in her name until the passage of the New York State Property Bill in 1848.[8]

Women's equality in marriage requires their ability to hold property; at the same time marriage is viewed by Stein as an inherently destructive institution that denies the self while remaining unable to eliminate the fundamental human experience of isolation. Although most of the opera is about marrying, it is clear that Stein's opposition is to the effects of marriage rather than the act itself: as Jenny Reefer says, 'I will not marry because if I did marry, I would be married' (p. 75). The linguistic play here is marvellous and underlines Stein's point effectively: the verb shifts from an active to a passive form, the past participle stressing the enclosing nature of the institution. But Stein wants to create a continuous present not only of language but also of self, an eternally renewing and transforming identity that cannot be confined to the permanent past of marriage. When Anne insists, hurt by Susan's denial of marriage, 'But I I have been, I have been married to what you have been to that one' (ibid.), her very language suggests the impossibility of arresting time. Anne has only been married to 'that one' – that is, what Anthony has been, and not what she is. The desire of marriage to freeze the other in a past time brings it inevitably into conflict with the need of the individual to change. As Susan explains to Anne, 'no one can be married to the present one, the one, the one, the present one' (ibid.). Although the evils of marriage are based on property laws and the inequality of the sexes, there is also something fundamentally impossible about the desire to make the impermanent permanent, a flaw that will mark the union of two women as much as that of a woman and a man.

This negative view of the relationship, with its clear parallels to her own long-term relationship with Alice B. Toklas, shows the extent to which Stein's late works reflect a major change in her thinking about the politics of sexuality. Her early male identification gives way here to a questioning of the entire drive to power over others, and makes The Mother of Us All one of her most politically engaged works. But the 'shift in sexual self-image toward greater acceptance of her gender'[9] can be traced back to the works of the 1930s, as she finds her way out of the trap of associating genius with masculinity and hence frees herself from adopting a 'mannish' role. The Mother of Us All is an acknowledgement of Stein's own indebtedness to her feminist progenitrixes and an affirmation of a fundamental right to freedom, now seen as the ultimate goal of the American Revolution, the Civil War and the women's movement.

Critics have been disturbed by what they take to be the opera's tone. Michael Hoffman claims that its language against men is 'vituperative',[10] and Richard Bridgman argues that what was merely 'contempt' for men becomes in the opera 'hostility'.[11] Such comments miss the point that what Anthony, and the text built around her life, criticise is not so much men as a patriarchal order. Stein's target is a way of thinking, one which has permitted the systematic exploitation of women and slaves for the benefit of white men, but one which has also paralysed men and made them into pompous cardboard figures of political oratory. Stein's linguistic practice is a way of combatting what Barthes calls the hierarchical maîtrise phrastique[12] or mastery of the sentence that links conventional style to patriarchal discourse. By a series of lateral movements, in which associated meaning or connotation (here extended by rhyme and sound patterns) comes to replace the linear order of fixed meaning, Stein liberates language from its service to Logos.

Male discourse is precisely that, male, as Stein shows. For instance, Daniel Webster addresses Susan B. Anthony in the third person as 'the honorable member' and employs the masculine pronoun when speaking of her. This is of course mere convention of parliamentary speech, and yet its use here, when Webster and Anthony are speaking only to each other, reveals the assumptions inherent in the 'generic' masculine. Speaking as he does, Webster must exclude women, since they have no access to speech. The language Webster employs is one in which fixed rules take priority over experience. Language in this form has ceased to function, and so quickly becomes the meaningless repeated phrases of patriotic speech. At the conclusion of a long speech into which he weaves fragments of songs such as 'The Battle Hymn of the Republic' and 'God Bless America', Webster answers Anthony's claim for the omission of the word 'male' from the Fourteenth Amendment by 'I say, that so long that the gorgeous ensign of the republic, still full high advanced, its arms and trophies streaming in their original luster not a stripe erased or polluted not a single star obscured' (*MOUA*, p. 82). Webster's claim for unity and preservation is based on simply ignoring women, on assuming that they are included in the generic, even though excluded in law. His abuse is as much of language as of human rights, for he makes the ideas of American republicanism over into empty signs. Language must retain its full playful sense of itself so that it can never be made over into rhetoric in this way.

If language can operate in this manner to inflate, it can also act to trivialise. The apparent term of affection 'dear' is applied to women in this way. Constance Fletcher's 'mad scene' of rejection, recalling Ophelia's, shows how such a repeated word of consolation, which becomes almost an epithet applied to her, comes to echo hollowly and ironically: 'be mine when I die, farewell to a thought, he left all alone, be firm in despair dear dear never share, dear dear, dear dear, I Constance Fletcher dear dear, I am a dear, I am dear dear I am a dear, here there everywhere. I bow myself out' (p. 56). Fletcher is a victim of such language and also a participant in it: she identifies with the very oppression that destroys her. When she speaks of Adams as 'this dear great man', Susan B. replies, 'Hush, this is slush' (p. 70). Although Adams adopts the language of infatuation to express his love for Fletcher ('I spill I spill over like a thrill and a trill') and claims that romantic love prevails over politics ('there is no cause in her presence' – p. 71), this is but the argument to the pedestal, which holds that men are really enthralled by women, and that women's power in love compensates for their lack of real power. But the truth of his position is expressed clearly when he transforms the opera's most famous words, Susan B.'s, 'When this you see remember me' (p. 59), into his own 'when this you see listen to me' (p. 71). If Susan B. counts on survival through memory and affection, he counts on survival through obedience. Language for Adams is power, and it is this kind of linguistic power that Stein's playfulness sets out to contest.

Much of the tone of the opera is delightfully comic, as in the appearance of the three political figures, Andrew Johnson, Thaddeus Stevens and Daniel Webster, as a 'Chorus of V. I. P.'

(p. 68). And yet the union of these historical figures is an indication of the way in which the interests of gender override all others. Probably the greatest crisis in the historic Anthony's life came when she realised that her campaign for women's rights, allied with a campaign for the emancipation of black slaves, resulted in a legal codification of the exclusion of women from the rights of citizenship. The *History of Woman Suffrage*, which Anthony co-edited, reports that she 'started for New York the moment she saw the propositions before Congress to put the word "male" into the National Constitution, and made haste to rouse the women in the East to the fact that the time had come to begin vigorous work again for woman's enfranchisement'.[13] The historical Stevens had in fact tried to include women in the Fourteenth Amendment,[14] but, as Stein depicts him, he is joined to the other men in their resistance to women's rights. The irony, which Stein places at the heart of her text, is that Anthony's fight for the rights of blacks leads to her own exclusion from public life. (As long as women were not specifically excluded from citizenship, they could perhaps claim it by implication.) Even black men choose to join their white male oppressors rather than the women who have fought for their rights. In Anthony's dream she sees a black man and woman:

Susan B.	Negro man would you vote if you only can and not she.
Negro Man.	You bet.
Susan B.	I fought for you that you could vote would you vote if they would not let me. (*MOUA*, p. 67)

This strong sense of historical betrayal underlies Stein's playful use of language and provides it with a dark context. The works of the last years of Gertrude Stein's life mark a significant modification in her attitude toward the relationship of text and world. It is as if the experience of the war had come as a terrible reminder of the degree to which language is embedded in, and a constituent part of, history. The formalist experiments of the Paris years in part gave way to a new literature of engagement, one which did not, of course, reject linguistic play, but one which sought to employ it as part of a critique of power. In many ways this amounts to a partial recuperation of the perspective of her early works, such as *Three Lives*, with its forceful expression of the oppressed lives of her female protagonists. There she had used her sense of a social reality as she had experienced it in Baltimore to give her access to a language that was inseparable from psychological truth, in a kind of thinking voice. The pursuit of that voice had been put aside in an attempt to capture the surface realities of experience, much in the manner of the cubists. But in her late works Stein once again saw language's potential to act as a means of power as well as a malleable source of pleasure. This did not lead her into a mimetic presentation of reality, but rather to a fractured form of representation, in which memory and dream are interwoven with fact, almost as if in a Marianne Moore poem. In *The Mother of Us All* her mostly 'real' characters are scattered across a largely imaginary landscape. By employing historical figures, Stein regrounds her art in the truth of experience, and thus permits her own linguistic strategies to perform their largest role as elements in a subversive strategy that challenges both patriarchal thinking and patriarchal structures.

In her figure of Susan B. Anthony, Stein gave expression to an historical struggle for emancipation – of language, of blacks, of women. By giving her psychological depth, Stein turned away from the traditional historical drama, or the Brechtian play of forces of history. Susan Anthony speaks as the lonely individual who has committed herself to a cause. At the same time she speaks for Stein's continuing belief in the necessity to preserve the self. Stein's reading of Anthony makes her into a figure of individual transformation, rather than of political change *en masse*. As Anthony reminds Jo the Loiterer, 'A crowd is never allowed but each one of you can come in' (*MOUA*, p. 70). This same belief in the centrality of the individual makes her wary of the process of co-option whereby even revolutionary figures such as Anthony (or Stein herself) are made over into safe figures of a public mythology. Thus Anthony's triumph, as marked by her statue 'in marble and gold', does not offer her satisfaction. For, as she asks herself, 'do I want what we have got' (p. 87). The 'success' of her movement brings about its end, and the achievement of a short-term goal (the vote) comes to replace the largest of objectives (the challenging of patriarchal authority ['Daniel was my father's name' – p. 53]). By obtaining male rights, Anthony wonders, do women simply 'become like men' (p. 81)? If so, what has been the point of her life?

Such questions had special meaning for Stein because of the extent to which she was herself 'male-identified'. Her belief that genius was by nature male had led her to identify herself as fundamentally male. At the same time she had retained a strong attachment to American political ideals of self-determination. In the last works, under the pressures of the Second World War, she attempted to look back both over her own career and over American history in an attempt to see both the potential and the failures. Her pageant for Susan B. Anthony is an attempt to assert a matrilineal heritage as important as that of the fathers who are usually taken to dominate American political discourse. She uses her opera to show that men have failed to fulfil the revolutionary potential of American history. She identifies this failure with a particular historical moment: the challenge of the first women's movement in the mid-nineteenth century. She offers in Susan Anthony a figure of maternal strength and constancy, but also a grieving mother mourning her children who have gone astray. Stein uses her opera to identify herself with her own traditions, at once American and feminist, and to recognise with sadness the difficulty in fulfilling them. Susan Anthony's final words suggest clearly that all one can do is offer up, as she has done, 'My long life, my long life' (p. 88). With those words, she rises out of history and into myth, in a radical revision of *das Ewig-Weibliche*. Anthony's career becomes another testament to the suffering, and heroism, of women throughout history and a statement of hope for some redemption from that historical nightmare.

Notes

1. Richard Bridgman, *Gertrude Stein in Pieces* (New York: Oxford University Press, 1970) p. 341.
2. Donald Sutherland, *Gertrude Stein: A Biography of her Work* (New Haven, Conn.: Yale University Press, 1951) p. 167n.
3. Michael J. Hoffman, *Gertrude Stein* (Boston, Mass.: Twayne, 1976) pp. 88–9.
4. See also the discussion in Sutherland, *Gertrude Stein: A Biography*, p. 133.
5. Bridgman, *Gertrude Stein in Pieces*, p. 345.
6. Walt Whitman, *Song of Myself*, 47.1233–4, in *Leaves of Grass*, 1855 edn, ed. Malcolm Cowley (New York: Penguin, 1976).
7. Ruth Evelyn Quebe, '*The Bostonians*: Some Historical Sources and their Implications', *Centennial Review* 25, 1 (Winter 1981) 95.
8. Ida Husted Harper, *The Life and Work of Susan B. Anthony* (Indianapolis: Hollenbeck Press, 1898) i, 46n.
9. Marianne DeKoven, *A Different Language: Gertrude Stein's Experimental Writing* (Madison: University of Wisconsin Press, 1983) p. 137.

10. Hoffman, *Gertrude Stein*, p. 90.
11. Bridgman, *Gertrude Stein in Pieces*, p. 341.
12. Roland Barthes, *Le Plaisir du texte* (Paris: Seuil, 1973) p. 81.
13. Elizabeth Cady Stanton, Susan B. Anthony and Matilda Joslyn Gage, *History of Woman Suffrage* (New York: Fowler and Wells, 1882) ii, 92.
14. Harper, *The Life and Work of Susan B. Anthony*, i, 250.

14

Three by Gertrude Stein

Edited by SHIRLEY NEUMAN

REALISM IN NOVELS

Of the three pieces published here, two – 'American Language and Literature' and 'Realism in Novels' – continue in the explanatory mode Stein had begun in 1926 with her first public lecture. Her method in these pieces is related to her method of characterisation in even her earliest novels: in that work she attempted to name and describe fully different categories of 'being' and different kinds of acting and much of the distinctiveness of the types comes from their implicit, and often explicit, comparison; in these late explanatory writings, she does much the same thing with national characteristics.

'Realism in Novels' was written in 1943. Stein wrote the beginning of a manuscript version of the complete piece in the same notebook as 'Look and Long', one of the one-act dramas she wrote for the local children during the war. ('Look and Long' is no. 545 and 'Realism in Novels' no. 546 in the 'Key to the *Yale Catalogue*, Part 4', as amended by Richard Bridgman in *Gertrude Stein in Pieces* – New York: Oxford University Press, 1970 – pp. 365–85.) She continued the manuscript on looseleaf sheets. I have identified this as 'MS 1' when noting variants. A second version of the end of the piece was written on looseleaf sheets; I identify this as 'MS 2'. A carbon copy of a typescript of the piece is in the uncatalogued Stein papers at YCAL. It is this typescript that I have followed in this transcription, noting the manuscript variants.

An excerpt from 'Realism in Novels' was printed in a folder announcing 'The Fifth Peters Rushton Seminar in Contemporary Prose and Poetry' (1952); this is its first complete publication.

After all there has to be realism in romance[1] and in novels. And the reason why is this. Novels have to resemble something and in order that they do there must be realism. The early novels and romances of America had to describe what they saw but they had to have a formula to express it and that formula came to them from England and from Spain. Romance as America lived it had at that time

something in common with romance as Spain had always known it
and as England knew it in the seventeenth and eighteenth century.
Until the civil war the literary influences were Spanish and English,
life was romantic as Spain knew it, life was romantic as English
sailors knew it. Then when the nineteenth century was well on its
way, life in America began to have a clearer logic, it needed
something that could be seen and known and could be the work of
one's hand.[2] And the romance, the fantasy of England and Spain,
the sentimental exageration of their humor, no longer had anything
to do with the clear outline and the logical exactness of American
life, and in the beginning of the latter half of the nineteenth century
the realism of French novelists[3] began to be more interesting to
them. De Maupassant's short stories and Zola's novels began to
mean more to them than the clouded fantastical imagery of England
and Spain, the young writers and the young readers wanted
realism. Of course they always had had a clear and resistant realism
and there France and America met, and there they had a great deal
in common.[4]

Then the American realism became harder and more brittle and
the French[5] realism became softer and more precious, and each
nation although knowing that they did have logic action and clarity
in common were troubled.[6] Then came the world war 1914–1918,
and America loved the clarity the force and the action in the
communiqués[7] and the ordre de jour[8] of the french the French
themselves[9] did not think they were literature, the Americans[10] did
and were impressed[11] and in the younger school of writers there is
the influence of these communiqués just as later there will be the
influence of Petain's messages[12] during the armistice, that[13] does
make literature to the American, but to the Frenchmen[14] it is too
much of their life's blood and so to escape they take to imagery and
fantasy, sur-realism and popular[15] things where fancy drowns
realism and realism tries to support fancy. It is easy to understand,
the Frenchman[16] does not want to look at his life-blood.[17] What the
future will do[18] of course nobody knows, nobody ever knows, all
that one does know is that it will be realistic, it has to be that, the
realism[19] that is real to each generation, but will it be the realism of
what they do, what[20] they win and what they lose or will it be the
realism of not wanting to know what they are and where they are,
this[21] of course nobody can know, but after they have done it they
will know, and it will be realism.

Notes

1. MS 1: 'realism, realism in romance'
2. MS 1: 'one's own hand'.
3. MS 1: 'french novelists'
4. MS 1:

> Of course they always had had realism writers and readers always have realism, after all, living is in a way always real, that is to say what one hears and sees, even what one feels is in a way always real, but the realism of the present seems new because the realism of the past is no longer real, and so the mental clarity of America and France in the years coming out of and after the french romantics to the french realists made french realism real to the Americans, who having a land with a clear light, manufacturing light and resistant steel, life needed a clear and resilient realism and there France and America met and there they had a great deal in common.

5. MS 1: 'brittle and the french'
6. MS 1: 'was troubled' (the second version of the ending begins after the phrase, 'in common').
7. MS 2: 'of the communiqués'
8. MS 2: 'ordres des jours'
9. MS 1: 'french. Although the french themselves'; MS 2: 'french, although the french themselves'
10. MS 1: 'think these were literature the Americans'
11. MS 2: 'Americans were influenced'
12. MS 2: 'messages to the french people'
13. MS 1: 'armistice, all that'
14. MS 1 and MS 2: 'frenchman'
15. MS 1: 'and other popular'
16. MS 1: 'a french man'; MS 2: 'the frenchman'
17. MS 1: a new paragraph begins here.
18. MS 1: 'will bring out'
19. MS 1: 'that, it has to be the realism'
20. MS 2: 'do what'
21. MS 1: 'are, all this'

AMERICAN LANGUAGE AND LITERATURE

'American Language and Literature' was written early in 1944 in the context of the imminent liberation of France by American troops and of Gertrude Stein's hope that she would soon be able to reassume her public literary role. The formula of its title harks back to the series of 'American' pieces she wrote in 1935 for the *New York Herald Tribune* with such titles as 'American Education and Colleges', 'American Cities and States and How They Differ From Each Other', 'American Crimes and How They Matter', and 'American Food and American Houses'. In this essay, she uses her preoccupation with what is 'American' in a literary-historical context to arrive, jubilantly, at the 'liberation' of American language and literature from their English models and at her own place in this 'liberated' writing. That the liberation of France is a central, if implicit, metaphor in the essay is clear both from the essay's conclusion and from the fact that its basic thesis (that 'every one is as their land is, as the climate is, as the mountains and the rivers or their oceans are as the wind and rain and snow and ice and heat and moisture is, they just are and that makes them have their way to eat their way to drink their way to act their way to think and their way to be subtle' – *WIHS*, p. 250) reappears in *Wars I Have Seen* in the 'What a day' passage about the liberation of Culoz.

'American Language and Literature' is written in a school notebook of the kind that Stein regularly used. This is the manuscript transcribed here. It is no. 548 in Bridgman's 'Key to the *Yale Catalogue*' (renumbered from Yale's no. 547a). The manuscript is somewhat hastily written; words in square brackets are my interpolations made for sense; frequently, they follow Alice Toklas's corrections pencilled in the manuscript, very probably, in preparation for typing it. Passages crossed through in the transcription are those Stein cancelled in favour of the passages which immediately follow them. There is no typescript among Stein's papers deposited at the Yale Collection of American Literature, Beinecke Rare Books and Manuscripts Library.

'American Language and Literature' was published in French translation as 'Langage et littérature', in *L'Arbaète*, 9 (automne 1944) 7–16. This is its first English publication.

Everybody is as their land is as their water is as the air above them is, as there are clouds or no clouds there, as the storms are and the wind is, as their food is, what they eat when they eat and how they eat, and the way it is cooked or raw, and what they drink, and how they drink. All these things make every one what they are, and generally speaking a nation is made up of a lot of people who more or less do and have all these things more or less in the same way. Then what everybody is is what their language is, their language is the result of where they are, how they are, what their land and water is, what their lakes and rivers and oceans are, and soil and seas, all these things make them having a language that fits them and not any other one.

In Europe the latin basis made the latin countries but in each one of the latin countries the air the food, the land the water the drink is different the spread of the land the height of the mountains and all that made it that each one of the latin countries being what they are each one of them twisted the latin tongue to suit them to make a language that could content no one but themselves. We have the same story with the Saxons, the English and the germans each changed the saxon tongue to suit their land their air their water their food and all the ways that are the result of land air water food and drink. The Slavs had the same history quite naturally enough. And it was quite easy for each one gradually to change the language to suit themselves because during the long years that these languages were formed the majority of those using them only talked them and in talking them nothing interfered with the language gradually changing particularly as each country was so to speak included within its own frontiers and practically never saw or heard the others who had a more or less similar language.

All this also was true of towns of pieces of the country even from one village to another, each developed their own patois, their own way of saying how they live every day how they eat every day how they drink every day how they die and how they live how they fight and how they love, all that special to themselves and only having it in common with all the other countries in that each one of them has a language. This is all very simple.

Now the situation in America was very different and for a very simple and excellent reason in all the years where the United States of America was becoming itself, slowly knowing itself for what it is it was of course talking English, but the great difficulty was that they were not only talking English, but that practically all of them from the beginning the great majority of them from the beginning knew how to read and write. So the conditions were completely different from those existing in Europe when each country was creating its own language. The immense majority of each country in those days could not read and write, but in America, it having so to speak really developed itself into a country in the nineteenth century when everybody practically everybody could read and write it made the situation very different. It was not only that they could read and write the language that they were speaking and living but they naturally were always reading and writing the language that the English were reading and had been reading and writing and as the English had been reading and writing it for many more years than the Americans naturally there was a great deal more language to have as a weight upon them.

This was the situation when the United [States] of America were slowly to themselves but compared to the long history of European and Oriental countries were very quickly making of themselves a nation.

Now the thing that is of the first importance is that the land and air and water the food the drink the kind of hills and mountains and rivers and plains in America having nothing in common with the same things in England nothing at all.

To begin with air, in England [air] is entirely different from air in America, in England as in most countries of Europe the atmosphere makes a cover over your head which we call the ~~heaven~~ sky but in America there is no such cover there is no ~~heaven~~ sky there is only air, and as far as you can look up that makes sky scrapers a natural form of architecture, there is no sky there is only air. That in itself would if the language had not been one that every one could read and write would have forced an entirely different language to exist, then there are the wide stretches of country, the violence of the climate, the tendency [to] terrible heat and terrible cold, blizzards, devastating storms and then our way of having hunger and thirst. ~~All this makes gayness and coldly logical~~ All this makes an entirely different way of feeling and living, of living and dying, ~~of dying~~, of dying and moving around, of moving around and staying still, of staying still and being always on the move, of being always on the move and being violent, of being violent and being very careful, of being very careful and not caring about anything, of not having any daily life, because life is of no importance and of not having any death because the earth is so dry and thin and everlasting, all these things make the Americans so completely different from the English that it can easily be understood that there is no sense at all in their talking the same language no sense at all. But there you are America came into conscious being when everybody could read and write and if you are [indecipherable word] reading and writing and there never was a country who read and wrote so much, the daily newspapers alone in the United States in one month could fill a fairly large sized library what could they do about it how can you change a language when it is being written and read so much so continuously any and every day.

Uncommonly from the beginning of American writing the American writer was face to face with this strange problem a problem that has never existed before because all other countries in the world made their language when everybody was not reading and writing it every day.

It did not take long for the Americans to know that they did not have the same things to say the same things to feel the same things to know and the same things to live as the English had who had made the language which was all the language the Americans had to tell their story. And what could they do. They had to do something because everybody does have to tell all of their story in their own way and from the beginning the Americans knew that they had a story to tell and it had nothing at all to do with the story the English who had made their language had to tell.

So what could they do. They could not change the language it was written too much every day and so from the beginning they began to see if by putting a sort of hydraulic pressure on the language they could not force it to become another language even if all the words were the same, the grammatical construction the same, and the idioms the same. So slowly by constant choice of words making some words come closer to each other than they ever had been before, in the use of the language, making a movement of the language that was steadily clearer more monotonous and fresher by thinning out the thicknesses, by pressure steady pressure they did not change the language but they did succeed they are succeeding in making it feel different very very different so different that it really can tell the American story and not the English story at all, so different that it has been having its effect on the way the English tell their story, it is making to a certain extent the English tell their English story in the American way to a certain extent and so we have the history of American literature, Washington Irving, Emerson, Hawthorne, Thoreau, Edgar Allen Poe, Walt Whitman, Mark Twain, Henry James Gertrude Stein Sherwood Anderson and then the first world war.

I have often thought that a war is very useful in making people conscious of the changes that have taken place in the point of view of a nation and most of the nation is not conscious of it until a war comes along and publicizes it, makes everybody and anybody conscious of it. In America [there] were four such wars, and now there probably is a fifth. The American revolutionary war, the American civil war, the Spanish American war and the world war. Each one of these wars made the nation conscious that in some way they had been liberated they and their language from something that had imprisoned them. The American revolutionary war not only separated America from England but it also by the orators and the writers of that period, however completely they had the pressure of writing which was English were beginning to feel that the story they had to right, the life they had to describe, the death they would meet, and the country to which they belonged had nothing to do with England.

They knew it and you feel the struggle with it from the orators of the Revolutionary Period, Patrick Henry, Jefferson Franklin, until Emerson, they knew they had a story to write that had nothing whatsoever to do with England and yet many of them had been born English and still felt English and certainly to a certain extent wrote as if they were English, but gradually they began to put the pressure on the language of which I have spoken and it began to feel different. It was English of course it was English but it did begin to feel very different, it began to feel quite a little American. Then came the enormous struggle between the north and south the question of slavery, the civil war 1861–65 the orators of the South who still continued to feel partly English and the orators of the north who ~~did not feel~~ practically did not feel English at all ending up with Abraham Lincoln who although still feeling the weight of English literature upon him nevertheless did force the language to tell an American story in such a way that the word English could hardly be said to be there at all. At the same time the writers Emerson Thoreau, Hawthorne Edgar Allen Poe and finally Walt Whitman who coming out of the civil war triumphantly shouted that he was all American not British at all, but nevertheless all the same a little the weight just a little the weight was there.

Then came the enormous industrial development of the United States from coast to coast, and a great many influences came, french literature and Russian particularly the realistic schools of both these countries and there was a large group of minor writers and some major ones like Mark Twain, who almost had no consciousness of the English having made the English language, Mark Twain on the one hand and Henry James on the other who came over to admire the English and took a further step in advance in making the language an American language. Then came the Spanish American war 1899 and that was another big step in making Americans American. We then knew that we could do what we wanted to do and we did not need ~~England~~ Europe to tell us to do what we wanted to do, we did not any longer feel that we were attached to Europe at all except of course pleasantly not at all as anything to dominate us. It was a decided liberation, that was when I began to write, and I found myself plunged into a water of words, having words choosing words liberating words feeling words ~~and the words were all mine~~ and the words were all ours and it was enough that we held them in our hands to play with them whatever you can play with is yours and this was the beginning of ~~having~~ knowing of all America ~~having~~ knowing that it could play and play and play with words and the words were all ours all ours.

Then came the world war and that produced a further liberation. We were now the arbiters we had that strength and so ~~it was for~~ was born a new generation of writers who did not have to think about the American language it was theirs and they had it and that was all there was to it, singing it or rag time Sherwood Anderson or Hemingway or Faulkner they all had it and now what are they going to do with it that is the question.

A POEM ABOUT THE END OF THE WAR

'A Poem about the end of the war' is a poem about wishful thinking and about the suspense, in spring 1944, of waiting for the end of the war. Stein begins the poem either just before or on 11 April 1944, a date given in the piece and one which matches the description of the same situation in *Wars I Have Seen*:

> It is now the eleventh of April the Tuesday after Easter-Monday and everybody had hopes that something would happen and in a way it has, bombardments have been bombing and the Russians have been moving and everybody is expecting everything to be happening and we all talk while we are out walking to find eggs and spinach and cake and everything, one does find everything.   (*WIHS*, p. 166)

The poem is worked on at different times through that spring and summer. The passage recording the buzzard's predatoriness, for example, is written shortly after the American landing in France: the buzzard carried off the chickens, *Wars I Have Seen* tells us, during the last days of the German occupation of Culoz (*WIHS*, p. 195). There is a blank of half a page just before the final 'paragraph', which was clearly added after the liberation of Culoz as comment on 'the end of the war'.

The manuscript is in the same notebook as the 1942 talk 'Conférence à Belley' (no. 540 in Bridgman's 'Key'); the notebook is turned back to front and 'A Poem about the end of the war' (no. 547) written on the back of the pages of the earlier piece. It is followed by 'A la recherche d'un peintre' (no. 557), a piece published as 'Découverte d'un peintre' in *Fontaine*, VIII (May 1945), 135.

'A Poem about the end of the war' has not previously been published.

We wish what.
We have to worry right up to the end.
We have to be afraid right up to the end
When the days are longer
And the sun is stronger.
And winter gives place to summer
And summer does not give place to winter.
Then but not till then.
They all say but when.
What can you wish.
If you wish
For a fish
What can you wish.
A fish is not dangerous.
Who said so.

What can you wish.
What can you.
I wish that is what they say,
I wish that to-day was anyway,
That is what they say,
They wish that thunder began to thunder.
They say that they wish that they were hungry and happy,
Who,
And they say who,
And then they say who who
And then they say to-day,
Lead away when you play,
That is what the children say
When they play marbles near the hay,
Believe it or not Tuesday is a day.
And it is not the eleventh of may
But of april.
Thank you for asking kindly after blemishes.
By which when it is not midnight it is eight o clock.
And then they were very uneasy all of this day.
    And what do they wish for, believe it dear me believe it what do
they wish for.
He,
They
Wished for what.
Not that eleven o clock came after one o clock.
Which it does
And no they do not
Did not.
Have to wish for that.
Not that.
Think well for what you wish.
Because you might get your wish.
So think well before you wish.
For what you are to get.
Supposing you wished for the end of the war,
Well you might get that.
And to-day and not yesterday,
Well you might get that,
So be very careful for
What you wish

Because you might,
You very easily might,
Get that.
Thank you kindly for yesterday.
That is a good wish.
Just like that.
What do you wish I guess,
I wish I could guess yes.
Wish kindly wishes six for kisses.

The end of the war will make a store of things to eat to wear and to treat, like anything that can be had good and bad.

Do they even think what they would like to have yes they do always think of what they would like to have, and have it, not halve it just have it. Any one thinks about that now. Have it.

Please ask the wind and the weather to go on, please do.

Oh yes thank you there is some news good news is news, yes thank you there is some news.

A little when they ask for puddings they get puddings.

Plums like potatoes to grow though everybody knows that nobody can care to say so.

Can you think that two makes three after a war.

Thank you for not troubling me before during and after a war.

They wish they could like bricks and wood and stone, they wish it.

Do they wish for cherries or for stones, both cherries and stones both stones and cherries that is what they wish they wish for cherries and for olives for olives and for cherries.

And then very likely they manage to be lively not very lively not lively that is what they wish.

I wish I was well I wish I was and they are and that is what we wish, a fish to swim and bird to skim and a frog to croak. Yes thank you and after that all all is well. Yes thank you so we wish. A happy birthday.

What she wishes it is bananas for which she wishes bananas and oranges and lemons yes and dishes, dishes wishes, and a buzzard has carried off three of our baby chickens, oh dear me.

Let us wish for what we have thank you very much.

Thank you for coming to-day which was yesterday thank you.

Which was that some would if they could thank them kindly.

If they go up and down well up and down, and now they are up and we up them thank you for wishing, we wish, we eat fish we do we do wish.

Meat is meat and butter is butter and honey is honey and fish is fish and we wish to say thank you for eating so much and perhaps we should eat less, yes well less. Thank you for your wish.

Yes yes thank you for cake when there is not bread, yes yes thanks.

Cake and bread bread and cake which do you like but, I kind of think there is good butter butter and bread bread and butter is better than cake, yet when there is no bread and butter there is cake. Marie Antoinette was very right about that.

For which we thank the boys at home who are over here just now. Thank you, we wish to thank you.

Let him laugh when he hears that what he sees is not what he says, but all the same we believe him all the same and that is nice all the same yes all the same.

Thank you [for] being so kind to me that she to he said he to she, thank you for being so kind to me.

And then they wished that they would like it when the war was over.

Not everybody does.

But now everybody does just as soon as it does then everybody does.

They will like it.

Is it so near or is it so far and wishes are are wishes are.

Leave it to me that is what they do not say because there is nothing to leave anyway. Nothing at all.

Which is not what they asked for they asked for what they got and they got what they had and it is very pleasant to have a new army with an old name or an old army with a new name.

Why should a truck be pulled by horses. Because there is no more gasoline. And when will there be more, after the others are in the war.

Any day yes any day there will be a victory any day yes. And we will not have to say thank you we will just be busy with a victory.

And with fruit, how fresh is fruit, how sweet is fruit how nice is fruit, if you are where fruit grows all is well but if you are not and there is no transport, well then there is no fruit and we want fruit, yes we do.

What do we want, what we have yes and wish wish wisely and

thoroughly and eventually and the moon will shine the new moon and wheat. That is why there is no vacation this summer.

And just then they began to wish for wishes.

Bet your life they are disappointed when they see that the cat can crow.

And when bread is the staff of life then we eat bread and butter yes we eat bread and butter.

Wishes wishes wishes.

Just imagine how scared they are just imagine.

What do you like to wish. I like to wish a wish.

We wish a wish well wish a wish, it is this wish, that we have our wish, which we wish.

We can have no more wishes because everything we wish is as we wish and therefore we are wishes.

Index

237